KING
RICHARD I

KING
RICHARD I

RICHARD PETTY
with William Neely

PaperJacks LTD.

TORONTO   NEW YORK

PaperJacks

KING RICHARD I

PaperJacks LTD

330 STEELCASE RD. E., MARKHAM, ONT. L3R 2M1
210 FIFTH AVE., NEW YORK, N.Y. 10010

Macmillan edition published 1986

PaperJacks edition published June 1987

Cover photo courtesy of STP

ISBN 0-7701-0649-8

Foreword

Richard may be the last of the thirties-type heroes we'll ever have in sports— the return of the all-American boy.

Richard Petty's chief asset has to be that he became a hero at a time when the popularity of American athletes began to fall because of drugs, high salaries, strikes, and the general impression that athletes had no time for their fans.

The peak of Joe Namath's popularity, for example, was also about the same time as the peak of Richard Petty's popularity. I guess this book is about why Richard has stayed so popular for all of these years, while the popularity of Namath and the others has relatively diminished. For one thing, Namath's era produced six- and seven-figure salaried athletes who ran down the courts and fields' at half-speed, while you could still find Richard Petty hanging around the track to sign autographs, totally accessible, two hours after a race was over. It didn't matter if it was the important Daytona 500 or a race at a half-mile dirt track in Columbia, South Carolina. In fact, it was after he had won the Daytona race for the first time that he opened his heart and his arms to the fans, and he's never closed them.

No person in the history of the sport—including Bill France, Sr., who started it all—has had more to do with its enormous popularity than Richard Petty. He has been its greatest salesman, simply because he let his presence be available to people, damn near twenty-four hours a day. This presence has to be mentioned. It's almost like a friend who shows up when a loved one has passed away. It's not necessary to say a word: just being there is enough. This sort of presence is nearly forgotten today in sports; it's confined to a boxing ring in Las Vegas, or the football field at the Meadowlands, or the Madison Square Garden basketball court. But Richard's presence went out of the asphalt lanes of *his* playing field, right out to the people.

Everybody in racing who ever asked Richard to make an appearance, or help this person or that charity, found him to respond much like the guy who pumps gas at the corner gas station. His humility and thoughtfulness are unparalleled. Why didn't the rest of the drivers do it—A. J. Foyt or LeeRoy Yarbrough or any of them? Well, perhaps they didn't feel comfortable with it. Who knows?

There is a great parallel between Richard and Arnold Palmer, if you look carefully. In the early days of Palmer's pro career when, suddenly, huge crowds began to show up and follow the golfers around the links, noise became a factor: cameras clicked, shoes shuffled, people even talked. Listen, they *yelled* at times. All of this took away from the concentration that is so important to a really serious golfer. Palmer made the decision to do something that may have influenced the way he played golf more than any single thing, and that was not to let the crowd bother him. Other golfers got real upset when anything happened in the crowd. Sam Snead did everything but pull a gun and start shooting into the gallery. To say the least, the response of most golfers antagonized and upset the crowd, compounding the original problem.

Richard reacted to what could have been *his* problem in exactly the same way as Palmer, perhaps unconsciously, when he got to the crowded racetrack, or anywhere for that matter. He was adored throughout the entire South; he couldn't go anywhere without being recognized and often mobbed. Everybody knew him. So maybe he said to himself, "I have to make this either part of my life or none of it." I think he decided right then to make it part of his life.

Compare our two athletes once more: say, Palmer is at the fourth tee of the Masters—a 400-yard, par four—and he hits the ball 275 yards, right down the middle. He's got one shot left to the green, and he's walking down the fairway; if the crowd antagonizes him, it will take his mind off the shot—but, then, after you hit so many golf balls, why do you need to think when you walk down the fairway? Maybe you need to get your mind off of it a little bit, so it might help to get out and banter with the crowd. He talks to the lady with the yellow hat and the guy in the madras pants. It loosens him up. Hell, he knows it's a seven-iron shot, so when he gets there, he takes his seven iron and he whacks it just right. Simple.

Richard Petty has done the same thing. He exists in the most hostile environment in sports—inside a 3,700-pound race car, around nearly unbearable noise and debilitating heat, dealing constantly with people who have to be the most aggressive in the world—just to survive. It's the name of the game.

I'm going to tell you right now, I've known Richard Petty for twenty-five years and I have never seen him lose his cool. Never. It may have cost him part of his stomach—we'll get to that later on—but it's why people like him so much, and, I assure you, it's why he has become the most successful race driver in history.

He has never made a single excuse for himself or in any way shown even the slightest hint of arrogance. In fact, he may be the last of the thirties-type heroes we'll ever have in sports. In case you don't remember, the thirties sports hero was anything but flamboyant; he simply went out there and broke records and then he sat down with the crowd and joked and talked. Maybe it was because of the depression. Richard may be the reincarnation of one of these guys: Red Grange or Bobby Jones or Wilbur Shaw.

Richard is far from flamboyant—nearly emotionless, if you want to know the truth—but he has captured the hearts of more race fans than any driver who ever lived. Perhaps, even in this "if it feels good do it" society of today, the vast number of Americans still believe in God, family, and country; maybe it sounds corny, but just maybe we don't hear from this silent majority. What we have in Richard is a different kind of hero— the return of the all-American boy. Jack Armstrong may not have left us after all. For all these years he has been alive and well in Level Cross, North Carolina.

It is truly incredible that someone can be in this pressure-cooker sport and still have as great an attitude, but I suppose that's what separates him from the rest of the pack. Example: I have never seen a formula-one driver who's not as nervous as a jackrabbit. Alan Jones, one of the Grand Prix greats, said of Petty: "I've never seen anyone that calm around a racetrack. The way he handles things and talks to people is unbelievable." He's right; when Richard's car has problems and maybe he should be stomping the brake, he just sort of shuffles off, as if everything was just perfect. Even the other drivers don't understand it; particularly the other drivers.

How did he act during his 1967 season, when he was on his way to an unbelievable string of victories? Just as calm as he did in 1965 when the Chrysler Corporation pulled out of racing and left him without a ride. Just another day's work: "Let's go out and do it again, boys." There was never any bravado or arrogance or rubbing it in. It was merely Richard Petty winning more races in a single season than, surely, anyone ever will. The fact that nobody had ever done it before didn't change his attitude one bit. The family was close then and he did a wonderful job. It was that simple.

A lot of his popularity—and maybe even his success—has to do with his tremendously high moral fiber. Here's a guy with absolute Hollywood-looks, who is in a sport that may well have invented groupies, and no one has ever seen him do a thing out of line or be connected with anyone who did. If it ever happened to him, I would eat my typewriter. He's the one who should be on the Wheaties box.

Don't get me wrong, this is not going to be a dull book about the other side of racing—the lily-white version. I promise you, Richard's rise to the top was a tough one. It came in a period that was so wild and woolly that just being there was enough to make it colorful. And Richard was right square in the middle of it. It was happening around him, and we are going to tell you about all of the colorful events of racing, right from the start, because that's when he came into Grand National stock car racing. It was a brutal sport, and we are going to take a look at how it got that way and how it has changed. We may dwell a little more on the early days because, well, because they were a lot more fun, if you want to know the truth. And, above all else, we want this book to be fun.

Richard knows why it has always been a dramatic and rugged sport; he will tell you that, but you won't hear him merely saying "I did this" or "I did that." He doesn't have to, because if you've picked up a sports page in the last twenty years, you already know what the man has done. And, after all, in this age of flamboyance in pro sports, which careens toward the bigger-and-bigger for more-and-more money with less-and-less work, it is refreshing to see why stock car racing has gotten more popular. Without Richard Petty leading the way, it might not have happened. We could easily have not had him and we would be light-years behind, because I'll guarantee you, nobody else would have given of himself the way Richard did.

If there is a moral in here, it has to be: Hard work really *does* pay off. If Richard had worked as hard at anything—pumping septic tanks or selling vacuum cleaners door-to-door, anything—he still would have become a millionaire. You see, nobody knows the thousands upon thousands of man-hours he's devoted to becoming a success.

It goes without saying that the man has enormous talent in what he does, but others have been highly talented and haven't set a record of 200 victories, which is a mark so far out there in space that it surely will stand forever.

Through it all, Richard Petty has been stock car racing's greatest ambassador. In the sixties, racing needed a shiny-toothed hero with roots strongly in the South to vault the sport to where it is today. I, for one, am glad he came along. I know my life is better for having known him.

As great as Cale Yarborough is, and as wonderful as Fireball Roberts and Junior Johnson and, yes, Lee Petty were, it was Richard who first got to the fans. And, you know, Kyle Petty is almost a clone of Richard. That's the greatest thing about this story: We have another generation of Pettys to look to. All Kyle has to do is follow the example of his daddy, on and off the track.

BILL NEELY

Preface

You'll have to understand that if winning wasn't the most important thing, none of us would be here.

When we started putting together the outline and the stories for this book, I was just winding up my twenty-eighth season of driving Grand National stock cars, and I was already starting to think about another season. I'll have to admit that my career is at the point where the first thing anybody asks anymore is "When are you going to retire?" Well, you probably won't find out in this book, because I don't know myself. You'll just have to be satisfied with "one of these days." For now.

For one thing, it doesn't seem possible that it's time to think of retirement. I mean, it only seems like a season or two ago that I *started* racing. I've gotten to this point so much quicker than I expected.

Listen, I can't even tell you exactly what my greatest thrill has been—the first race I drove, the first race I saw, the first race I won, or the two-hundredth time I won. I guess it's all of that. *Racing* is a thrill to me—everything about it—and when the fun and excitement begin to lean toward boredom or, worse yet, work, that's when I'll walk away from it. I'll put my helmet in the Smithsonian Institution, along with one of my old race cars that's already there, and I'll turn the whole shootin' match over to the new generation, which just happens to include my boy. They can have it at that point.

But I'm not turning myself out to pasture just yet. I promise.

Certainly not while I feel as competitive as I do. I can still win races, I guarantee you.

I guess, in a way, this book is about being competitive and why it's so important to all of us in racing—why none of us want to lose. Sure, I want to tell you my life story and I want it to be interesting, but, more than that, I want to tell you the story of an entire sport. I might have been a little kid when it all started, but I was there, in the grandstands at first, yelling my head off for Daddy, who was driving in the very first Grand National race. Later on, I was in the pits. So, from that first race, I was right there, in one place or another. I was a real part of the early days of racing. Or maybe I should say that racing was a real part of *my* early days—whatever. What I'm trying to say is, age doesn't matter—any more than it does now that I'm on the long side of the racing hourglass—experience is what counts. I'm going to try to prove that in the following chapters.

Kyle is a third-generation racing Petty, but you probably knew that because you've been hearing about the Pettys for a long time. You see, Daddy came close to being the first household name in the sport. That's why it's important to take a close look at his racing career, too. It's really where mine started, and you can't separate the two. It's always been a family deal—the *Pettys*, not Lee Petty or Richard Petty or Kyle Petty. Besides, if we didn't go back to those days I wouldn't be able to tell you about the wild years of racing.

Those early days of NASCAR were tough—I can tell you that right off the bat—but they were colorful and exciting, too. I'll have to admit that we weren't much a part of the hell-raising because we were usually too busy working on the race car, getting it ready for the race that night or getting it put back together for the next one. But I was there and I knew what was going on. I saw it, because Daddy carried his family to the races, just like I've always carried mine.

I want to spend more time with the fifties, sixties, and seventies than I do with the eighties because you probably know what's going on today; you can pick up any paper or magazine and read that. But it hasn't always been that way; there weren't any accounts of the races back then, so I hope this book fills in the part that schoolteachers call "history." That's what it's called when there aren't many people left who were there when something happened the first time. If I were more of a politician, they'd call me an elder statesman, so if you want to refer to me as an elder statesman of racing, it's all right.

There aren't too many people, for example, who remember the dirt tracks and their "Saturday night heroes," like Ralph Earnhardt, the Flock boys, Red Byron, and a whole bunch more who were tough drivers but never got much national recognition. Those were the days when you banged somebody good if you expected to win. Oh, we still bang somebody out of the way from time to time, but it's not like it used to be. You had to be more than good then, you had to be good and *tough*.

This book is not going to hop from race to race, picking out the ones I won. Everyone knows I've won a lot of races, otherwise I probably wouldn't be writing this book in the first place. You can look up all of that if you really want to know. There are books out that have all the records. What this book is going to be is an inside look at what makes a race driver tick—what we're really like if you peel off the outside layers. I think you'll be a lot more interested in what the good ol' days really were all about than in what happened last week or last season—although we'll have a little of that, too.

You hear all of us talking about the good ol' days every chance we get, because all of us in racing have a tendency to look over our shoulders a lot. I guess it comes from the constant fear of somebody coming up from behind to pass us, about the worst thing that can happen to a race driver. You'll have to understand that if winning wasn't the most important thing, none of us would be here. We'd be running a hardware store or a dry cleaning shop. I'd be willing to bet that when Kyle writes his book twenty-five years or so from now, the eighties will be the good ol' days he talks about. Look on it as an occupational hazard.

I'm sure you've heard about how dangerous and exciting racing cars really is, and I guess it's true, but I'm not going to overplay that part either, because I'm just not that excitable a person. I don't have a death wish. I hate to disappoint a lot of the shrinks out there, but I don't. And I don't wave my own flag a lot—there are plenty of other people out there doing that. But I am going to tell you what it was like growing up in the Piedmont region of the South, and what it was like being around race cars morning, noon, and night.

I want to tell you about the South of my youth, not the industrial giant of today. Life was a lot tougher than it is today, particularly where I grew up. I remember reading one time what Chet Atkins said about growing up on a farm in eastern Tennessee: "We were so poor, and everybody around us was so poor, that it was the forties before anybody knew there had *been* a depression." Well, we weren't that poor, but we didn't have a whole lot more than anybody around us had. I mean, we never lacked for shoes if we needed them, but we only had one pair and we wore them until they were worn out. I never had to go to school barefoot. It might have made a better story, but I *did* have shoes. Still, what Chet said sums it up pretty well for us, too, even though I grew up after the depression. It's just that if anybody grew up that way today, they'd sure call it a depression—or worse.

I'm going to tell you how we pulled ourselves up out of the darkness of the old South and into the sunlight of the new South: by racing cars. Now that I think about it, I guess it does seem like a long time. It just doesn't seem like it's been as long as it really has.

*KING
RICHARD I*

1

You can't imagine the fear a six-year-old boy has when he's standin' there, watchin' his whole world burn up.

I didn't qualify well for the Southern 500 at Darlington in 1985, so I was way back in the field when the starter dropped the green flag —twenty-fourth position, if you must know. The car handled like a tank the first day we got there, but the crew and I worked out most of the problems by the time I qualified. I still wasn't what you would call "competitive," but it sure wasn't the first time I had started back in the field at the track everyone says is "too tough to tame." In fact, the truth is, I've never had much luck at Darlington, and I'm sorry about that because it's the one track where we all want to look good: the granddaddy of all stock car superspeedways.

I *had* won there before, so I wasn't about to give up just because I was way back in the pack. Anytime I'm out there, I feel like I can win; it doesn't matter where I am. If I didn't feel like that, I wouldn't be out there at all. Besides, starting back that far gives you a good chance to see what's going on up front; sort of an opportunity to let the cars get sorted out. You see, I do some rationalizing, too. But 500 miles does give you plenty of time to work out your problems and get up front, no matter where you start. I guess that's why I've never been too concerned about how I qualify.

The start of the race was smooth for this track. Everybody got through the first couple of turns without any problems, so I figured maybe this was going to be a good day after all.

I moved up a couple of places on the first lap, but it looked like it was going to take some doing to win this one. For one thing, I could see the leaders—Bill Elliott, Dale Earnhardt, and Harry Gant—pulling away from the rest of the pack. They were turning laps like their cars were on rails. My STP Pontiac felt a whole lot better than it had on Thursday, when they rolled it off the truck, but I was still having to manhandle it through the tight, narrow turns of the Darlington racetrack. After twenty-eight Southern 500s, you get so you can *make* a car handle, even if it has other ideas: that's where experience counts.

I watched Earnhardt blow by Elliott; he sort of dirt-tracked it, going through the third and fourth turns, and for a second the good ol' days flicked past my eyes. I had a flash-image of Dale's father, Ralph, on a dirt track a long time ago, and I remembered how much fun those tracks were to drive—back in the dawn of NASCAR. That's about all the time I had to daydream, because a car in front of me got a little "sideways" coming out of the fourth turn, and I had to drop down a little from my high groove. I could tell that if he didn't save it, he would spin right in my path, so I moved down. But as we say in NASCAR, he "gathered it up." There probably wasn't a fan in the place who even noticed what almost happened. You have no idea how many times during a race cars *almost* crash. People are only aware of the ones that do.

My uniform was already soaked from sweat, even though the race was only twenty-five laps old; you see, driving a 3,700-pound rocket we call a "stock car" at speeds approaching 200 mph in the straightaway is hard work, believe me, particularly here in South Carolina on Labor Day when the temperature is close to 100 degrees outside. You can imagine what it's like inside one of those tin cans. You get used to things like that when you've been racing for as long as I have—you learn to live with it—and this was my 978th race. That's a lot of green flags and a lot of checkered flags and even more wild and woolly things in between.

I worked my Number 43 race car past two more cars, but the leaders continued to open up the margin between themselves and the rest of us. My car was doing what I wanted it to and there was still a lot of time. As tough as it might appear, I still had confidence. At that moment, the caution flag went out. A car, way up in front of me, had blown its engine and dumped oil all over the track. I eased off the accelerator just the slightest bit and started to slow the car down. It's not something you do fast, unless you have no choice. But this wasn't an emergency. I had plenty of time, so I backed off little by little, and I kept my eyes open for the oil I knew would be there. If you hit oil at high speed . . . well, I don't have to tell you what happens.

Other than fleeting thoughts, like the one I had about Ralph Earnhardt, the only time you can let your mind rest is when you're running under caution—when the cars slow down and you can't pass anybody. You almost always go into the pits for fuel and tires, but there are a few laps after that when you're out there for a Sunday drive, tooling along at about 90 or 100 mph. You can let your mind wander for a minute or two and you can think about something other than winning and crashing, which is what it's all about—in that order.

When the yellow is out at Darlington, I always think about the past. Maybe it's because I grew up thinking that the Southern 500 was about as important as the World Series, the Kentucky Derby, and the Indianapolis 500, all wrapped up into one. This caution period was no exception. Keep in mind, I wasn't up front or close to it, so I sure didn't have much race strategy to get in order. There was a better day somewhere in my memory. Feel the flashback coming?

As we circled the 1⅜-mile oval, lap after lap, while the crews tried to dry up the trail of spilled oil down the front straightaway, everything got sort of hazy around the edges, and my thoughts drifted back to 1967, the year when everything went right: the year when we broke all the records.

The Southern 500 in 1967 might have been the most important race of my career—I know it was up to that point. I had tried seven times to win this one, but it had always managed to escape me. Two times I had that rascal won and I fell out of the race with mechanical problems, with less than ten laps to go. In 1966, I was leading and had a flat tire—with six laps to go. Man, that's enough to *discourage* you. And that's only part of it: Daddy's luck there had been as bad as mine. The jinx started for him in the very first race they had at Darlington in 1950. He never did win it.

You could write a book about the times Daddy and I had bad luck at Darlington. Although I don't know why you'd want to—you see, racers don't like to talk about bad luck. But we knew it was going to be a different story in 1967; all of us could just feel it the day we got to the track. For one thing, I had already won twenty-one races that season and the Plymouth was running like Jack the bear.

Everybody was talking about who would run second to me, but I wasn't going to take any chances—not with my record at Darlington. I got the pole position, but I still continued to practice, lap after lap, examining every inch of the track at racing speed, trying to determine where the car ran with the least amount of effort. As strong as that car was, and it may have been the single best race car in history (it's in the museum at Darlington now), I wanted to baby every part of it, if you know what I mean.

Even when the race started, I was skeptical. I held back a little, just to make sure everything was running right, and I hoped there wasn't the usual madness that's around for the start of almost every race—when people are nervous and careless. It's the most dangerous part of racing.

Buddy Baker, who started on the outside of the front row,

beat me to the corner, and I dropped in behind him. I followed him for a few laps, trying out the speed and handling of my car from time to time. Everything felt perfect, so I passed Buddy on the back straightaway on the seventh lap. I didn't have any trouble staying in the lead. I had to pit on lap 65, and David Pearson took over the lead, but I got it back two laps later when he went in for tires and fuel.

By the time we got to lap 80, I was a full lap ahead of the entire field. You'd think at this point I would have been able to relax a little, but I couldn't. I guess when you get stung so many times, you get a little leery. And it's a good thing I was alert and trying so hard because just as I roared into turn four I saw it, right there in my path—a major crash. There was smoke from tires and parts from cars flying everywhere. Dick Hutcherson apparently had gotten a little sideways and Sam McQuagg had plowed right into him. Sam's car smashed into the concrete wall on the outside of the track, careened across the asphalt, and hit the wall guarding the pits. The car flipped into the air, skidded all the way down the front straightaway on its top, and then did another flip and landed on its wheels. Man, there were parts of the cars spread all over the track.

There was a big part—I never did find out what it was—right in front of me, so I got off the accelerator, eased the car slightly to the left and held my breath. I wasn't sure I could miss it completely, but I didn't dare turn the car any more or get on the brakes, or I would have spun. I missed the part. There was another one a few car-lengths' ahead and I steered around it, too. By then I had scrubbed off enough speed that I could use the brakes a little, and it was easier to weave through the rest of the mine field. There were other cars doing the same thing, so it was a lot like a dodge-'em car show.

I managed to get through the mess, and, when I went into turn 1, I let my breath out for the first time since I had seen the crash. All of it had taken only a few seconds, because I was probably still going 125 mph, but it seemed like it had been in slow motion. That happens at times: It all seems to slow down and give you a world of time to think. Again, that's where the experience-part takes over. You just seem to do it all by reflex action at times.

There are other times, of course, when you do it all wrong. One of those times just popped into my mind. There wasn't anything else going on out there at the moment that needed my attention, so I guess you could call this a flashback within a flashback:

It happened in 1970, the year I scared 70,000 fans to death. Man, it was spectacular, I'll tell you that. I felt the rear end let go when I came out of turn 4, and then the car rode up against the wall, sending it spinning toward the pit wall. When it hit, I remember seeing about a six-foot section of the concrete wall give way and collapse. You always feel an impact like that in every bone of your body, but this one was worse. I knew it when I saw the wall crumble. I also knew it wasn't over. I felt the car start up in the air, and I knew the flips were about to start—they always do. I can remember, just like it was yesterday, trying to steer that car, mashing on the brakes. You know, it doesn't do a bit of good to steer or brake when you're upside down, but I do it. I do everything I can to try to land that rascal.

I remember the first flip, but that's all. I guess I was knocked out on that one, but I've seen the movies of the crash, and I've counted the flips: five. It's just that I don't remember anything after the first one; it seems like it was happening to someone else, like I wasn't even there. In the films, I could see my arm and shoulder hanging out the window. I was limp as a rag as the car flipped. The car, needless to say, was a total wreck when it was all over.

They took me to the track hospital in an ambulance—unconscious—and I guess everybody thought I had bought the farm. But I came to in the hospital pretty quick and I talked to the doctors.

"How's the race car?" I asked.

"Not too good," one of them said. "What's more important, how do you feel?"

"My shoulder hurts," I said.

"No wonder," a doctor said. "It's dislocated. But you're lucky."

I knew that.

I had crashed before, and I always felt lucky when it was over. That's what gets me in the car the next time. But crashes don't dim my enthusiasm one bit. I forget all about them. Just as soon as the pain goes away.

We all have days like that.

Let me get back to the daydream that started all this—the *good* year at Darlington. When we left the 1967 race, I was sailing along, without a care. It was lap 125 and I had a two-lap lead over everybody else. Another dodge-'em show took place, this time on the front straightaway. Bobby Isaac sideswiped H. B. Bailey's car, and then Elmo Langley and Buddy Baker came around and ran into the first two cars. Again, all I could see was a spinning junkyard in front of me. "Oh, boy," I thought, "here we go again."

There was a little bit of daylight up close to the wall, so I sort of sucked up my breath and hunkered up my shoulders a tad, as if it might help me get through, and I headed for the hole. I got past Buddy, but Elmo was still sliding, heading right for the outside wall: my path. There was only one place to steer—right *at* Elmo's car. I didn't know how far he was going to slide or exactly where he was going to be when I got there, but I knew where he *wasn't* going to be, and that was exactly where he was at that moment, so I aimed right for him. It's what you do. By the time I got to where his car had been, Elmo was ten yards away. The rest was easy. The other two cars had stopped and were sitting down near the edge of the track, smoking and steaming.

That was the last real excitement of the race. That is, if you don't count the three or four times someone got squirrelly in front of me but saved it. I was ready for anything, because I was sure the old track was going to bite me again; I know it always tries. But in 1967, it was worse. That was before they redesigned turns 3 and 4 and, man, they were treacherous. Not only were they narrow and fairly flat, which makes it hard to drive anyway, but they were sort of catty-wompus: You actually had to tap the wall between turns 3 and 4, just so you could get the right angle coming out. You really had to hit the wall on purpose; if you didn't do it, you didn't make good lap-times. The reason those turns were so narrow is that when they were building the track, that's all the room they had. There was a catfish pond down there, and they figured catfish would be a lot more profitable than race cars. They were wrong, of course.

What they did was make it necessary for the drivers to invent a maneuver called the "Darlington Stripe," and if you didn't do it, you didn't win. It was that simple. Or, worse yet, if you hit it too hard you crashed—it had to be just right. By the time the race was over, the wall had every color of paint on it that there was on a race car, and the cars had their right rear-quarter panels ground down to about the roll bars—the fast ones, at least. Darel Dieringer said one time that when you came out of that turn and tapped the wall, it sounded like someone had dropped an armful of kindling in the back of your car. And that summed it up pretty well, because it really did sound like you had completely torn up your car, every lap. You had to do it 367 times.

So here I was on my hard-luck track, running along with a five-lap lead with only fifty laps to go. You won't believe what happened to me at this point—I got bored. That's right, I was so far out front that there wasn't any challenge anymore, and I have to have a challenge or I lose interest. A sure thing just doesn't have any appeal to me.

All I had to do was stay out of everybody's way and I had it won. I could have stopped for a sandwich and still come in two laps ahead of everybody, and I was sleepy. I guess you could call it another occupational hazard. I would rather win by a car-length than by five laps. It takes all of the excitement out of it when you feel like you're out for a drive in the country—even if the drive is at 170 or 180 mph. You're just not as alert.

With ten laps to go, I began to perk up. This was the "critical" time for me at Darlington, the time when everything had always happened, so I got back in the swing of things. I held the steering wheel a little tighter, looking farther ahead for trouble than I usually did, but I stayed on the accelerator. The car was running best at full throttle and I didn't want to interrupt its rhythm. Crazy thoughts like that were helping to keep me awake.

There were five laps to go. Ol' Blue was running like the champion it was, but it seemed like every car on the track was running straight *at* me, and I began to hear strange noises in the car, sounds of every part starting to break. I guess I was getting paranoid. With two laps left, I could see cars smoking, up there ahead of me, so I gave them wider berths as I went by, hoping their motors wouldn't let go before I got to them. The last thing I needed was an oily track.

The starter waved the white flag the next time around. One lap to go. I went high into turn 1 and drove down off the slight bank, heading straight for the outside wall in turn 2—that's what you have to do. I roared down the back straightaway and headed for turn 3. One more brush with the wall there and Darlington would be mine. This time when I hit it, it sounded like the whole rear end of my car had come off. I checked the rearview mirror, just to make sure. It was all there.

I could see the starter holding the checkered flag over his head as I headed down the front straight. It was my seventy-first career victory, but by far the most important one to me.

Believe it or not, those are the kinds of things you think about when you're running under yellow, particularly when you're having a day like I was having at Darlington in 1985. At other times, you're so busy getting into the pits and watching what the other cats are doing that you can't even take your mind off of it for a second. There are races—most of them, in fact—when you can't let down for one second. You have to keep your mind going 200 mph for four or five hours, even during the few times the car isn't. I guess it's why you're plum wore out when it's all over.

We finally got the signal for one more lap under yellow. The race was about to get back to the frantic, full-speed action again. When I saw the green flag, I got the jump on two more cars and I took dead aim at another one. Lap by lap, I worked on the cars that were slower and the drivers who were less experienced, but, as hard as I tried, I couldn't pick up any time on the leaders. The truth is, I was losing ground on them. The outcome was inevitable: It wasn't going to be my day at Darlington. I was used to it.

You have to be philosophical about racing—often. I mean, you can't run strong at every track. There are times when you do everything exactly the way you did it the week before—you know, the week you *won*—and this time you're not even in the ball game. Nobody can explain it. I swear, at times I think cars have more bad days than drivers have. They just don't run as well on some days or on some tracks as they do on others, and they don't run as well at certain temperatures or with a particular tire compound. Cars are temperamental creatures. Even in 1967—the year we finished forty times in the top ten in forty-eight races—there were days when that supercar didn't run a hundred percent. I think my momentum and mental attitude won some of those races.

But this definitely was not one of those days. I didn't have any momentum. I'll tell you, it's tough for me when I'm out there, running a couple of laps behind and just keeping up. It makes for the longest day in the world, and I just keep hoping for the race to end so I can take a shower and go home.

I'll let you in on another thing, right up front: I only re-member the crashes when there's something to trigger the memories—like being at Darlington with nothing to do but aim the car. I never dwell on what bad thing happened here or there or on being scared or anything like that. If you want to know the real truth, I have never been scared in a race car in my life—I swear. The crashes or spins or near-misses all happen so fast that I don't have time to be scared. When it's over, it's too late. I just thank the Lord that I'm all right, and I go on to the next race. It's that simple. Honest.

A lot of people—including some shrinks that track pro-moters and magazine people have brought in over the years to try to find out why we do the crazy things we do—have suggested that maybe I don't know what fear is. Well, I've got news for them: I know what fear is. Are you ready for this: I'm afraid of high places, for one thing. I am. Listen, I don't feel comfortable on anything higher than the heels of my cowboy boots.

Riding in those elevators on the outside of hotels takes my breath away, and, I promise you, I never go up and look at the city from the top of a building. I'd rather see it from the subway.

Let me tell you about when I was helping build my house. It's two stories high in the middle, and I was up there helping nail rafters in place. At first, I held on for dear life to anything that was solid. I'd ease off with one hand and put the nail in place and then I'd hit it right quick and grab hold of what I was hugging before. After an hour or so, I was holding on less and hitting more. By the second day, I was running around up there like a squirrel. I get over my fear quick, that's one thing; it's just that it's always there the first time I go up high.

I've been in free-flight balloons and helicopters and the Goodyear blimp and every kind of airplane there is, and I'm not the least bit scared of them. If I'm not connected to the ground, I'm okay. I could go to the moon, and I wouldn't mind racing airplanes, but put me on something high that's hooked to the ground, and it always feels to me like it's going to fall over.

That's about it for fear. Oh, I've never met a tiger in the jungle, and I think that would definitely get my attention.

While we're on the subject, this is as good a time as any to tell you about the first time I ever remember being afraid. I was six years old when it happened. It was 1943 and it was winter.

We lived in a frame house, just down the road from most of my relatives. It was a tiny place, but Mother and Daddy always kept it looking real nice. It was freshly painted and the grass and shrubs around it were all trimmed and neat. It was home.

On this particular morning, everything was rolling along on schedule. Daddy had left early to haul some lumber up North. I was in my bedroom, getting ready for school and fighting with my little brother, Maurice, who is two years younger than I am and wasn't in school yet. We fought every morning—and evening. I wasn't there during the day.

Mother came into the bedroom and said the same thing she said every morning: "Boys if you don't stop this roughhousing, I'm gonna tell your daddy when he comes home, and he'll tan your hides. Now, get ready, Richard."

"Yes'm," I said. When she was out of sight, I threw a shoe at Maurice and it hit the wall with a thud.

"Boys! What did I tell you?" came from the kitchen.

Then there was an explosion. Mother screamed, and we ran to the door. There were flames shooting out of the old wood-burning stove in the middle of the room. She always tossed some kerosene in the stove, so it would be easy to light; for some reason, it had exploded this time.

Mother ran to the other side of the kitchen, away from the flames that were leaping out of the iron door of the stove. She stood in horror, with one hand on the bucket of drinking water.

It was useless; the flames fell to the floor and crawled along the linoleum like a fiery monster. Within seconds, the whole kitchen was ablaze.

She ran around the edge of the flames and scooped us up, one under each arm, and she carried us outside to the front yard. Nobody said a word. Nobody moved. We stood there and watched as the flames licked out the front door. I've never seen anything like it; the whole house was engulfed within minutes. The flames were dancing into the winter sky and sparks were flying everywhere. Ashes were drifting down, making everything a dull grey—the lawn and the trees and us. I thought about my toys and my clothes and the big, old Zenith radio in the front room, and the pictures in oval frames with convex glass: old, brownish photos of men with long beards and women in black dresses buttoned to their chins—family pictures. I watched as the outside walls fell into the flames and were eaten up by the monster.

It couldn't have been more than ten minutes until my whole world was nothing but a pile of glowing ashes.

People started rushing up in pickup trucks and cars to see if they could help, but they all did the same thing; they ran for a while, and then they sort of went into slow-motion. They could see it was too late. Pretty soon, the yard was filled with people just standing there, not saying a word.

I looked at the blackened forms of the cookstove and the Burnside stove that had caused the whole thing and at the bedsprings and the old metal cabinet that had been our wardrobe. The doors were open, and the hangers were still on the steel rod, but there were no clothes on them anymore. All the forms looked like skeletons, standing in a sea of glowing embers.

Maurice and I stood beside Mother, and she held us tight against her hips. One by one, the people went away.

Unless you've been through it, you can't imagine the fear a six-year-old boy has when he's standing there, watching his whole world burn up. That's why I've never let the psychologists and the writers tell me I don't know when I'm afraid.

I know what fear is.

I can see right now that I'm not going to be able to tell you how things are today without jumping around all over the place. I mean, after a while, none of it will make any sense, what with all the flashbacks and stuff, so I might just as well go back to the beginning and take it from there, just like all the other books. After all, even the racing part of my story starts with my family.

We've always had strong family ties . . . but you'll find that out.

I'll try to keep everything in order, but don't hold me to it. I always skip around a lot when I'm telling stories.

2

*We had a swimmin' hole over on Pole
Cat Creek, where the water was cold
as ice.*

There's not a whole lot to see in Level Cross, North Carolina.
Let me just tell you what's here (it won't take long, I guarantee
you): Let's see, there's the crossroad of old U.S. Route 220
and Branson Mill Road, the fire station that now has "Fire
Company 43" on the front of it. You see, they asked for that
number because that's the number on my race car. Petty Enterprises is right down the road. Across from the fire station
there's a general store and some houses, and right across the
road from that there's a ball field, and that's about it. When
I was a kid, we didn't have the fire station and the ball field.

Level Cross is four miles north of Randleman, the place
where I went to grade school through high school. We still
shop there because they've got a lot of stores. Listen, they've
even got restaurants and neon signs and all that stuff. The
population is only two or three thousand, but to us in Level
Cross, it's a city. Greensboro is about ten miles to the north.
It really is a city.

The country around here is slightly rolling, with little bitty
hills and great big trees—mostly white oak and long-leaf pine.
The streams run clean and clear, all the way to the ocean,
which is about 150 miles away. For a big vacation, we go to
the beach.

It's warm around here a lot more than it's cold, and we
hardly ever get any snow, so I suppose it's as good a farming

15

area as any place in the country, although not too many people do much farming anymore. They mostly work in the textile mills around Randleman or the furniture factories over in High Point. But when I was a kid growing up around here, farming was about all there was.

They put in a new section of U.S. 220 a few years ago, a four-lane that runs from up near the Virginia line down to below Asheboro. It bypasses us and leaves old 220 a quiet country road with little roads leading off it to where all the farms used to be. They're mostly housing developments now.

They call all of this area the Piedmont region. It was never a poor section, but nobody had a bunch of money either. I mean, there weren't ever any silver spoons in any mouths around here. Most of the men—including my daddy—had as many jobs as it took to make a living. Everybody had the necessities of life, but not a whole lot more. It meant that nobody spent money foolishly. If anybody did, the rest of the people talked about it.

The houses were adequate to keep the family dry and warm. Of course, not many of them had things like indoor plumbing, but they were well kept up. Oh, yes, there was one other thing: There usually was a junk car sitting around someplace on the property. Everybody kept them because they figured they might need them for parts someday, even though they almost never did.

The Piedmont is pretty country. It's where the low coastal land starts to hump up a little before it gets to the mountains to the north and west of us. I think it makes it interesting to look at, particularly with all of the trees we have and the big, open fields of tobacco and beans and corn. There might not be as much farmland today as there was when I was a kid, but what we have is nice.

It's the kind of area where everybody speaks to everybody else. I'll bet life is as simple and pleasant here as any place in the world. I know that if somebody gave me a world atlas and told me I had my choice of any place I wanted to live, I wouldn't even have to open it.

We all lived a pretty sheltered life around Level Cross, particularly when I was growing up during World War II. It was made up of work and picnics, and work and church socials, and work and visits with other members of the family. Did I mention work? Well, I can't stress work too much, because it's the first thing parents taught their kids. From the time they were big enough to walk, kids in our area did whatever they were told to do, in the way of helping with the farm and house chores. As you got bigger, you took on bigger duties.

Next in importance to working were your manners. I lived smack in the middle of a world of "yes ma'am" and "no sir" and "thank you" and "please." A world where kids were to be seen and not heard. Don't get me wrong, I'm not complaining about my upbringing; I'm glad I was taught some respect, and I sure am glad I learned at an early age that work won't hurt you. They have been important lessons in life, and ones I've tried to teach my kids.

The Pettys were like most of the other families around the Piedmont: They had been there for several generations. I guess my ancestors came over from Ireland a couple of hundred years ago and settled right here. You see, North Carolina was one of the earliest areas to be settled, and I don't know for sure, but I'd be willing to bet that my people were among the first.

The stories I remember hearing most were about my great-grandfather Petty, who may well have been the first racing Petty. He was an old man, and I don't mean just from a kid's eyes. He was an *old* man, ninety-eight, when he was still racing around the countryside in his stripped-down Model T Ford. There wasn't much there, except the frame and engine, and that old man sitting up there on the gas tank with his long, white beard blowing in the wind, hell-bent for leather. Then one night he didn't come home. It was winter, but he was still out in that old Model T—or maybe on it would describe it better. They found him next morning in a ditch. He had frozen to death. They said he had gotten pretty lit up and he was wrecked. Now, you'll have to admit, it wasn't a bad way to go. Particularly at ninety-eight.

Granddaddy Petty was just the opposite. Judson Petty was a quiet, God-fearing Quaker gentleman, who was sort of dominated by Grandmother Petty. I don't think I ever saw him without his hat on, except at the dinner table. He took it off just before he sat down to pray, and he put it on the minute he got up from eating. Grandmother said that it was the last thing he took off before he put on his nightshirt. He hung it on the bedpost and put it on the first thing every morning.

Daddy told me that they moved a lot, too—I mean, lock, stock, and barrel moving. Since Granddaddy Petty was like the rest of the family and did everything from farming to carpentering, there were lean times every once in a while. When times were good, they moved to the city, and when the times were bad, they moved back to the country, where they could grow food.

In 1928, when Daddy was sixteen years old, he traded his bicycle for a Model T. Bikes were worth more than a lot of the cars back then, so a kid could make a trade like that. In fact, a bike was a luxury and most cars weren't. Daddy said you could buy a Model T that would run pretty good for, say, twenty dollars.

The first thing he did was strip down the Model T and race it all around the countryside. You'll have to admit that he was living up to his heritage. That car lit the fire for a love affair with speed that has consumed every bit of energy of every Petty who has come along since (or will come along, I'd be willing to bet).

I guess it's why my earliest memories include cars. There was always a car in the front yard or the side yard, or wherever there was a shade tree to work under. And it was always apart, in one stage or the other, being modified to make it run faster.

It didn't matter if it was a brand new car or an old one, Daddy was never satisfied with how fast it would run. All of my uncles and cousins were the same way. It must be in the Petty genes.

When Daddy and all his friends weren't driving flat out on the highway, they were loafing in the general store in Level Cross that my uncle Bob ran, or they were down the road a mile or so in a place my uncle Bud ran—it was actually a beer joint, but the guys all played cards down there. I never got to go to Uncle Bud's place very often, but I did spend a lot of time at the general store, and I used to love it. I sat around on the nail kegs with Daddy and his friends, right there around the old stove—winter or summer, it didn't matter if the thing was lit or not, everybody sat around it—and I listened to the stories they told. The conversation was always about cars, not politics or religion or anything else: cars.

There was a cardboard box next to the stove that everybody used to spit their tobacco juice in. Every once in a while, somebody would miss and hit the stove and there would be a sizzling sound and a puff of steam. It was part of the storytelling routine. They usually put the box in the fire at night and started out the next day with a new one. There was a lot of ritual.

Uncle Julie had a garage up toward Greensboro, and Daddy used to take me up there, too. In fact, it was there that the racing bug bit us all, because some of the fellows around there used to bring their race cars in to work on them. Well, they weren't exactly race cars; they were jalopies, really. But to me, they were about as impressive as an Indianapolis 500 car.

There was a little, old, quarter-mile dirt track between Level Cross and Greensboro. You went up old Route 220, turned back to the right, and drove into the pine woods. We used to pass the sign all the time, and I pestered the daylights out of Daddy to take me there. He finally gave in.

I'll never forget that first race with Daddy and Uncle Julie. It was nothing but a little old track that had been scraped out of a pasture field with a road grader, leaving a red clay oval, but it just about thrilled the pants off me. There were some wooden bleachers along one side and a little bitty concession stand underneath where they sold hot dogs and pop—nothing else, except maybe popcorn, but I don't remember anything but hot dogs and pop. That's what I had.

There were a few big, old truck tires, half-buried along the outside edge of the turns, to keep the cars from getting knocked out into the field, and there was a low board fence along the front straightaway, near the grandstands. There was an eight- or ten-foot-high wire fence behind the board fence to keep the cars out of people's laps. That's all there was to the place, but it was heaven to me.

There were twenty-five or thirty race cars, maybe more, I'm not sure anymore, but I know it seems like there were a lot. They were mostly Ford and Chevy coupes that the guys had gotten from junkyards or out of their own front yards. They got them running again and raced them. It was where most guys started their racing careers.

The race cars were just regular old cars with their fenders off and some bumpers made out of pipe and welded right to the frame. They didn't have mufflers, so they sounded powerful. As I look back at it, the total cost of most of the race cars was probably about fifty dollars a car, and the total purse for the evening probably wasn't much more than that either.

When the guy waved the green flag for the start of the first heat race, I couldn't believe it. The whole deal was just as wild as I had expected. There were only about half a dozen cars in that first race and they all ran together in the first turn. They restarted the race and the same deal happened again. It took three tries before they ever got the first lap in, and then it was slam-bang the rest of the way.

I didn't know any of the drivers, so I didn't really cheer for anybody. I just enjoyed the whole deal.

"That sure was good, Daddy," I said. "Can we come back sometime?"

"Come back?" Daddy said. "It's not over. There are four more races tonight."

"Wow!" I said. "This is the best place I've ever been."

And it was.

They watered down the track between races, but it was only a couple of laps before there was so much dust you could hardly see the cars. In fact, I had no idea how the drivers could see where to aim their cars. From up in the grandstands, I couldn't even pick out one car from the other. There was a cloud of dust that just hung over the whole place, and it settled down over everything, including the hot dogs I was eating, but that didn't matter to me; those hot dogs tasted better than any ones I ever ate—before or since.

I just sat up there in the stands and cheered and chomped and drank pop. There was so much dust that the little beads of condensation on the Pepsi bottle would make tiny rivers in the dust as they ran down the sides. I was hooked. From then on this was the sport for me.

I looked forward to Friday nights like I never had before.

After the fire I told you about before, we moved in with Grandmother and Granddaddy Toomes, who lived a couple of miles away. They had a nice big house with a front yard that was as big as all outdoors. The grass was always cut neat and there were a lot of trees around. Man, it was like living in a park. Maurice and I used to roll in the grass and run around like a couple of Indians, and I've often wondered if my grandparents knew what they had gotten themselves into. We were pretty wild kids. But they seemed to like having us there as much as I liked being there.

It wasn't the first time we had lived there. In fact, that house had a special feeling for me: I was born there. Mother and Daddy lived there with my grandparents for the first few years of their marriage, until they could afford a place of their own.

So it was more like coming home than it was like moving in with somebody.

Granddaddy Toomes was like all the other men around our part of the country: He did a little bit of everything to make a living, but most of the time he farmed and ran a sawmill. They moved it from place to place, wherever they could buy a good stand of trees to cut down and saw up into rough boards.

Daddy hauled a lot of the lumber, and sometimes he took it all the way up to Virginia or over to Raleigh.

Granddaddy's house was on part of the original 180 acres of land that had been in the family for generations. He had moved over onto the edge of the property and sectioned off thirty-five acres or so for his place, and then he cleared the trees, moved his sawmill in, and sawed the lumber for the house. Mother was thirteen years old when the house was built.

We stayed there for several months before Daddy made enough money to get us another place. You see, not many people had luxuries like fire insurance in those days, so the fire had cost Daddy a lot. It took a long time just to get enough money to buy new clothes for all of us, not to mention all the other things a family needs to get along.

When we did move, I hated to leave, partly because I was so happy there, and the rest because the place we moved into wasn't quite as nice. I'll have to be honest with you, we moved into a trailer. And I don't mean the kind you see in trailer parks, I mean the kind you see on the back of a tractor-trailer rig—part of an eighteen-wheeler—that kind of trailer.

There was a good reason: It was 1944 and we were right smack in the middle of the war. There weren't any houses to buy or rent and you couldn't get enough construction materials to build one, so people had to take what they could get.

"Well, why don't we just stay with Granddaddy?" I pleaded.

"I wish we could, son," Daddy said, "but we need to be in a place of our own. And Granddaddy and Grandmother do, too. You and Maurice'll like our new place."

I wasn't so sure about that. But I knew I had to make the most of it.

He moved the ten-by-twenty-foot trailer over on the edge of our old property, and then he jacked it up and built a cement-block foundation under it, so it wouldn't be rickety. When he took off the wheels and let it down on the foundation, it was pretty sturdy. I was still skeptical about the whole deal.

He put a door in the back and a window over where the kitchen table was going to be, and then he paneled the whole thing inside with plywood and painted it. You know, it actually started to look like a house.

But he wasn't finished. He built another room onto it, up in front. It was about the same size as the original trailer so, all of a sudden, we had twice as much space. He cut a door in the front of the trailer, so that we could get from one part of the place to the other without going outside. We had a long, narrow house that looked a lot like a motel.

There was one bedroom, which we all shared, and, man, I mean *bedroom*. That's all there was in it: wall-to-wall beds. Mother and Daddy had a double bed and Maurice and I had cots, so there was just room to squeeze between the beds in there. You walked in and you lay down—that was it. The dressers and the clothes closet were out in the other room, so we were ready for bed when we got in there.

It probably comes as no surprise that Maurice and I got into a whole lot of trouble by not going right to sleep once we went to bed. But, after all, we were little boys, so we poked and picked at each other and giggled and carried on. We couldn't help it; our beds were just too close together for us to resist pestering each other. We usually got a spanking before we settled down to go to sleep. You could count on it.

The house didn't have indoor plumbing, but Daddy dug a well and put in a pitcher pump so there was at least some water for the kitchen sink. We could pump water to heat up so we could take a bath. We might not have had running water, but we had the next thing to it—it ran as long as we pumped.

There was a stove in the main room that heated the whole place, but it was always so cold in there when we got up on winter mornings that I would lay there in bed with the covers pulled up under my chin and hope that I could stay there until the fire warmed things up. It never worked. Either Maurice was pulling the covers off me or Mother was calling us, "Get up and get ready for school, boys—now!"

I can still feel that cold linoleum on my feet. There's nothing that gets your attention in the morning any quicker than cold linoleum on bare feet, unless it's a trip to the little brown house out back. Listen, I broke all speed records getting out there, doing what I had to do and getting back. When I got back, I would get up so close to the stove that my clothes would start to smell scorched. Then I'd toast the other side.

Now that I look back at it, it really was fun growing up in that little place. There are a lot of happy memories: like the support beams Daddy put in the kitchen that were so low he couldn't stand up straight. He was constantly hitting his head. It got to be a family joke—well, with everybody except Daddy. I can remember hearing him get up to go out back at night, and I could predict what was going to happen. He would run into both of our beds, trying to get out of the bedroom and then trip over something we had left on the floor, and then I waited until he got to the kitchen. There was a dull thud, followed by "Damn it!" and then I heard the back door open. It was the same deal every night.

We never thought much about the way we lived because those were unusual times—the war years—and everybody lived a different kind of life than they had before. I've never known any time since when people were as close together—everybody. We all had a common cause, and you almost never heard anybody complain about doing without this or that. It was just the opposite, in fact; everybody was so happy when they *did* get a pound of sugar or a loaf of sliced bread or a pound of coffee that there was a sort of celebration. People even called their friends to tell them when coffee or sugar got to the stores—if they had a telephone. I know Mother about went crazy when she got to buy a pair of nylons.

We lived by ration stamps and determination, and everybody I knew did his or her part. The women got together and folded bandages to be sent off to the battle zones, and the men ran scrap drives to collect aluminum or copper or steel or anything that was needed to help build planes or tanks or whatever.

I was happy all the time, even when I went to school. Well, maybe I'm getting a little carried away—I wasn't all that happy about school, if you want to know the truth. It was about a mile walk to where I caught the bus, and then a long ride to Randleman because the bus wound around everywhere. It took forever to get to school. I was ready to come home by the time I got there. But I still remember the smell of the bus. It was a smell of sandwiches wrapped in waxed paper and stuffed into brown-paper sacks, and of bananas and apples and wood smoke from the kid's clothes. I always hated it when it rained, because the smell of wet wool isn't one of your great all-time aromas, I'll tell you.

We all yelled and carried on and we *always* ate our lunches before we got to school. That would give us more time to play at the noon recess.

The only thing that marred that period of our lives was Maurice's illness. He got awful sick and the doctor couldn't figure out what it was, so they took him to Duke University Medical Center, where they found out he had polio. He was four years old at the time, and he had to stay there for several months.

Nobody knew much about polio then, so it took a long time and a lot of whirlpools and therapy for him to get the use of his legs back again. Eventually he got to come home, and little by little he learned to walk again, although he never completely got over it. He still dragged one leg a little, but that didn't slow him down much. Now that I think of it, it didn't slow him down any.

The whole thing must have been hard on Daddy financially because I know it cost him a lot—it had to. After that, Mother would never let us even give a penny to the March of Dimes because they didn't help us a bit. She felt it wouldn't have hurt them to.

My cousin, Dale Inman, who was a year older than I was, was always at our place. He and Maurice and I were like triplets. He lived a mile or so down the road, but we played together all the time and he helped work on the race car or whatever we happened to be doing when he got there. But, no matter what we started to do, we always ended up at the ol' swimmin' hole.

Every kid that grew up in any rural area—I don't care if it was the South or out in the wilds of Wyoming—had a swimmin' hole where he and all his buddies went. I'd bet on it. We were no different. Ours was half a mile down the road, right in a big bend of Pole Cat Creek. I'm not making that name up, I promise you, it really is Pole Cat Creek—I know it sounds just like it came right out of *The Adventures of Tom Sawyer*, but it's the truth. It was on the Peeler farm and three of their boys—Hoppy, Wade, and Nathan—always went with us. We stopped by to get them on the way to the creek. And Tommy Milliken, who lived on the other side of us, usually came along, too. At times we had a whole bunch more kids with us.

The water in the creek was as cold as ice. I mean to tell you, when you jumped in there, it was like somebody had hit you in the stomach. You couldn't get your breath for a while. It's a wonder one of us didn't drown from getting cramps or muscle spasms or just plain shock. The reason it was so cold is that it was spring fed. It came all the way down from up above Greensboro, and I'd bet that in the fifteen or so miles it flowed before it got to the Peeler place, there wasn't a total of a mile where the sun ever shined on it. Trees grew out over it all along the way because farmers didn't cut their pastures all the way down to the creek bank.

There was a four-foot waterfall that spilled over into a seven- or eight-foot-deep pool and we slid over it all the time, because it wasn't really a drop off as much as it was a natural rock slide. Man, it was fun. And a big grapevine hung from a sycamore tree right at the edge of the water. We yelled like Tarzan every time we swung out and dropped into the water—every time.

You got the full effect of the cold water from that swing. So it wasn't so much that we wanted to sound like Tarzan, we knew what was in store for us when we hit the water. But, after we were in for a while, it wasn't too bad, as long as you stayed in. We only got out long enough to run for the vine or to slide down the rocks. The sliding was a little rough on our bare behinds, but it would have been against the "Rule Book of Kids" to even think of wearing bathing suits at a swimmin' hole.

There was a sawdust pile on Granddaddy Toomes' place, and we played in that a lot, too. Let me tell you, if you've never had sawdust down your back and in your pants, you don't know what agony is. I mean, it will drive you crazy. When we couldn't stand it any longer, we headed for the creek at full speed. By the time we got there, there was a trail of T-shirts and jeans, and the hills echoed with screams as we hit the water. It sounded like bloody murder.

There were a few snakes around, but they didn't worry us half as much as we worried them. Cuts and bruises and poison oak and stubbed toes were a lot more of a problem, but that didn't even bother us much. It was all part of growing up. Listen, iodine and calamine lotion were a way of life.

3

I could slide through the turns on my bike and the other boys couldn't get around me.

I can honestly say that the thought of being a race driver never entered my mind when I was a little kid. In fact, I didn't want to be a fireman or a cowboy or any of those deals kids are supposed to dream of. I was content with growing up the way I was, whatever that was going to be. But, you know, now that I look back at it, Maurice and Dale and I raced everything we got our hands on. It's just that we never talked about becoming race drivers when we grew up.

The first racing started when we were real little, maybe seven or eight. We dug out elaborate racetracks in the dirt and pushed toy cars around them. Most of the time, we even built the race cars. Not many kids around there had store-bought toys, so you had to be pretty inventive. We discovered that you could make a pretty good race car out of wood, with wheels made from pop bottle caps. If we put a nail through the center, they actually turned. We even painted them—if there was any paint around.

We spent hours playing in the dirt, but as I got a little older, that kind of play got so it bored me. I looked around for something more exciting: I found out that I could coast my wagon clear downhill to the swimmin' hole. When Maurice and Dale saw that, they ran after their wagons. The next time, the three of us coasted down the hill. Dale got to the creek first and I remember, just as clear as day, thinking, "There's something bad-wrong here someplace." It didn't take me long to figure out that I would have felt a whole lot better if I was the one who got down there first. I had lost a race, that's what it was.

"I'll be right back, boys," I said. "I've gotta go up to the house." I guess they figured I had to go to the bathroom or something, because they didn't even question me.

"We'll just coast down the hill some more," Maurice said.

"Go to it," I said. It didn't matter, because when I got back I was going to blow their doors off. I had a plan.

I went straight to the reaper shed and got the can of axle grease from the shelf, and I took off each wheel and greased the daylights out of the axles. Then I went back out there and said, "Okay, boys, let's try it again."

Dale and Maurice didn't know they were in a race; they thought we were just playing, but I meant business. I beat both of them by a country mile. "Now, that's more like it," I thought, as I got out of my little red Radio Flyer.

Racing Lesson Number One: If you can get an advantage, take it.

"How come your wagon's so much faster'n it was?" Maurice asked.

"Beats me," I said. "Maybe I got a tail wind."

"Tail wind my butt," Maurice said. "Lemme see that wagon."

"Whatta ya mean?" I said, looking as innocent as I could. But Maurice grabbed the tongue of my wagon and turned it over. It was easy to see the fresh grease all over everything.

"Look at this, Dale," he said as he pointed to the shiny evidence. "Ol' speedy here's greased the wheels."

"So what?" I said. "I just didn't want to wear 'em out." They didn't buy that, of course, and I learned an important lesson that day: If you are going to do something to a race car, you have to be neat about it; otherwise, all the other guys will be doing the same thing. Sure enough, Dale and Maurice went straight to the reaper shed and greased their axles.

So much for my advantage.

While they were busy copying my discovery, I was studying the situation. There had to be something else I could do. And there it was, sitting over in the corner in plain view—a steel plate, just the right size to lay in the bed of my wagon. I knew the extra weight would help me go faster down the hill. So when the boys got their wagons all greased up and they started back for the downhill racecourse, I said, "I'll be right there, boys, I'm gonna put some more grease on mine."

When they were gone, I put the weight in my wagon and covered it over with a burlap sack.

It didn't work. Maurice took one look at it and said, "What're you coverin' up with the sack, Richard?"

"Nothing," I said, indignantly, "it's just a cushion."

"Sure," Dale said. "Let's see under it."

Maurice jerked the sack off. "Get the weight out," he said. "Man, we can't take our eyes off you for a minute."

"You cats sure make up rules fast," I said, as I dumped the weight out on the ground. But I still beat them the next time down. From then on it was racing every day. Well, actually it was more like war. We dug out some of the bumps and made a pretty good racecourse with turns and everything. And crashes—let me tell you about one of the major ones.

On about the fifth day of the wagon-racing season, we all had our racers honed to perfection, so the competition had gotten pretty furious. In this particular race, I had gotten off to a good start. You see, our rules allowed us to push with one foot to the first turn, and then we had to coast the rest of the way, so I was leaning on the one knee in the wagon and kicking like mad with the other leg, and I was going good.

I had beat them both off the line this time, but Maurice caught me about halfway down the hill, just as we were going into one of the sharpest turns—the one that went between two trees. Well, he got right up beside me and we sideswiped each other. We could have avoided the trees if either one of us had dragged a foot, but I guess we thought we could make it—

wrong. Maurice hit one tree and I hit the other. Both wagons stopped real quick, but we didn't. Maurice went flying through the air, out through the woods in one direction, and I sailed out the other way. There were two big thuds and two groans. Man, I was sure I had broken every bone in my body. I just lay there in the leaves for a long time. I wiggled my toes first, and then I moved my arms. I raised my head. Maurice was motionless.

"You all right," I said.

"I'm dead," he answered.

Then we heard the laughing; first a giggle, and then yelling, screaming, laughing. Dale was out of his wagon and rolling around on the ground, pounding his fists into the dirt.

"Listen," I said, "we might have killed ourselves, and you think it's funny."

"It is funny," he howled. "Can y'all do it again? I'll stay right here where I can see good." And then he broke up again.

Racing Lesson Number Two: If you can possibly avoid a crash, do it.

It didn't take long for other boys to start bringing their wagons around, so pretty soon we had some real races. Man, we had heat races and everything. It went on for the rest of the summer, and, I'll tell you, I sure hated to see school start. But I figured we could spend the whole winter planning and getting things ready for the next summer.

It was the last time we ever raced wagons. By the following summer, we had moved on to bigger and better and faster things—bicycles. Dale and I had gotten bikes during the winter—almost-new ones—so the first thing we did when the weather got warm in March was take the fenders and the baskets and the rear carriers off. We got them right down to "racing trim." You could have predicted that, right? Of course, it made them look about ten years older, but it also made them look a lot racier, and that's what we were shooting for.

Right after we got them stripped down, we automatically

started peddling for the racecourse. We didn't have to discuss it; it was the next logical step. Maurice didn't have a bike, so he tagged along behind, kicking at everything and generally being a nuisance. We promised him he could take turns on our bikes, so that made him feel a little better. Not much, but he didn't throw rocks at us anymore.

I'll tell you, that first run we made down the course was something. For one thing, the bikes were about three times faster than the wagons, so that meant that we hit the bumps harder and took the turns faster. I was off the bike more than I was on it. It was clear I was going to have to have practice just to stay in one piece, as well as to win races. Oh, I guess I could have slowed down until I got the hang of it, but that wouldn't have been as much fun.

By the end of the day we all looked like we had been sorting wildcats. And you can imagine how the bikes looked. When I got home that evening, Daddy took one look at my bike and said, "Where's your bike?"

"This is it, Daddy," I said, trying to cover as much of it with my body as I could.

"Stand aside so I can see," he said, moving me out of the way. He looked puzzled. "*Your* bike had fenders and a basket and it had paint on it. This looks like something you got out of the trash heap."

"Well, uh . . . I, uh," I stammered. "You see, we've got this racecourse and I, uh, I wanted to make it look like a racin' bike, so we took a couple of parts off."

"A *couple* of parts?" he said. "You took everything off but the wheels."

"I didn't want to skin up the paint on the fenders and those other parts," I said. "Yeah, that's it—I didn't want to skin it up. And we're gonna put them back on. Soon."

"Well, see that you do," he said, walking away, shaking his head. I could tell he didn't want to know anything else about it.

Maurice pestered the daylights out of Daddy until he gave

in and bought him a bike, too. We helped him strip it down. And then we set out to build a new road course. The one to the swimmin' hole just wouldn't do. We needed something more challenging. We got it, I'll tell you that.

The new course had everything—uphill and downhill sections, twists, turns, jumps. It went all the way down to the tobacco barn and back, so we could make as many laps as we wanted.

We worked for about three days, whacking out underbrush and putting jumps in here and taking them out there. When we finished, we had about as neat a bike racecourse as there was. In fact, as far as I know, we had the only bike racecourse back then. We were years ahead of our time; it was like the BMX courses kids have today—you know, the ones adults build and supervise. We definitely didn't need adult supervision.

Let me tell you, an adult would have passed out if he had watched us. I mean, we really got some speed up on that course, particularly the steep downhill section, just before we got to the barn. But we didn't wreck half as much as we had on the old course; the new one was really well designed.

We had kids coming from miles around, and we really had some wild races; that was good, because it was a lot more fun to beat a whole bunch of kids than it was to outrun just Maurice and Dale. I won most of the time, because I was the one who never held back a bit. I mean, I pedaled as fast as I could, even downhill. Of course I wrecked from time to time, and, I'll have to admit, when I did it was a dandy. I spent about half my time repairing my bike, but that's about the formula for any kind of racing, I was to find out.

It didn't matter, I wouldn't have slowed down for anything, because I liked the feeling of winning.

You probably won't be surprised to learn that, after a couple of weeks, the new course got too tame for us. It was time to make it even more challenging, so we studied the situation and decided to add some bigger jumps and a mud section, right at the bottom of the steep hill—just to make the whole deal more interesting.

We dug up the dirt so it would be soft, and then we carried washtubs full of water from the pump at the barn and poured it in. What we ended up with was the biggest and deepest mud hole in Randolph County.

Man, it was sensational. When the bikes hit the hole, mud flew in all directions. And, for the first couple of days at least, so did we. It was hard to keep the handlebars straight, but if you let the front wheel get the least bit sideways, it was flying time. You went right into the mud hole—headfirst. It's a good thing we had the swimmin' hole; it became the laundry, bike wash, and public bath. While we swam, our clothes dried in the sun, and we didn't look like ragamuffins when we got home. If nothing else, it kept us from getting a whipping every day. I don't think Mother ever figured out why we were as clean when we got home as we were when we left.

"Lee," she said one day, "the boys are sure a lot neater than they used to be."

He looked at us, with one eyebrow raised, and said, "Yeah, I wonder what they're up to?"

He knew there was more to it than met the eye.

There were six or eight bikes racing on that course all the time, and I practiced even when the other kids weren't there—particularly when the other kids weren't there. I worked at it, but it got tougher, because some of the other kids were getting pretty good, too. It was harder to win, so I had to start using some strategy. For one thing, I found out that if I got out front early, it was easier to stay there, especially if I got through the mud hole first. The course was tighter after that and it made it harder to pass. I could slide through the turns and use up most of the track and there was no way to get around me. I remembered that from watching the guys drive the old quarter-mile dirt track up toward Greensboro.

If anybody tried to pass in the tight part of the course, it usually meant both bikes crashed, and if the two lead bikes crashed, the rest of them piled into the first two. There were lots of times when bikes were spread everywhere and kids were scrambling around like mad, trying to get them untangled and be the first back on the race course. You didn't have time to think about being hurt. At least, I didn't. The desire to win far overcame the pain.

The bike racing period lasted all summer—well, for most of the summer, anyway. It would have lasted longer if Daddy hadn't come down to watch the races one day. After seeing what was going on, I guess he figured one of us was going to get hurt bad, so he eliminated a lot of our free time—he gave us more chores, "just to save our lives."

There was always a lot of work to do—I mean, it had never been just play—but, all of a sudden, there was more work than usual. One of the first jobs he gave us was picking up rocks.

It looked like it had rained rocks around our place, so we gathered them in our wagons and put them in the mud holes on the long drive that led up to the house. I felt like I was on a chain gang.

Maurice and I always fought like cats and dogs when we were kids anyway, so putting rocks in our hands was a mistake; a *big* mistake. The minute one or the other of us said something that could be taken the wrong way, it was *thunk!*, and the rock fight was on. Not only that, all of the rocks were scattered all over the place again. And when we ran out of rocks, we threw whatever was handy.

One of us usually got hurt, but you couldn't "go tell Daddy," because Daddy would have hurt us worse than the rocks. I've still got a scar on the back of my head where Maurice hit me with a wagon wheel, and he's got one between his eyes where I hit him with a rock.

It was only when there was blood drawn that Daddy knew we had been in another rock fight, and then he'd lick us both. You couldn't win.

Tobacco-cutting time saved us from further bodily harm—

if you can call that being saved. If nothing else, it was a lot safer than the rock battles. In rural North Carolina in those days, everybody worked in the tobacco fields—and I mean worked. There is nothing in the world that is as hard as messing around with tobacco, any part of it.

Some people might think tobacco is pretty, growing out there in the field with those big, velvety-brown leaves, and I guess it is to them, but if you've ever had to work around it, you sure don't see much beauty in it. It's backbreaking, that's what tobacco farming is.

All of my uncles grew tobacco, so we had plenty of fields to work in. I went down the rows, making holes in the ground with my finger and filling them with water. Then I set the plant in and packed dirt tight around it. I'll have to admit that I enjoyed the mud part. I don't know why I liked mud so much in those days, but I did. If things hadn't turned out for me the way they did, I might have made a crackerjack mud wrestler.

Once the tobacco started to get big, it had to be suckered. I hated that part. It's where you take the little leaves off the stock so the big ones will grow faster. It's also when the whole deal starts to get messy. I had tobacco juice all over me; I mean, it was on my hands, so I wiped them on my pants and shirt, and then on my face. I couldn't even touch anything or it would stick to me. Man, by the time I got home, I was a mess. Mother made me take my clothes off outside and wash off at the pump. The water was always as cold as the swimmin' hole.

But the suckering wasn't the worst part—the worming was. About the time the plants got full grown, the tobacco worms moved in. If you've never seen a tobacco worm, don't bother because they're uglier than sin. They're about four inches long and green. Man, they're not pretty. I had to go down each row and pick them off by hand; that's how you did it then, because nobody could afford the chemicals to kill them.

The ground between the rows was hard because people had to walk up and down there all the time to do one thing or the other, so I'd pick those dudes off and slam them to the ground. *Bam!*, I'd pop them on the hard, old, red dirt.

When you got past the worms and dry spells and all the other things that could happen to tobacco, it was time to prime it and string it on poles. After that, it was put in the tobacco barn to cure. In the fall, when it got damp out, the tobacco softened a little and the leaves could be tied into bundles we called "hands." The last step before it was sent off to Greensboro or some other tobacco auction was putting the hands together to form bales.

There are a lot of things I've missed about childhood, but working in the tobacco fields is not one of them.

Now that I think about it, there *was* one thing about it I liked—dinner. Like I said, it was a family deal, so we had a big washtub to wash our hands in, and when we got the tobacco juice off, we'd sit down in the dirt and eat Vienna sausages and crackers and drink Pepsi. It was my favorite dinner, and, you know, it still is.

I liked the "family" part of growing up. As far back as I can remember, we always did things together—both the Pettys and the Toomeses. I mean, there was a lot of visiting back and forth, and we had lots of picnics and family reunions and every excuse you can imagine to get together. We went through a lot of family rituals. For example, we always had Sunday dinner at Grandmother Toomes' place. And, do you know, there's hardly a Sunday that's come along since that I don't think of her fried chicken and black-eyed peas and candied sweet potatoes.

There was always so much to eat—pies and cakes and, on special days, homemade ice cream. When we left her place, with everybody so stuffed they almost couldn't move, we went to visit Grandmother Petty. It was understood that we were going to eat before we got there and she always promised "not to go to any trouble." But every Sunday when we pulled up, she came out on the porch to greet us, and she said, "Now, y'all can eat just a *bite*, can't you?"

"No, Mother," Daddy would say, "we've already eaten. We couldn't eat another mouthful." Maurice and I held our stomachs and moaned. Mother said, "No, thank you, Grandmother."

She would turn around and say, "That's nice, children. Now, y'all come right on in to the dining room and I'll give you a nibble, just to tide you over." She didn't hear a word any of us said, so we followed her into the dining room, where there was a full Sunday dinner.

Sunday was the day when we never stopped eating.

That all ended when Daddy started racing, because there were races almost every Sunday. And, you know, as much as I've always loved the racing Sundays, the warmest memories are of the Sundays of my youth.

I'd give a lot to sit down at either grandmother's table again. Listen, I'd be the happiest person alive to sit down at both of their tables again.

On the same Sunday.

4

Call it the "law of the West," but those moonshine runners had an honor about them.

To say that I was a product of my environment would be the understatement of the century. I mean, I grew up in a world of fast cars and the constant talk of racing. And, since there was always a car around our place that was in one phase or another of being souped up, I spent a lot of time watching how it was done.

Mother said one time, "Lee, why can't you just leave a car alone? Aren't you ever satisfied with the way they come from the factory?" She knew the answer, but still she never stopped wondering.

"Elizabeth," he answered, "you know I'll never be able to leave a car or an engine alone. Besides, I'm improving it." At which point, Mother shook her head and went back in the house. The same conversation took place about once a week for as long as I can remember, always with the same dialogue.

You know, I think he was making them better, because the feel of power in Daddy's cars was unlike that in any others I ever rode. Keep in mind, this was a long time before he started racing—on the track, at least. But I'll never forget the power of those cars. You could feel it in the seat of your pants first. When he stood on it, there was a heavy vibration that started on your bottom and worked it's way up your spine. By the time it got to your shoulders, the hair on the back of your neck was standing up. It was like summer thunder that you hear off in the distance—the kind you can feel on your skin.

Daddy had a way of driving a car on the highway that gave people confidence, and it's a good thing—otherwise, he would have scared the tar out of all of us. He drove fast, I don't have to tell you that—why else would he spend all that time souping up the engine?—but he drove safe, if you know what I mean. You can tell the minute you get in a car with someone whether or not he can drive. Well, it didn't make any difference if Daddy was going 30 or he was going 90, you felt comfortable. Not many people can make you feel that way.

Of course, all of this was leading Daddy and Uncle Julie closer to the track themselves. They had been going to races all over the area—even up to Martinsville, Virginia—for a long time, and you could see them getting the bug. I guess they were filing away everything they saw from the grandstands, putting it back there in the memory banks for future use.

When the race was over, they got back in Daddy's car and drove back home, faster than any car they had seen race that night. But that was Daddy's favorite deal; he loved to drive those old back roads at night, making the tires *sing*. I'll bet nobody from the races could have kept up with him on those roads.

They carried me along at times, but if I didn't get to go because of it being a school night or something, Daddy always told me about the race the next day. I loved the racing, but now that I look back at it, I realize there wasn't a whole lot of organization to stock car racing. Most of the time, a bunch of guys just got together and planned a race or maybe a promoter dreamed up the idea and had some signs printed, and he put them in stores and gas stations, and some drivers showed up and raced.

It was really the Wild West stage of racing: It was about as unrespectable as a sport could be. At times the hustler/promoters took off with the gate receipts before the race was over, and a few times the race continued over the Carolina highways, late into the night, with the race drivers, madder than wet hens, in hot pursuit of the guy who had run off with the money.

Auto racing was a rough-and-tumble sport—everything about it, from the tracks to the drivers. Even the fans were tough, and there were fights breaking out in the grandstands all the time. I'm not sure if it was more dangerous out there on the track or in the stands. At least on the track you knew what to expect; everybody else was out to run you over.

The tracks were little old dirt deals—they weren't planned, they were just built. There wasn't much to them, but most of the guys racing thought they were on their way to Indianapolis, which was about the only thing anybody could hope for. It was the only race that anybody knew of that was truly organized.

The best tracks we had around the South were the fairground tracks, but, since they had been built for horse racing, they were flat and narrow. That's why there were so many crashes, and it's also why the cars ran right through the rickety, wooden fences all the time. They stopped the horses, but they didn't even slow down the race cars.

But, man, let me tell you, the races were exciting, even if they weren't too professional. Nobody would give an inch, and if one guy didn't get out of the way, they would run right over him. When the green flag was dropped, you'd think war had been declared. They went anyplace there was an opening—in the grass, down through the pits, through the infield, everywhere. There were cars crashing into other cars all over the place. I don't have any idea how they knew who was leading.

Once in a while, a guy showed up who was a lot better than the rest, and he ran away with everything. But the next race, the hooligans ganged up on him and wrecked him. It didn't look like racing would ever get beyond the demolition derby stage.

Daddy and Uncle Julie must have seen more promise in it than I did, because they talked all the time about building a car for the track. Even though I was only about ten years old,

I wasn't sure if it was a good idea to have Daddy out there with those wild men. I mean, it was one thing to sit up there in the stands and laugh and cheer while everybody bashed everybody else to pieces, but it was something else to think of your daddy out there in the middle of that mayhem. But, deep down, I had a feeling that he could take care of himself.

I think the only thing that kept him from jumping right into the roundy-round racing deal was the fact that he was becoming king of back-road racing around the Piedmont.

As Daddy's cars got better, his reputation grew. He had outrun about everybody around Randleman, so there wasn't anybody to race for a while. But, one by one, the guys drifted down from Greensboro to sit in on the bull sessions at Uncle Julie's garage. I couldn't begin to count the times I heard "Put your money where your mouth is." It meant that there was going to be a race that night between Daddy and the latest challenger.

There were good stretches of road around our part of the country, sections where you could really open up a car. There was one down toward Asheboro, for instance, that had a straightaway that must have been five miles long. It was like the world's longest drag strip. Like it? It *was*.

They always raced at night, because they could tell from the headlights what was coming down the road at them. Of course, there was a lot less traffic at night—and fewer cops. Anyhow, they had a much better advantage if a cop ever did show up. Those guys were used to running wide open at night on those roads, and I doubt if there was a cop around who could catch them. They could run with their lights *off* if they had to.

Daddy carried me along if it was on a weekend. I stood right there along the side of the road, with all the older guys, and I was as proud as I could be, because I knew Daddy was going to blow their doors off.

Here's how it went: They got out there on the highway, lined up side by side, somebody waved a handkerchief or an oily rag or something, and it was Katie-bar-the-door! The rubber smoke boiled out from under the rear tires, and the cars were off into the darkness.

The sound of Daddy's car was different from the rest as it disappeared into the black hole, probably because he was turning more RPMs than the other guy before he shifted, or maybe it was just the brute strength of his car. Just about the time I was sure it was going to explode in first gear, you could hear the sound drop to a lower-pitched roar, and I knew he had shifted. There wasn't any pause at all; the sound just changed. When it happened again, you knew he was in high gear and his foot was mashed to the floor until the race was over.

Most of the other guys backed off when they saw a curve coming up, but not Daddy. You could see his brake lights flick on for a second and you knew he had tapped the brakes to bring the front end down and help the car steer better. And then you heard the tires scream as he went through the corner.

It didn't make any difference if it was a road race or a drag race, all the money was on Daddy, because everybody knew how good he was on those back roads.

It wasn't long before guys started coming over from as far away as Raleigh and Charlotte—and then Atlanta. It got so he was making pretty good money as a semi-pro race driver. I'll guarantee you, he was making more than those cats on the track. He would have cleared a lot more if he didn't have to put a lot of it back into the car, but he had to do it. You see, the competition was getting tough, so he had to constantly keep modifying the Dodge he was racing.

They always worried about the cops finding out about it, so they changed the location all the time. They had to, because a lot of people showed up. As the crowd grew, the bets got bigger. Listen, there was as much as $1,000 bet on some of those moonlight races, and Daddy won so many races that he had to repaint his car every week or so, just so the other cats would race him. He knew they wouldn't keep losing to the same car, so he had a different color one all the time.

"Where's your other Dodge, Lee," they'd ask.

"Blew up," he told them.

And then he took their money again, with the very same car. I don't know why they didn't put two and two together—his cars always smelled like new paint.

But if he fooled the other guys, he sure didn't fool the cops. Every trooper and every sheriff in the state knew his Dodge, no matter what color it was, so he had to start driving pretty careful in the daytime. The cops were always on the lookout because they wanted to catch him so badly they could hardly stand it. He knew if they did, they'd lock him up and throw away the key.

The cops tried to catch them a few times at night, but that was a lost cause. I mean, how could they? The cars the guys were racing probably had twice the horsepower of the police cars, so they would just nail it and they were gone. The last thing the cops saw were the two tiny taillights, fading off into the darkness. Those cars were like rockets, so I don't know why the cops even tried.

It's a wonder somebody didn't get hurt—or worse—but I don't remember hearing of anything real bad ever happening. Oh, there were times when they ran off through the woods or rolled, and there was even one guy who drove through a barn, but nobody ever got hurt. Except maybe their pride, but that could be repaired with a new camshaft or some different pistons or any number of things that would give them hope for the next race.

It was at about this time that moonshine runners came into the picture. If you haven't heard about whiskey runners, let me tell you some of the stories I heard from Daddy and his racing buddies. You see, a lot of the early race drivers in the South actually got their start runnin' 'shine. One of my favorite stories was about Bob Flock and the Lakewood Speedway in Atlanta. I guess so many of the drivers had been arrested that the speedway announced that nobody who had ever been convicted for anything could run there. They even went so far as to have a couple of cop cars there, just to keep the moonshine guys from trying to race anyway. Well, that didn't stop Bob. He waited outside the track, until the race had started, and then he just entered the race from the gate on the back straightaway.

He was moving right up through the pack, because Bob was a good race driver. That was his mistake. They noticed him right quick, but like most race drivers, he would never have been content to just hang back there; he had to get to the front as quick as he could. The cops got in their cars and took after him. Right on the track. Here came the race cars and, right behind them, were two police cruisers, lights flashing and everything. It was like the Keystone Kops.

They made several laps and finally Bob signaled to one of his guys in the pits that he wanted to go out the next time around, so they opened the back gate and out he went. The cops went after him. They actually chased him all the way through downtown Atlanta before he ran out of gas.

They gave him a ticket for speeding—in a race car. But it was the only thing they could charge him with, because there really wasn't any law against moonshine runners racing cars on a racetrack.

"Hell, I coulda won the race," Bob said, "if those cops had stayed out of it."

If you want to know the truth, many of the best drivers to come out of the South in those days were guys who had learned their skill behind the wheel of a car hauling moonshine. These "wheelmen" could drive wide open on about any kind of road—as long as there was a reason, be it a fed on their tails or a big bet to win. You can imagine what some of those races between them and Daddy were like. It's a shame they couldn't have raced in some arena, where a lot of people could have watched, because there was probably more skill displayed in those races than in any thrill show that ever was.

You may have heard about a lot of those moonshine runners in later years because some of them became famous as race drivers, but there were others nobody ever heard about again. I guess some of them ended up in jail or they got killed or went straight. There was a guy named Otis Walker, from up in Virginia, everybody used to talk about, and I guess he was a pretty good driver, too. He ran 'shine up there, but I heard a lot of the stories clear down home.

I guess Otis would let a fed pull right up beside him, and then when he figured the guy was going about as fast as he could go, he'd look over and grin, and that's the last the fed ever saw of him. He was gone. He'd do it every time, and nobody ever had any idea what kind of motor he had in his car. He wouldn't let anybody see under his hood.

One of the fellows who used to come into Uncle Julie's garage was a retired fed who had chased Otis a few times. He used to tell the same stories every time he came in, so I had them memorized. I could repeat them as good as he could, and even though I never got to meet Otis Walker, I felt like I knew him.

"I was chasin' him one night," this retired fed would say, "and stayin' up with him pretty well. I had already figured on just runnin' him till he broke, because he was really loaded with 'shine—the springs were really saggin'—and I figured that if I chased him long enough, he would blow a supercharger or something. But all of a sudden, we came up on this running block. You know what a running block is?" he would always ask and, without waiting for an answer, he'd always explain:

"A running block is where they get four cars out on the road, two in front of you and two behind you, and they just block you in and keep slowin' down until they get you stopped. They set the whole thing up with two-way radios. Well, we came up on two cars in front—they were state troopers—and they were doin' maybe 90. They didn't know who I was, because my car sure wasn't marked. In fact, it was a '40 Ford coupe, just like Otis'. I looked in the rearview mirror and here came the other two cars up behind us. I guess they figured we was both runnin' whiskey.

"I thought, 'I don't want ol' Otis to get caught this way,' but I didn't anymore than get the thought in my mind when I saw these two balls of smoke come from behind Otis' rear wheels and I knew what he had done. He had caught second gear, and he was headin' right for the front two cars. He hit the one on the right first, and then he hit the one on the left in the same place. Well, they had been driving about four feet apart so they could use up all the road, and when Otis hit them, one went in one ditch and one went in the other. It was the damnedest piece of driving I've ever seen.

"I figured right then that if a man's good enough to do that, damn if I'll run him till he's crippled. So, when he put it into a broad slide and skidded off to a side road a little farther on, I stayed right on the main highway. The two cops who had been behind us came around the turn and saw me and took off after my Ford. I stopped a few miles down the road and showed them my badge. 'I was chasin' him, too,' I said, 'but he got clean away.'

"I saw Otis a few days later," the fed would say. "He wasn't carryin' any 'shine, so he stopped and said, 'I really 'preciated that. You know, when I slid in that side road, every tire was cryin' a different tune.' "

The only reason I went into that deal is that it sums up the whole thing better than any story I ever heard. You see, it became a game of cops and corn—moonshine, that is.

The wheelmen built fast cars. The feds built fast cars. The wheelmen drove the back roads at night with their lights off. The feds learned to drive with their lights off. And when a runner didn't have a load of 'shine, the feds left him alone. It was a respect competitors hadn't had for one another since the time of the World War I fighter pilots. But just let the feds see sagging rear springs, and the chase was on. And if they caught them, they went to prison.

Otis never got down our way to race, because he died when the drive shaft dropped out of his Ford at about 120 mph. But as the fed said, Otis was really something. "He drove with one hand—two fingers, really. He's the only man I ever saw who drove a wet road just like he drove a dry road."

He and Daddy would have put on some show.

This whole deal of moonshiners and back-road racing gives you some idea exactly where stock car racing was at this point. All of the drivers weren't moonshiners, but they had that same devil-may-care attitude, and the racing reflected it. I'm just glad that, even though I was a kid, I still got to know some of them and got to hear some of the stories. Listen, I could go on forever with the stories, but I won't—I promise. I'll just tell you a couple of them.

There were a couple of guys from Greensboro, I can't even remember their names anymore, who got caught for making and selling peach brandy. The cops arrested them and confiscated their car. Well, these guys got out on bail and broke into the compound area behind the police station, stole their own car, and raced it that weekend.

You know, though, they were nice guys to talk to. They had their own code. Call it the "law of the West," call it what you want, but they had an honor about them. Like Buddy Shuman, who was one of the first really great drivers to become well known after the war. Well, Buddy was from Charlotte, and he had been known to run a little whiskey in his time, so he was out driving one day on the back roads near his home and a deputy sheriff started chasing him. I guess the deputy had recognized Buddy and figured he might be running some 'shine.

Buddy took off—not because he had any whiskey (he didn't), but, would you believe it, because he didn't have his driver's license with him and he didn't want to get a ticket. So he gave the sheriff a real run for his money, until he came to a washed-out bridge. That was definitely the end of the chase. As it turned out, it was almost the end of Buddy.

That deputy was shaking like a leaf when he got out of the

car, and Buddy smiled a great big smile at him. But the deputy pulled a pistol, stuck it right up to Buddy's throat, and pulled the trigger. Nobody could ever explain it, but the bullet didn't hit any arteries or anything. It was some kind of miracle. Buddy carried that scar the rest of his life.

They put Buddy in a chain gang, and he served the time. He could have gotten off because he had a lot of influential friends around—he was a popular race driver, everybody knew him—but he didn't want anything to do with probation. He wanted to serve his time and be completely free when he got out. He was determined to do it right.

So the people who didn't know the race drivers thought they all were a bunch of desperadoes, but they really weren't. Oh, some of them were, I guess, but most of them were guys like Buddy Shuman and Bob Flock and, I'm sure, Otis Walker. They were fun-loving guys who made their living with a car, one way or another.

It was only a matter of time before the circle-track deal finally got to Daddy. The only thing that surprises me is that it took as long as it did. I guess Daddy was doing so well on the back roads that he didn't have time to build an actual race car. Not that his street machine didn't have more power than any of the modifieds on the tracks—it did—it's just that you didn't race a new car on a track. You raced old cars there, because they got beat to pieces real quick.

Right after the 1946 season had closed at most of the tracks, Daddy bought a 1937 Plymouth coupe, and he and Uncle Julie started planning on what kind of engine they could put in it. They decided that a Chrysler straight-eight would do the job, and they just happened to have one in a car out back of the garage. They took it apart and completely rebuilt it, reboring, restroking, and generally doing everything they could to make that dude powerful. It was fun watching the coupe being turned into a race car.

I don't think either of them realized how much money they had put into the car until they were finished, and then they took stock.

"You're gonna have to win ever' race, just to break even, Lee," Uncle Julie said.

"Well, I plan to," Daddy said. "Whatta'ya think we built the car for?" And then he looked at me, sitting on top of the toolbox, and added, "Uh, Richard, it's not necessary to tell your mother any of this, you know."

I put both hands over my mouth.

Daddy had so much confidence in himself that it rubbed off on everybody else. I figured he was going to win every race anyway, so it didn't really matter how much they had spent. But I also knew that Mother would have had a fit if she found out. Daddy had a small trucking business, and she knew some of the profits were starting to be eaten up by the race car. She had no idea how much. But she knew she might just as well try to stop the sun from rising as to try to talk him out of going racing. She didn't even try.

The first race they entered the car in was in Danville, Virginia. All of us were excited about it, even Mother, although she never would admit it. Daddy carried us up there in his Dodge, towing the race car right behind. Daddy and Uncle Julie were in the front seat and Mother and Maurice and I were in the back. I kept looking out the back window at the race car, thinking, "That has to be the best race car in the world."

It was a good car, but the kind of racing Daddy was stepping into was a cut above what they had done on that little track near home. If it had been baseball, Daddy would have been going into at least Double A.

There were a lot of cars at the track when we got there and Maurice and I were all eyeballs. "Man," I thought, "every race car in the world is here." It was, "Wow! Look at that one" and "Oh, boy, look there!" for the first five minutes.

Maurice and Mother and I went up in the grandstands and Daddy and Uncle Julie took the car to the pits. I knew it would be a race to remember. I had watched several of those kind of races before, but this one was going to be different: I had a hero to cheer for.

We got hot dogs and Pepsis and waited for the first heat race. In fact, that night Maurice got a nickname that stuck with him for life. We were waiting for our hots dogs at the concession stand window. The guy handed them to Maurice and said, "Here you go, Chief."

"*Chief*," I said, "gimme my hot dog."

When the cars lined up, Daddy was about in the middle of the pack. I was halfway through my second hot dog, and I don't think I took another bite until the race was over. I was just out there in space, somewhere between bites.

It was a twenty-lap heat, but he got to second place within a couple of laps, and he spent the rest of the time working on the lead car. On the last lap, he went into the first turn, down low. He gunned it and shot past the other guy, and then he crossed up his race car and used up all the track so the other guy couldn't get past. Dirt from the tires was flying up into the stands, and I thought it was the most beautiful sight I had ever seen. It was just like I used to do on my bike course. I knew what he had done.

Maurice—er, Chief—and I jumped up and down. Even Mother was cheering. She tried to make it appear like she was a little disinterested, but it didn't work. I could tell she was hooked, just like the rest of us.

Daddy came up to where we were sitting, so he could watch the next heat race.

"You won, Daddy, you won," I yelled. "It was great! Chief here even liked it."

"Of course, I won," he said, trying to act as matter-of-factly as he could, but we all could tell he was pretty excited about it, too. I will have to admit that he really did expect to win.

It finally soaked in. "Chief?" he said.

"Chief," I said, jerking a thumb in the former Maurice's direction.

After the second heat race, he went back to the pits to start getting ready for the feature. "Good luck, Daddy," I said.

He looked at me and winked. He had me convinced. I mean, I was sure he was going to win the feature.

They lined the cars up for an inverted start in the feature, which means that the cars that did the best in the heat races started in the back of the pack. That's supposed to make the races more interesting or something, and I guess maybe it did, because when they started the race, Daddy and three or four other cars that were on the tail end of the field, blasted past about a fourth of the pack and started banging away at each other and at all the cars in front of them. Two cars got past Daddy, but he was right on their tails and, together, the three of them worked their way to the front. By midway in the race, Daddy was running second.

I could tell what he was going to do next. He dropped down low, ready to broadslide past the leader. He was lined up just right, but just then, one of the slower cars got into the fence and hit another. That started a chain reaction, which eventually involved about a fourth of the field. Cars were spinning everywhere, including Daddy. He slid down into the bottom of turn 1 and hit the rubber tires they were using as a fence. He bounced right back into the middle of things, and somebody hit him from behind.

When the dust had settled, he was still running—although the car was bent up pretty bad. That beautiful race car. He had lost about five positions. After they got all the cars off the track that wouldn't run anymore, the starter waved the green flag again, and Daddy shot past two cars before they got to turn 1. After that, everything just seemed to go his way. The Plymouth was running like a charm. He picked off car after car and, with ten laps to go, he was in first place. I was steering and broadsliding and dodging cars, right with him.

He won goin' away.

I doubt if there was anybody who ever started in a new kind of racing who pulled off the first race with so much ease. All the way home, all he and Uncle Julie talked about was what they were going to do the following week, so they could make it even easier to win. There never was any talk about losing.

They raced at Roanoke, Virginia, the following Friday night, and all week long Maurice and I looked forward to going. I had a lot to be excited about, so by the time we got there, I was charged up. When Daddy won his heat race, I figured, "Man, this is going to be easier."

He started in the back again in the feature, and he worked his way up front, just like the week before. But this time a car flipped in front of him. In fact, it came down on top of his car, but aside from the top, which got bent-in real bad, the car was still all right. He was still running. I figured it could have been a lot worse. We had some extra work to do the following week at Uncle Julie's garage, that's all.

He really had the car moving on the restart, and he was right back up to second place in no time at all. But that was as far as he got. He just couldn't get past the first-place car. He finished second.

When you look at it, it really was an incredible performance—a first and a second in his first two races—but you would have thought he ran dead last. Neither he or Uncle Julie said a word on the way home. Man, it was like a wake.

We dropped the bent-up race car off at the garage and went home. When he got out of the car in the yard and started for the house, I said, "Daddy, you did real good tonight." What else could I say? He did do a good job.

"Good?" he said. "You call that *good*? Hell, I lost."

"But you finished second," I said.

"Richard," he said in that tone I knew so well, the one he always used when he was going to tell me something that was for my own good, "there ain't no second place. You win or you lose. That's the only two parts there are to racing."

It was strange, but I knew what he meant. I was a kid, but it's exactly how I felt when I lost a bicycle race.

"I know," I said to him. He stopped walking, and he looked at me. We both knew that I understood completely. It was maybe the first time I had ever really communicated with him and I did it with two words:

"I know."

5

I guess the country needed the wildness of stock car racing—I know the South did.

Daddy finished third in his third race. It was at Lynchburg, Virginia, and I knew what was going to happen. He didn't even have to say anything. When we got back from the race, Daddy said, "Just park the damn thing out back, out of the way, Julie. We won't be needin' it anymore."

We were out of the racing business.

As he walked up the steps to the house, he mumbled something about "probably finishing *fourth* next week and then *fifth* . . ." He was really dejected. Mother hadn't gone with us to this race, so when she came in the room, she also didn't have to say anything. She took one look at him as he walked past her and she knew.

" 'Lo, Elizabeth," he said. "I'm goin' to bed."

When he was gone, she looked at me and whispered, "Second again?"

"Worse," I said and shrugged my shoulders. "Third."

"Oh, Lord," she said, "did he even bring the car home?" You see, Daddy was predictable.

"I think it's retired," I said. "It's over behind the garage."

None of us thought for a minute that he would stay in retirement, but we did wonder what the next step was going to be. I figured he would be up early the next morning, feeling better about the whole thing, and the race car would get moved back into the shop, where they would start working on it again.

Mother agreed. But he fooled us all. He didn't go near the car again for several weeks. It just sat over there behind the garage.

It turns out that he was right. There wasn't much point in pouring good money after bad in that car. It wasn't as competitive as a lot of the other cars, mainly because they had never built that kind of car before. The only reason he had done so well was because he drove the daylights out of it. The other drivers knew what to expect from him after the first race, and they had more experience, so they did whatever was necessary to keep him from winning. Lack of horsepower and lack of experience give you two chances to win: slim and none.

With Daddy, racing was a combination of excitement and economics. Now that I look at it, everything was. You see, I understood this because I was turning out to be an awful lot like him. I guess that's why I'm spending so much time talking about his racing. I didn't know it at the time, but I was learning a lot from him and from this primitive stage of racing. I knew he was going to change his mind, and that we would be back in it, but this time it would be on our own terms.

Here's why it didn't add up: For one thing, Daddy and Uncle Julie had made $900 from the three races. That might not sound too bad, but, considering the fact that they had spent $4,000 on the race car, it didn't take a Harvard Business School graduate to figure that this wasn't going to cut it. That, combined with the fact that he was accustomed to winning races—you know, the back roads—just didn't make good economic sense to him and he was right. He never came right out and said it, but I knew that he wouldn't have been happy finishing second and third, even if he did make money at it— a ton of it.

"Why, I can make more than this racin' at night on the road," he said. "Besides . . ." and he stopped short.

"Besides what?" Mother asked.

"Nothing," he said. "Nothing."

I knew that the rest of the sentence would have been "I can *win* those races."

All that winter, they raced inside; the car still sat out back. Chief and I didn't go near it. I don't know why. I guess most kids would have been inside it, going *hoodin! hoodin!*, and playing like they were racing it all over the place. But we never did. I still didn't think I ever wanted to be a race driver. I loved hearing about racing and I really liked going to the races, but I was a lot more interested in how a car ran than how a car felt.

Nobody believed me. People were always patting me on the head and asking dumb questions, like, "You gonna be a race driver like your Daddy when you grow up, Richard?" The head-patting part is what I hated most.

"No, sir," I'd say. "I'm gonna be a mechanic and build the cars for Daddy." They always looked at me like I was a little on the strange side, but it was the truth. I wanted to see what made a car run; I didn't want to drive it. Oh, I wanted to drive on the highway, don't get me wrong. In fact, my whole life was aimed toward the day I could get my driver's license. No matter what anybody said, that was the day a boy became a man, as far as I was concerned. It was the track I wasn't interested in driving on.

I spent hours at the garage, watching them work on cars. A lot of them were race cars that other guys brought in to see if they could get some more horsepower out of them. I'll bet I asked a million questions, but I was learning a lot about cars and engines. It would come in handy someday.

It wasn't long before I figured I could take an engine apart and put it all back together again, with all the parts in the right place. As I showed more interest, Daddy gave me more chores around the place. I put parts back on, cleaned grease off, ran after tools, and I filed it all away. I had a dream: It would be painted on the side of Daddy's race car someday, right there in big, bold letters:

Chief Mechanic: Richard Petty

I suppose that's what I was trying to say back there when I said I was a product of my environment. I'll bet any shrink would agree with me, too. And why not? From the time I could walk, I always felt a car was something you took apart—in your front yard, if that's the only place you had to work on it, but you took it apart. And you put it back together—right. You only drove it between the times you were doing all those wonderful things to it.

Why wouldn't I want to be a mechanic?

While my interest was growing in the nuts and bolts of racing, something was happening 500 miles away that would have the greatest effect on all of our lives of anything that ever happened: A real racing organization was formed in Daytona Beach, Florida. We read about it in the *Greensboro News*. They said the new group would "bring some order to the chaos that had been called stock car racing." It was named NASCAR, which was short for the National Association for Stock Car Auto Racing. You're going to hear a lot about it from here on.

Bill France, Sr., and a bunch of guys who had been around stock car racing for most of their lives formed the group. Some of them were drivers and some were track promoters. I had met a lot of them around the racetracks I had been to.

"Maybe we better hold off buildin' another modified until we see what these guys are going to do," Daddy told Uncle Julie.

"I didn't know we were going to build another modified," he answered.

"Aw, c'mon, Julie," he said, "you didn't think we were goin' to quit while we were behind did you?"

Racing Lesson Number Three: Only quit when you're ahead.

The deal that really interested all of us—and I want to tell you right here, I keep saying *us* because I mean us, because

I was a part of it: I lived and breathed what they were doing—was the talk that the new NASCAR group was doing about racing a late-model stock car division.

"Strictly stock," they said and it made a lot of sense. It was right down Daddy's alley. For one thing, it wouldn't cost as much to build a race car, and, for another, everybody would have a more equal shot at winning. The truth of the matter is, we figured Daddy would have a better shot at it because we figured he could outdrive the other guys. If everybody started out with the same amount of experience—none—well, you can see the rest. NASCAR was made for us.

I read the sports pages everyday, the Greensboro paper and the Charlotte *Observer* and every paper I could get my hands on. NASCAR announced that their first race would be held on the old beach course at Daytona. It was going to be a modified race, but they said that the late-model plan was still afloat.

Even though I had never been there, I knew exactly what the beach course was like. I had heard about it from some of the other drivers, and I had read everything that was written about it in the newspapers. Let me tell you about it: It was supposed to be about the most exciting racecourse in the world, mainly because it had a long straightaway down one of the Daytona streets, where the cars went plenty fast. Then it made a big turn, right in the sand, and went back up the beach. There was another turn in the sand, and the cars did it all over again. It was a little over two miles long and the race was going to be 150 miles. The newspaper said all that, but I could just picture the whole thing.

Everybody I knew was talking about it. You know, I guess the country needed the wildness of stock car racing—I know the South did. The seriousness of the war had passed and everybody was looking for heroes to worship. They found them in stock car racing. One in particular was Red Byron of Atlanta. I mean, he was perfect for the role. Even before NASCAR was formed, Red had taken the first step to becoming a real hero in the South, in the 1946 Daytona Beach race. I read it in a magazine somebody brought to the garage. Byron was a wounded war veteran, a tail gunner whose leg had been so badly mangled by Japanese flack that he had to wear a steel brace. His mechanic had to design a special clutch for him. In fact, his left shoe was actually bolted to the clutch. To make things more dramatic, his mechanic was another redhead from Atlanta, who was to become one of the best-known "wrenches" in the business—Red Vogt.

Now, let me tell you, what happened to me next was the biggest deal in my young life: Daddy decided to go down and see the Daytona Beach race. He said he was going to carry all of us down there with him. Man, this was the best deal yet: We were going to Florida. Now you have to keep in mind that people around Level Cross didn't travel much. A trip to Raleigh was a big deal, and the ones we had made up to Virginia to watch the races, well, that made me almost a world traveler with the other kids.

Florida made me something like Lowell Thomas.

Dale and some of the other kids came over the day we were leaving. It was almost like we were going to the Belgian Congo. They waved and yelled as we loaded into the car and headed south. It was a long trip in those days, because they hadn't even thought about interstate highways yet, but we drove straight through. Oh, we stopped for gas, but that's about all because Mother had packed the usual trunkful of food and iced tea for us—enough for the entire trip. So, it didn't take all that long. About 500 how-much-farther-is-it-now-Daddys, as I recall.

We stayed at the Silver Beach Motel, which was just a mile or so north of the racecourse and right on the beach. I hadn't seen the water until we got up to our room on the third floor, so the first thing I did was go over to the big picture window and look out. I didn't say a word. I quietly went over to Chief, got him by the arm, and dragged him over to the window.

"Holy cow," he said, "that's the Atlantic Ocean."

I had never seen so much of anything in my life.

The next morning, on race day, there were people everywhere. The man at the motel office told us that we would be better off walking to the race because there wouldn't be any place to park down there. It turned out to be a good idea, because it was a mess; there were cars stuck in the sand everywhere.

We got out tickets and started right through the sea oats and sand toward the bleachers in the South Turn. There were some signs that bothered me. "Daddy," I said, "uh . . . what about that sign?" And I pointed to the biggest attention getter I had ever seen: BEWARE OF RATTLESNAKES.

"Aw, don't pay any attention to that," he said. "That's just to keep people from sneakin' in."

"You sure?" Chief asked.

"I'm sure," he said.

"*How* sure?" I asked.

"Listen, the guy at the ticket booth told me we could go straight through here. Don't worry 'bout the signs. He *told* me."

We didn't get snake bit. If there were any snakes in there, I'll guarantee you, they left the country once the race started. There must have been seventy-five cars running. I can still see them flying down the beach section, with big, old rooster tails of sand spewing up behind them. Even though it was a long track, they crossed the cars up before they got to the turns, just like our guys did on the short dirt tracks. I got to see Red Byron and all the big names of racing. Of course, I had seen a lot of them before, but never so many in one race.

Late in the race, the turns got all dug up and rutted and a lot of the cars crashed and rolled over right in front of where we were sitting. Some of them flipped in the ocean. Mother was a little uneasy, but I could just see Daddy itching to get out there. Maybe that's why Mother was a little uneasy.

I still have a newspaper account of the race in the twenty tons of clippings I've saved over the years, and, while we were working on this book, I looked it up. The way the writing is, it sounds like it happened a hundred years ago. I'd like for you to read it. Here's what it said about the race; it's from the *Illustrated Speedway News*, which isn't around anymore:

How the drivers escaped in one piece at the South Turn will always be a mystery to the fans who watched the race from that vantage point. It was at the sharply banked, quarter-of-a-mile South Turn which connects the beach and the road where the major crashes occurred.

Ralph (Three Wheel) Sheeler was the first to miss the treacherous approach to the turn and go spilling over the edge of the bank into a sand dune pit twelve feet below. Tex Callahan smashed up on the eighth lap in the identical spot and landed kerplung atop Sheeler's car. In the ninth lap, Glenn (Fireball) Roberts missed the turn completely and capsized. Jack Ethridge, a star driver, lost control of his car at the deceptive South Turn in the eleventh lap and hung on the edge of the sand drop. To make it a full house, Turk Atkins came barreling around the turn in the fifty-fourth lap and he, too, bashed into the other wrecked cars.

The hole neighboring the South Turn resembled a junkyard, three of the cars upside down and demolished.

One crackup at the North Turn occurred in the early phase of the race. Max French drove his car piggy-back on another speeding buggy and flipped over.

That's colorful, but here's what happened in the race:

While all the wild stuff was taking place in the turns, there was even more action in the straightaways. Marshall Teague, who started from the front row, took a big lead early in the race. He was about half a straightaway ahead of everybody else. But by about thirty-five or forty laps, Fonty Flock caught him and passed him. Then Fonty built up a big lead, but that didn't last too long. He came flying down the beach—I mean he was *motoring*—and a wheel came off. His car started flipping down the beach, and every time it hit the hard sand, parts flew in all directions. It must have flipped four times, and it wound up sitting in a palmetto grove about a hundred yards off the track.

Marshall was back in the lead, but Red Byron caught him on about the sixtieth lap and that was it. Red was a smooth driver and you could tell that Red Vogt had his '39 Ford coupe built up real strong. It reminded me of one of Daddy's cars.

And here's something interesting: Marshall ran the whole 150-mile race without a pit stop, but he ran out of gas as he crossed the finish line. He ran second.

One of the best showings all day was put on by Bob Flock, Fonty's brother, who started fourteenth. He was clear up to fourth by the twenty-fifth lap, when his motor blew. Well, Bob jumped out of the car and flagged down his buddy, J. F. Fricks. I guess they had a deal worked out before the race, but Bob took over his car, which was running way back in the pack, and he finished third. That's the kind of driving we all expected to see in the new league.

It had been one of the wildest races ever. There were only twelve cars running at the finish.

It looked like NASCAR was rolling. The organization had been created to help overcome some of the problems in racing—things like the great disappearing acts of some of the promoters and racing conditions in general, to name a couple.

Bill France and Bill Tuthill took over the reins and they started contacting race drivers everywhere to try to get them into the organization. I saw the letter Daddy got. It sounded to me like the new group might help some, and, I'll tell you, anything would have been a help, because there really was nothing but chaos to racing, just like the newspaper said.

The first spring meeting of the new group was held in Charlotte, and they sent Daddy another letter, telling him that they wanted him to come so they could let him and all of the drivers know about their plans for the coming season.

Daddy and Uncle Julie were right there, and they helped in the decision to have a late-model, strictly stock car race in Charlotte. They voted and everything, Daddy told me. It would be the first time that current-model cars would be put on a racetrack against one another—no modifications, just *stock* cars.

It wasn't hard to see the appeal this kind of racing would have. I mean, people could identify with this. With any other form of racing—it didn't matter if it was an Indianapolis car or a hooligan stock car race—the cars weren't anything like you ever saw on the street. This new kind of racing would take street racing to the track. The fans would be watching cars compete that were exactly like the ones they had come to the race in. They'd eat it up.

The thing that sounded particularly good to most of them is that it put the burden of proof right on the shoulders of the driver, where it really belonged. Think about it. If you put two guys in exact Fords, the best driver of the two was going to win. Every driver figured it was going to be him. That's how race drivers are. They may not be long on money, but they sure are on confidence. I guess it's what makes them different from bus drivers or street cleaners, or almost anybody, for that matter.

So many people around home were talking about the late-model deal that there wasn't any doubt in my mind that it was going to be the best thing ever to happen to racing. The arguments had even started. The Ford owners were needling the Chevrolet people and they, in turn, were putting it to the Pontiac fans and the Plymouth crowd. Everybody was convinced that once and for all it was going to completely settle the argument that had been started when they built the second automobile.

Daddy was just like everybody else, he could hardly wait for the race, which was set for June 19, 1949. The purse was going to be $6,000, an unheard amount of money for a stock car race in those days. But I don't think the money attracted Daddy half as much as the idea of driving strictly stock cars. It was like bringing his kind of racing out of the closet. The only question he had was "Which car do I race?"

He finally decided on a 1948 Buick Roadmaster that belonged to a friend of his. He had driven it a few times on the highway—at top speed, I might add—and he figured the big straight-eight engine and the weight of the car would make it perfect for the job. The only thing he had to do was talk Gilmer Goode into lending him the car for a race. It sure wasn't the sort of thing you ask too many people, but Daddy must have had a pretty convincing story, because he sold him on the idea. I heard one end of the telephone conversation. It went something like this:

"Hello, Gilmer? This is Lee." Pause. "Lee Petty. That's right, over in Level Cross. Why, I was wonderin' if I could borrow your Buick in a couple of weeks?" Another pause.

"Well, Gilmer, I'm goin' to Charlotte with it." Then he added the clincher; why the guy didn't hang up on him with the next line, I'll never know: "To race it," he said.

There was a real long pause, and then Daddy said, "Listen, we're gonna not only make you some good money, we're gonna make that Buick the most famous car in the country. Why, people'll be stoppin' you for autographs."

Chief and I were in stitches. "You wanna blow the whole deal?" Daddy said, with his hand over the mouthpiece, motioning for us to shut up.

Would you believe, he talked the guy into it? Well, he did. He even had him convinced that there wouldn't be a scratch on it after the race. "At least nothing we can't touch up right quick," he said.

It was one of the best jobs of selling I ever heard.

When they got hold of the car, Daddy and Uncle Julie took it out every night and raced anything in sight, trying to get used to the way it handled. They were convinced it would do the job.

NASCAR rules said you couldn't do anything to the car except take off the hub caps, tape over the headlights—and take the muffler off. After all, they wanted it to sound like a race. Fans love noise. I don't base that on any study, I just know it.

Daddy had a sign painter come over to paint a number on

each side of the car with paint they could wash off after the race. After all, it had been a street car and would be one again after the race.

"What number you want on it?" the guy asked.

"I don't know," Daddy said. "How 'bout thirty-eight." He doesn't even know why he picked it.

Daddy had used Number 42 on the other car. He picked it by looking around the garage until his eyes stopped on the license plate of his passenger car. Four and two were the first two numbers, so that was it. Somehow there should have been a more exciting reason for picking the number that someday would become one of the most famous in NASCAR history; even though there was a slight detour in the number department in that first Charlotte race.

On the day of the race, we went out and got in the Buick and Daddy drove to Charlotte, about two hours away. Just like on a normal day. When we got to within about five miles of the track on Wilkerson Boulevard, we wound up in maybe the world's biggest traffic jam. We weren't the only race car with that problem. We saw several others with numbers on the side of them, so we figured they couldn't start the race until we got there. There wasn't anything to worry about.

I was really proud to be in that Buick with a number on the side of it because there was just something about this race that made it seem more important than the rest of them. It wasn't called "Grand National" yet (that name was to come a little later), but it was the first Grand National race any way you look at it, and it was important to the outcome of stock car racing. It was Triple-A, easily.

When we finally got inside, Mother and Chief and I went to the grandstands and Daddy and Uncle Julie went to the pits. There were 13,000 people there, and they were wild about the practice and qualifying. I'll have to admit it was exciting. I mean, most of those guys had never even been in a race car before, so they were spinning and crashing—in practice. I could imagine what the race was going to be like.

There was a major problem, almost immediately. The minute the race cars got on the track, and there were a bunch of them, they created the biggest dust storm in the history of North Carolina. It looked like an atom bomb had gone off. There was a mushroom cloud of red dust that reached a couple of hundred feet into the sky, and I guess it was settling over everything in southwest Charlotte. Cars were crashing into each other on Wilkerson Boulevard, and the highway patrol told the track officials that they were going to have to find some way of controlling the dust or they couldn't start the race.

They found about fifty bags of calcium chloride that somebody had bought for a motorcycle race in a storage room under the stands, and they loaded them into a pickup truck that belonged to one of the fans. They drove around the track, dumping the calcium chloride over the sides of the bed. Then they got a big piece of wire, hooked it on the back bumper of the truck, and dragged it behind, spreading out the stuff that was supposed to keep the dust down.

Daddy came up to see us while he was waiting for things to get rolling, and he told us that some of the drivers were still looking for rides. The race would be starting soon, but they hadn't given up hope.

Tim Flock, the third Flock brother, had spotted a couple, watching everything from their brand new 1949 Olds 88 and, do you know, he actually talked them into letting him race it? He qualified third, in fact.

Glenn Dunnaway went through the pits, with his helmet in his hand, until he ran across Hubert Westmoreland, who had a '47 Ford. He needed a driver, so Glenn signed on right there.

"It's probably a whiskey-runnin' car," someone told him.

"Well, it won't be the first time," Glenn said.

By the time everybody had begged, borrowed, and even maybe stolen all the cars they could get, there were thirty-two cars ready to race.

When the starter dropped the green flag, Bob Flock, who had started from the pole, immediately took the lead. Right behind him was Red Byron and then Bob's two brothers, Tim and Fonty, who were relative newcomers to racing. There were two other new names to racing in that area—Curtis Turner, a whiskey-running timber man from Virginia, and Buck Baker, a Charlotte bus driver. Before the day was over, their names would be added to the list of Southern stock car heroes. So would the names of Julian (Tim) Flock and Lee Petty.

I don't know how they did it, but the cars all got through the first turn. They were driving everywhere, trying to find a spot where their stock machines would stick.

One of the first incidents happened when one of the cars spun off the track and into the infield, right into a clump of bushes. We didn't know it for a while, but the car had flipped into a nest of yellow jackets. The driver didn't get hurt in the crash, but the yellow jackets almost killed him before he got out of the car. Everybody figured the car was on fire, the way he ran away from it, and, just as quick, as the yellow jackets would take after anyone who would run over there to see what was wrong. In a few minutes, there were people running all over the pits, and the fans, who didn't know what was going on, thought everybody had lost their minds. They never did get that car back in the race.

But out there on the track, Daddy was moving up through the pack in that Buick. He was just about to take the lead from Bob Flock when the radius rod broke. That left him rolling along at about 80 on four coil springs with nothing to hold it down. The car got to bouncing so bad that it finally flipped, four times. There were parts flying everywhere.

This was another time I was scared. I said I'd never been afraid in a race car myself, but I sure was afraid when I saw his car flying through the air and coming crashing down to the track every time it flipped. It seemed like it was never going to stop; and when it did, it just lay there on its side. I couldn't see any movement inside. Nobody in the stands said a word. Finally, Daddy's head appeared from the driver's window, and he pulled himself up through the opening and jumped to the track. He waved to the crowd. And, man, they cheered louder than they had all day. I never told anybody how scared I was when that crash happened—until now.

With Daddy out, it became a battle between Red and Fonty and Glenn Dunnaway, with Jim Roper from Kansas right behind them. Glenn finally took the lead and the other guys just couldn't seem to get around him. His car stuck better in the turns for some reason.

Glenn hadn't had a single lap of practice in the borrowed car, but he won the race.

The new rules said that every car that won a NASCAR race had to be inspected afterward. That's when they ran into the probem. They found that the car Glenn was driving had altered rear springs. There was a wedge between each of the rear-springs, which was an old whiskey runner's trick. It limited the rear spring movement and kept the body straighter in the turns. The guy who told Glenn that it looked like a whiskey car was probably just joking, but he couldn't have been more right.

They declared Jim Roper the winner, with Fonty second, Red third, Sam Rice fourth, and Tim fifth. When Fonty heard the news, he rounded up the other drivers and told them, "Look, what the hell, Glenn drove the car and actually won, and he didn't know anything about the springs. I mean, it wasn't his fault. And it moved all of us up a spot, so why don't we each take some of our winnings and throw it in and give it to old Glenn."

As it turned out, Glenn got more than he would if he had won the race. It's just that his name didn't go in the record book as having won the first NASCAR strictly stock race. But the gesture showed what the other drivers were really like.

I figured that racing was all over for us. I think Uncle Julie did, too. Daddy said Uncle Julie was as white as a ghost when he climbed out of the car and went over to where he was standing. But the first thing Daddy said was, "Hey, Julie, if we're gonna make it in this here late-model deal, we're gonna have to have a lighter car. That Buick's too heavy."

It took two wreckers to haul away the Buick, because it was beat up so bad that none of the wheels would turn. There wasn't a spot as big as your hand, anywhere on that car, that wasn't bent. Man, you talk about "total loss," that was it.

Gilmer Goode just about went into cardiac arrest when he saw what was left of his car.

"We were doing good 'til the radius rod broke," Daddy said. "After that it sort of went to hell."

Gilmer just stood there, looking at his car, and he didn't even speak.

It may have been the least profitable partnership in the history of racing. Well, not exactly—if you want to know the truth, there have probably been more like that one than anybody wants to admit. But there was no doubt whether or not we were going to stay in racing. Daddy had liked the strictly stock deal so well that, as far as he was concerned, we were in it for good.

He bought a 1949 Plymouth business coupe the next day. That was about the lightest car on the market. It also was one of the cheapest.

The business coupe was the deal salesmen used in those days—the kind that didn't even have a backseat, just a big trunk where they could haul their line from town to town. He figured this would work just fine for them, too. What it lacked in horsepower—I think it had 97—it would make up in dependability. A light car would be easier on parts, he figured.

"If I get out there and take it easy on the car and let those other cats blow up their cars," he said, "then I'll be around at the end of the race when they aren't. You know, they pay first-place money to the cat that's leadin' the race at the checkered flag. It don't matter when he got there."

It was a whole new concept for him, and one even Mother had to agree with.

There wasn't much they could do with the car to get it ready, but he still took it all apart and put it back together: the Petty way. Was there any other way?

He worked on it in the little barn out back of our place. It wasn't much more than a shed, and he couldn't even get all the car inside, so he got some lumber and I helped him build an extension on the barn, so he could at least get in out of the rain. The car was right there; he could fiddle with it any time he wanted to.

I liked the idea, because I could also spend a lot of time out there. But not as much as I wanted. Mother made me keep up my homework, which was a real drag. For the life of me, I couldn't see why I needed any more education than I already had. I was going to be a race car mechanic and they sure didn't teach that in school. If they had, I might have been an "A" student.

I told Chief I was through studying.

"You ain't gonna get by with it," he said.

"Sure I will," I told him. "Daddy'll back me up. I mean, I'm his assistant."

I figured wrong. Daddy agreed with Mother one hundred percent. Can you believe that?

"Your mother's right," he said. "You march right in there and do your homework, boy. You're gonna graduate from high school, and then you can think about bein' a mechanic—if nothing better comes along."

I couldn't believe what I was hearing. *If nothing better comes along?*: What kind of career guidance was that? What did that Roman cat say: "Et tu, Brute!"

"I tol' you," Chief said.

Somehow they managed to get the car done without my full-time assistance. They did a pretty good job on the car, I will have to admit, and I still felt a part of it, even if I was going to be a scholar.

Daddy's theory paid off. He ended up the 1949 season in second place in the point standings, right behind Red Byron.

He drove that Plymouth hard, but not too hard to break it, and when the smoke had cleared in a lot of those motorized gunfights, the fans were surprised to see the little coupe in first place.

A lot of people looked on it as a miracle. They didn't see how anybody could win with that little car, particularly against the big Hudson Hornets and the strong V-8 Oldsmobiles and Fords. But it was simple: He just outdrove them and out-thought them.

And that brings us right to when I got to be Daddy's crew chief.

At twelve years of age.

6

*That's what racing was in those days:
little bitty dirt tracks with a whole lot
of two-lane blacktop in between.*

You could buy a new Plymouth business coupe for about
$1,300. A Ford was maybe $100 more. And if you found a
dealer who wanted his name painted on the side of the car,
you could save another couple hundred dollars. Things were
simple in those days.

That's how it was in NASCAR in 1950, when we got into
racing to stay. There was no doubt in anybody's mind: The
Pettys would never break away from it again, and we were
going to do it *right*—make every race and run for the championship.

Daddy stopped driving the race car to the races. He towed
it on the ground, behind the Dodge that had once blown
everybody's doors off on the back roads of the Carolinas. Towing the car made a lot of sense, because racing was starting to
get pretty rough. There were a lot of cars badly damaged every
race, so he figured that if his car got beat up bad, we would
at least have a way home after the race.

But towing wasn't without problems; nothing was in those
days. I mean, we pulled the car through the mountains and
across some of the worst roads in the country. They were
crooked and bumpy and something was always happening:
parts were shaken off, the car came loose and nearly got away—
you name it, it happened.

There were times when the roads were so slick that we

couldn't get up the hills. You see, the tires we had were almost always worn down, so they didn't get much traction. Worn down? They were bald, if you want to know. More than once, one of us had to get in the race car, fire it up, and actually push the tow car to the top. I volunteered every time. Sometimes I got to do it, and, man, it was fun. The rear tires would be spinning like mad on both cars. It sounded neat, sort of like an airplane coming up the mountain. When I got to do the pushing with the race car, I really felt like I was an important part of the team. Daddy would signal to me when to give it gas and when to coast.

I was in my glory.

Let me tell you why the tires were always bald. To get the car to handle right on the track, they put caster in the front suspension, which means they angled the wheels so that the car would turn left easily. Most of the tracks were so short that the cars were in an almost constant left-hand turn anyway, so caster was the hot set up. But it caused a serious problem in towing; it wore out the front tires on the race car, because it was literally trying to run down the highway sideways, in spite of the fact that the tow car was pulling it straight. So it also wore out the rear tires on the tow car. Daddy bought used tires by the truckload. It was the only economical thing to do. And let me tell you, we economized in every way we could.

It suited me fine. I got to drive the race car because of it. Even if it was only on a back road at night, pushing the tow car, it was still driving. I used to sit up high in that car and wave to people, whether they noticed me or not. I figured I was pretty important.

Another job I had was putting gas in the race car, which was something we always did on the way to the track, at a gas station along the road. Daddy told me exactly how much to put in so he would have enough for practice and qualifying and running the race—not a gallon more. He filled the tow car and I put gas in the race car. The reason he didn't want the race car filled up is that the less gas we had in the car, the lighter it was, and that was important with the Plymouth. With that car, we needed everything going for us that we could get.

One of Daddy's races at Heidelberg, Pennsylvania, turned out to be another highlight of my life, mainly because he asked me to go with him. Nobody else—just me. It was early fall, which is tobacco-priming time and the rest of the family had to stay behind and help Uncle Bud in the fields. It was just going to be the two of us, all the way to Pennsylvania, and I'll have to tell you, I was happier than I had ever been. I'll bet there wasn't a kid in the world who felt as important as I did that morning we left.

It was about four in the morning when we pulled out of the drive to head up north for what was to be the first of many adventures with Daddy. I was back there in the race car, steering, and Daddy was driving the tow car. I knew it was going to be a long trip, but that made it all the better. It was going to take all day, and I loved the thought of that. All day with the race car, out there on the two-lane highway. In fact, that's what racing was in those days: little bitty dirt tracks with a lot of two-lane blacktop in between.

But Heidelberg was different. Like many tracks up north, it was fast, big, and smooth. I figured Daddy could show those guys up there what driving a race car was all about.

That race put my racing dedication to the test. Daddy qualified pretty far back in the pack because there were a lot of really fast cars, but that was no problem. I've already told you about the lack of speed of the Plymouth and Daddy's ability to make up for it. It was a hundred-mile race so there would be plenty of time for his driving skill to get him to the front, which is exactly what he was doing when the crash happened.

It was about midway through the race. Two cars got together in the back straightaway, right in front of Daddy as he came out of turn 2. He had to swerve to miss them and his car got a little sideways. That's all it took. Some other guy came barreling out of turn 2 and hit Daddy in the rear. It drove him right into the wall, tearing the whole right front suspension off the car. They towed it back to the pits on the back of a wrecker.

It was so messed up that we couldn't even tow it, so something had to be done. We had to get the car home. The only problem was, where do you find parts at ten o'clock on a Saturday night? It turned out that this wasn't the first time there had been a problem like that, so one of the guys in the pits told Daddy about the junkyard across the street. He said the guy who owned it would probably come down and open it up. I guess he sold more parts on Saturday nights than he did all week.

"Run over there and get the telephone number that's written on the gate in front of the place," Daddy said. "They said it's down there near the lock."

I took off for the junkyard. As I got close, I could see the little sign that was tacked to the wood frame of the gate. I could also see something else. I was about to learn about junkyard dogs. Inside the gate was a dog that looked about as big as a Shetland pony. No, he *was* as big as a Shetland pony. He had his lips curled back to about his ears, and I had never seen teeth like that in my life. There was no question in my mind that he could bite through that wire without even trying. The heels of my shoes dug into the dirt as I slid to a stop. There was no way I was going any closer, but I couldn't read the phone number from back there. I had a problem: If I went any closer that dog was going to come right through the gate and make a meal out of me; if I didn't go any closer, I couldn't read the phone number and Daddy was going to skin me alive, because at this point, he was in about the same mood as the dog.

I eased forward, an inch at a time, saying, "Nice doggie, nice doggie," and praying a lot. My heart was pounding, but I finally got close enough to get the number and then I hightailed it back to the track, breaking all speed records. I could have qualified for the race—on foot.

"Have any trouble gettin' the number?" Daddy asked, as I ran up.

"Naw," I said. "There's a dog over there that's about as big as a Pontiac, but he didn't scare me. I ain't afraid of dogs."

The man came down and opened up the place. "There's a couple of Plymouths over there," he said, as he pointed into the darkness. Daddy turned on his flashlight and started out.

"Bring the tools," he said.

"Where's the dog?" I asked.

"Thought you weren't scared of the dog?"

"I'm not," I said, looking all around. "It's just, well . . . uh . . ."

"I put him inside the shed," the man said. "He can't get out."

"Aw, that ol' dog don't worry me," I said. "Let's get those parts."

It took us an hour to get the A-frame and the other front end parts we needed, and then another hour to get them on the race car, but we finally got it put back together. It still wasn't perfect, but we could at least get it home. As long as I held on tight to the steering wheel. It was no problem, I was big for my age and I knew I was strong enough to wrestle that old race car all the way back to North Carolina. I was Daddy's crew chief and getting the car home was part of the bargain, no matter what it took.

The weather was another matter. It was about two o'clock in the morning when we got started back and it had gotten cold, so I thought I was going to freeze to death. Oh, did I tell you that the crash broke the windshield out of the car? And that the cars we found in the junkyard also had broken windshields? Well, it did—and they did, too. The trip up there might have seemed quick, but I'll tell you right now, the one home sure didn't. I was learning another rule of racing (they call it Murphy's Law now): Just when things are as tough as they can get, they get tougher.

I know one thing: I'll never forget how cold my hands got.

I held the steering wheel with one hand and blew on my other hand; then I reversed the procedure. I was sure I was frostbitten and that gangrene would set in any minute. Well, it may not have been quite that bad, but I don't remember my hands being that cold ever again. I can still feel the millions of tiny needles in each hand. Nobody ever said racing was easy.

After that, Daddy tried all sorts of towing techniques, but there was hardly ever a time when we went to a race that we didn't have trouble. And we weren't alone; everybody had trouble. In fact, if you want the truth, Daddy's racing operation was a cut above the rest. It might not sound like it, but it was a first-rate operation. You have to remember that it was the dark ages of NASCAR. But like I told you, it's important to my story. Important? It *is* my story.

As unlikely as it might seem, speeds went up and competition got tougher. The drivers got more experience, and you could tell it on the track. I mean, those races got to be something. But the extra excitement on the track meant that there was more to do to the race car when it came off the track. It got pretty beat up in every race. Daddy gave Chief and me more and more to do, but it didn't matter what it was, we loved doing it. And Dale was always there to help, too, so we made him an official member of the Petty Racing Team. Among other things, the three of us were in charge of keeping the car clean, which was a job in itself. After every race, we must have scooped out two five-gallon buckets of dirt from the car. That's how dusty those tracks were. We changed the oil before every race, repacked the wheel bearings, and, in general, did everything that kids could do. Of course, we didn't think of ourselves as kids; we were the crew. There's a big difference. But no matter how you looked at it, it sure wasn't play.

When we got to the track, Chief and Dale and I unhooked the car and took the tools out of the trunk and got everything ready. You can tell that racing was still pretty simple, because we could haul everything we needed in the trunk of the car.

It was at this point that NASCAR threw us a curve. The guys that ran it decided that kids had no place in the pits. It wasn't aimed at us, just kids in general.

"Kids get in the way," they said. "Besides that, somebody's gonna get hurt." Daddy tried talking to them and telling them that we weren't in there to play or roughhouse, we were there to work.

"It doesn't matter, Lee," the NASCAR guy said. "If we make an exception for you, we'll have a hundred kids in the pits. They can't come in."

That would have put an end to it for most people. For *most* people. But all it meant to us was that we were going to have to slip in now, instead of riding right in where everybody could see us. At times we got in the trunk with the tools, and at other times we hid in the backseat, down on the floorboards. Where we rode depended on how much traffic was backed up at the pit gate. Sometimes they just waved the race cars through. It got more complicated, naturally. NASCAR started requiring pit passes to get in.

It was tough to keep ahead of them.

Every crew member had to have his own pass, so that slowed us down again. But only for a while. Daddy wasn't about to let them get the upper hand because he felt we had a right to be in the pits. "After all," he said, "those boys help me all week with the car, so they should be able to go to the races with me, too." So he went around the pits after the race and picked up discarded pit passes, which he put in an old cigar box. They only had about four different colors and they alternated them from race to race, so it wasn't long until Daddy had a complete collection. He would sign in and find out what color pit passes they were using, and then we would wait until it got real busy at the pit gate, and up he would drive. There were a bunch of arms sticking out the windows, each with a pit pass in the proper color for that race. The guy at the gate was so busy at that point, he never even looked at us. He waved us right in.

After we were inside, it was a battle to try to stay there. It wasn't easy, because if one of the NASCAR guys spotted us, he chased us out. But that wasn't much of a problem; we just ran around behind the grandstands and got back to the pits before he did. Most of the time it was Bill France, Jr., who ran us out and that made it worse, because he was only a few years older than we were. But he was the son of the man who ran all of NASCAR. Even then it made a difference who you were.

What a way to grow up! Man, it was fun. You know, it's hard to think of a time when I *wasn't* having a ball. The whole family was, and maybe that's the part I liked most. We were still doing everything as a family. Even Mother was bitten by the racing bug just as bad as the rest of us. She went to almost every race with a picnic lunch and enough food for an army. It got so other drivers and crew members would come over to our car to stand around and talk. They talked, but they had their eyes on the fried chicken.

"Would you like some chicken?" she'd say.

The answer was always the same: "Oh, yes, ma'am, Miz Petty. It wouldn't be a race without some of your fried chicken."

If there was ever a kid in the world who grew up doing exactly what he wanted to do, it was me. Those were exciting, fun-filled days, and I almost couldn't wait for the next race.

We went to Peachhaven Speedway in Winston-Salem and the Charlotte fairgrounds and Columbia and High Point and Greensboro and Richmond—I mean, all over—anywhere there was a Grand National race. Most of the tracks are gone now, and I'll bet a lot of people don't even remember that there were Grand National races at places like High Point and Raleigh, but there were—good races.

About all of the tracks were small, but everything was improving—the tracks, the crowds, and particularly the drivers. Men like Fireball Roberts, the Flock brothers, Curtis Turner, Herb Thomas, and Cotton Owens were starting to make names for themselves. They were getting a real following. But no one had more fans than Daddy. And I was his biggest one.

As far as I know, nobody in racing had ever heard of Darlington, South Carolina, let alone gone there, before they started building the speedway. But all the newspaper stories said that the new track was really going to be something—the "Indianapolis of the South," they said.

I could hardly wait to see it and neither could Daddy. On the next trip to Columbia, we went by way of Darlington. Let me tell you, the track was impressive. It looked so big that I figured there might be different seasons at each end of it, and the banking in the turns was steep. It looked like a race car might just slide right down off of it. It wasn't that big, of course, and the turns weren't that steep, but to a kid who had been used to fairly flat tracks, it was a monster.

The track wasn't paved yet, but the machinery was there, ready to start. The bleachers were almost done, and it looked like they would hold every race fan in the world. I couldn't imagine what a race there was going to be like.

From then on, Labor Day 1950 was marked in red on my calendar. That was to be the day of the first race.

I think I realized from that first visit that racing was going to become big time. We were about to move up to the major leagues.

For the time being, though, racing went on in its usual fashion. We raced every weekend, and sometimes once or twice during the week, and we still hauled everything in the trunk of our car. That's about all there was to it. We had a couple of tires back there from Sears Roebuck and the old bread box Daddy used for his tools—and fried chicken and potato salad. There weren't any spare parts, except spark plugs and fan belts.

If something broke, we went to the Plymouth garage and

got a new one, whatever it was. We were beginning to get on a first-name basis with every Plymouth parts man in the country. But that didn't help, we still paid full price for parts and everything we got. The car companies still didn't see much benefit to them from this new kind of racing.

But I knew there was a future to it, even if a lot of people didn't. And I couldn't help but think that after the stock cars raced at Darlington for the first time, the world would look to the South, and they would see what a lot of us had known for a long time: Grand National stock car racing was as real as any sport in the world—and a lot more exciting.

I was convinced of it.

7

"Leave the taxicab here; I'm gonna race it."

—JOHNNY MANTZ

I never saw anything like it in my life. The traffic must have been backed up to East St. Louis. If the number of cars out there on South Carolina Highway 34 to Darlington was any indication, the first Southern 500 was going to be a success. There were license plates from states I had only seen in a geography book.

And none of the traffic was moving.

We all just sat there and baked in the sun. Car radiators were boiling and cops were trying to get things moving, but it wasn't working.

We had been in Darlington for three days. It was the first time that there had been a race where practice and qualifying were on different days. Before that, we had been like a pack of gypsies; we rolled into town, put on a show, and then moved on. It was almost like a carnival. But this one was different, right from the start. It was big time, there was no doubt.

We stayed at a tourist home, out near the track. I liked tourist homes because they were always nice, friendly places. It was almost like being in your real home, because you always felt like family. We had breakfast there before we went to the track every day; I can still remember those big platters of scrambled eggs and bacon and toast.

The house was a big, old, white frame place with a porch that ran clear across the front. There were three huge rocking chairs on the porch and Chief and I used to sit out there in the evenings and rock away. When we came back from the track we had to sneak up stairs, because there was always some guy in the parlor, listening to the radio. I wanted to yell at the top of my voice, just to make him jump out of his hide, but I figured Daddy would skin me, so I resisted the temptation.

The trip was good from the time we pulled out of the driveway and headed over to U.S. 220 South. Daddy had borrowed a pickup truck to tow the race car because, for the first time, we took extra parts. Extra parts? Listen, we took along an extra *motor*.

"Nobody's ever run a 500-mile stock car race before," he said. "It may go on for days."

He figured that the Plymouth could win, and even if it did blow a motor, he would get into the pits and change it; he knew he would be one of the few with a spare. He would be a step ahead of everybody.

"There's no way a motor is going to last 500 miles at full speed," he said. "So we'll just dump this fresh one in, and we'll be sittin' in the winner's circle at the end of the race. It's that simple."

It made sense to me.

Chief and I rode in the back of the pickup, with the engine and the spare parts and the suitcases. It was a great feeling. Most of the time we stood and leaned on top of the cab. The warm air blowing in my face felt good, except for the times when a bug hit me and then it stung like mad. I learned fast to keep my mouth closed—bugs don't taste all that good. It was a lot more fun, if you want to know, than riding in the backseat of a passenger car.

After we got a room, we went straight to the track, and I'll tell you, my heart was in my mouth when we got there. Cars were coming from all directions and it seemed like every one of them had a race car hooked on behind it. Daddy went into the little shack that had a sign over the door that said "Drivers

Check In Here." When he came out, he was smiling, so I figured everything had gone all right. He looked at us in the back of the pickup and held up the pit passes. "Well, boys," he said, "let's go racin'."

He drove around to the back of the track, where the signs said to take the race cars, and we went through the tunnel under turn 3 and right into the infield. When we came up on the other side, we were smack in the middle of heaven.

Man, it was big. It looked twice as big as it did the first time I saw it because now it had this big ribbon of jet-black asphalt running around it. "Oh, boy," I thought. "We've made it to the top."

There were some race cars on the track and even more in the pits. People were unhooking cars and pulling out toolboxes and running around like mad. Everyone seemed as excited as I was. You have to realize, this was a gigantic day for everybody in racing.

I jumped out of the pickup. Chief was right behind me. The minute Daddy stopped backing up, we began to unhook the race car. He got the toolbox out of the back of the truck and sat it in the pit area where the race car was, and he moved the pickup out of the pits. Mother stayed in the truck while we got things organized, which didn't take too long because there still wasn't much you were allowed to do to a race car. You towed it to the race and you raced. This might have been the biggest stock car track in the world, but the rules were the same.

As long as I live, I'll never forget the feeling I had when he pulled that Number 42 Plymouth out onto the racetrack. I don't know whether it was mostly pride or mostly excitement, but it was probably a mixture of the two because, you see, I really was proud of Daddy. It was great to be a part of racing, particularly at a track like this one.

There were a dozen other cars on the track when he went out there, so we had something to gauge his performance by. None of us were too excited by what we saw. The Fords were much faster, you could see that. Daddy would come roaring down the front straightaway at 90, probably, and they would go right past him like a freight train passing a bum. And then, the couple of Cadillacs that were there went out on the track. They sailed past the Fords. Then the Lincolns and the new Olds 88s with the overhead valve V-8s came out. Man, there were some mighty quick cars out there.

When Daddy brought the car in, I ran over to where he stopped in the pits and started blabbering at him, even before he got his helmet off.

"How's it feel out there, Daddy?" I yelled. "What's it like? How come the Fords are so fast?"

"Hold on," he said. "I can't even hear you with this helmet on." He took it off. "Now what're you goin' on about?"

"What's it like?" I said. "And what about the Fords?"

"The Fords won't be any problem," he said. "We'll be runnin' at the end when they're sittin' right here in the pits. And, as for the track, it seems mighty narrow when you're goin' into turn 3 wide open."

All of the other drivers said the same thing, particularly Red Byron, who seemed to be going the fastest in one of the Cadillacs. As modern as the track appeared, there seemed to be a design flaw in it, right from the start. There was pretty good banking in turns 1 and 2, but turns 3 and 4 were pretty flat, so the cars really got squirrelly when they went in there at speed. Daddy told me that it felt just like you were going to be sucked right into the wall. He found out real quick that the closer you let the car get to the wall, the better you could come out of it in turn 4.

Curtis Turner and a couple of other drivers actually rubbed the wall between turns 3 and 4, but they managed to gather it up and, you know, they looked pretty good. They seemed to get the best line on the straightaway. Everybody was talking about it.

Daddy didn't practice all that much because he didn't really need to. His strategy was simple: All he planned to do was get out there and run about 75 or 80 and stay out of trouble. At the end, he would be exactly where he wanted to be, but he knew that he had to take care of the car for 500 miles.

For one thing, he didn't think the tires would stand up under the high speeds and even higher temperatures. He was right, of course. Some of those cats were blowing tires in practice. So he parked the Plymouth and we went back to the room.

When we went to the track the next day, we were surprised to see another Plymouth in the pits. Johnny Mantz, who had finished seventh in the Indianapolis 500 the year before, entered the car. It was the only time I think that Daddy showed any concern. He knew that Mantz had the same advantage as he did: He was an experienced race driver and he would be doing exactly the same deal, staying out of trouble and waiting for the end of the race.

"That Mantz is gonna be tough," he said. "You watch."

"His Plymouth can't be any faster'n yours," I said, "can it?"

"I don't know," he said, "but just look at those tires sittin' over there in his pit," and he pointed to four tires that looked just like any others to me.

"They're tires," I said.

"Yeah," Daddy said. "*Race* tires."

At that point in my life, I didn't even know there was such an animal as a race tire. Neither did most of the other guys. But Daddy knew the difference, and he knew that he wasn't too pleased with the situation.

Mantz had them shipped down to him by one of his buddies in Akron, Ohio. They were the old five-rib Firestones that had been used on a couple of the cars at Indy. They weren't the best Indy tire, but they had been built to stand high speeds, so they were probably better than the Sears All-States that we had. It meant that Johnny was the only one that had anything that even resembled a real racing tire. It would be a definite advantage. But the Plymouths wouldn't be as hard on tires as the other cars, so I didn't think it would make that much difference. Still it concerned Daddy. After all, he knew more about Plymouths than anybody.

The whole Mantz deal was a funny one. Let me tell you how he happened to enter the Plymouth in the first place: Johnny had come down to Darlington with Bill France and Curtis Turner. They drove Curtis' race car, the Ford, so they stopped in Winston-Salem at a Plymouth garage that was owned by a friend of Curtis. And they bought a black two-door sedan, just so they would have something to run around in while they were in town. They used the Plymouth pretty much like a taxi. Anytime any of them needed to go any place, they jumped in it and took off.

Well, Johnny had expected to get a ride in a good race car, just on the strength of his Indy experience alone, but everybody who had a car at the track wanted to drive it himself. The lure of that big new track was more than any of them could handle, so Johnny couldn't get a ride. He went back to the motel. Bill France was there.

"Where's the Plymouth?" he asked.

"Curtis took it to the Elks Club," Bill said. "Why?"

"Because I'm gonna race it," Johnny said.

"You're gonna *what*?"

"I'm gonna race it," he repeated. "So tell Pops to leave the taxicab here when he gets back; I'm gonna race it. I gotta qualify it today."

It was that simple. Johnny entered the taxi. There wasn't anything else for him to drive, and it wouldn't have mattered if was a real taxicab, with a meter and everything, he would have raced it. He hadn't even told Curtis or Bill about the racing tires at this point. I guess he was saving that until he found a car.

Well, Curtis laughed so hard when he heard that Johnny was going to race the Plymouth that he didn't even pay any attention when Johnny told him about the tires.

"It don't matter if you're usin' racing tires or steel tractor tires with that car, Johnny," he said as he howled and slapped his thigh. "You better call your buddies up there and have them send you a racing engine, too." And he went away, laughing his head off.

When Daddy and Johnny qualified in about the middle of the pack, everybody immediately forgot about them. It's like they weren't even there. The big talk was whether or not Fireball Roberts in his superhot Olds 88 Rocket could keep up with Red Byron's Cadillac, which had been entered by Red Vogt, who was one of the mechanics from the beach racing deal. And then there was Curtis and the Flock brothers and Bill Blair and a lot of guys who were running very fast.

It didn't bother me. I was sure Daddy was going to win, so I didn't even pay any attention to all the talk around the track.

That's how things went through practice and qualifying. The newspapers said that this race would make a national hero out of the winner and double the sales of the winning car. (I figured they were right.) People would be flocking to showrooms all over the country to buy a car "just like the one that won the Southern 500."

And now it was race day and we were trying to get to the track. Little by little, we moved closer to where we could turn off and get to the tunnel to the infield. I could see that the lines to buy tickets were about as long as the line of traffic we were in. There were card tables set up all over the place, with people selling tickets like they were going out of style. Every card table had a cigar box on it, and every box was crammed full of money.

We finally got inside. The guy on the public address system said that there were thirty thousand people at the race—to me, it looked more like thirty million. The grandstands weren't covered then, so there was a sea of people, all baking in the sun. I figured most of them were going to look like raisins by the end of the day. But they were a lot like me: They didn't care.

Mother and Chief and I sat in the grandstands for two good reasons. Reason 1: I wanted to see the race and I knew I couldn't see a thing from the pits. Reason two: They wouldn't let kids in the pits on race day—which, of course, was the *only* reason for two more reasons. Reason three: We had gotten in there the first couple of days only because they had so many things to think about with the big, new track that they didn't have time to worry about who was in the pits and who wasn't; you could have gotten a water buffalo in. And reason four: Daddy didn't need us.

Uncle Julie had come down the day before the race and brought along a couple of friends from home, so they had a pit crew, even if they were just guys who hung out at the general store. They knew as much about being a pit crew as any of the others. Up to that race, there really had never been a need for a crew; one person in the pits could do fine, because there wasn't any reason to pit in the first place. But in a 500-mile race, it was important. None of us knew how important it was going to be until the race started.

Seventy-five cars started that race. It was unbelievable. You've probably already figured out what happened in the first few laps. Cars were spinning and parts were breaking and tires were blowing. It sounded more like the Fourth of July than like Labor Day. There were times when there was a crash on the front and the back straights at the same time. I mean, it was like watching a tennis match. You never knew where to look. One by one, the field was being narrowed down.

Curtis Turner got out front for a while and then Red Byron and Fireball came on strong. Each time one of the really fast cars got in front, something happened. Either he blew a tire or somebody hit him (you can't imagine how wild it was). And while all of this was going on, there was something happening that even the most diehard race fan couldn't believe: Daddy and Johnny Mantz were moving up to the front of the pack.

By the halfway point, Johnny was in the lead and Daddy was right behind him. The race had turned out exactly as Daddy had predicted. The big heavy carts, like Red Byron's Cadillac, were clearly the fastest ones out there, but here would come Johnny and Daddy, tooling along at about 75. Red or Curtis or any number of other fast drivers would blow by them and roar down the straightaway, and then by the time they got to the corner, you'd hear *blooey!* A tire had let go, so into the pits they went and the two Plymouths would continue in the lead.

Curtis said after the race that he knew exactly how many pit stops he had made because he counted the number of blown tires in his pits: twenty-seven. In addition to the racing tires, Johnny had one other advantage over Daddy. Being a veteran of Indianapolis, he was used to pit stops. For one thing, he knew to pit under caution, when it didn't cost much time. You see, if you got into the pits while the yellow flag was out and got back on the track before the pace car came around, you didn't lose a lap or anything, but if you pitted under green, you might lose a lap, or even two. The crews were slow for a very good reason: None of them had ever changed a wheel or fueled up a car under pressure before. But Johnny picked up probably four or five laps on the field by pitting under yellow. Like everything else, it always works better when you know what you're doing.

By the time Daddy realized what Johnny was doing, it was almost too late. There was no way he could catch him.

Johnny Mantz won that first Darlington race by two full laps. His average speed was 76 mph. I know, it doesn't sound like much by today's standards, but it was one of the best examples of driving strategy in racing history—so was Daddy's. Nobody ever again laughed at a car because it was underpowered, not after two Plymouths wound up in the top ten in a race like the first Southern 500. I'll have to say that Daddy drove one of the best races of his career, and I saw them all. Just

avoiding all of the spinning cars had to be some kind of mon-
umental task, but he did it—and, just like he said, that was
the key. He was just wrong about *which* Plymouth was going
to be in the winner's circle. I still think that he would have
been there if he had known as much about pit stops as Johnny.

You can imagine how the hot dogs like Curtis and Fireball
felt after the race. They were madder than wet hens, that's
how they felt. Red Vogt was so mad that he demanded that
Johnny's Plymouth be inspected. He had the right to protest
under NASCAR rules, so they had no choice but to take it
apart.

"There's no *way* a Plymouth can beat a Cadillac, boys,"
Red said. "No way."

I guess the inspection took all night. Daddy went over there
the next morning and they had the car completely torn apart.
Red was pacing the floor, muttering, "No way . . . no way."

The carburetor was torn apart, the exhaust system, the head—
everything. The pistons were out, the valves were all over the
place, even the gas tank was off. They had been to the local
Plymouth dealer four times to compare parts—valve springs,
head, and pistons. They even compared the mill marks on the
head, to see if they were turned in the same direction. Listen,
they got the poor guy out of bed twice.

When they had taken everything of that would come off, Bill
Tuthill of NASCAR told Red, "We've checked it as much as
we can, Red, and we're declaring Johnny the winner." And
then they dumped all the parts in the backseat of the Plymouth
and told Johnny to get it out of there.

As they all left, Red was still saying "There's no *way* a
Plymouth can beat a Cadillac."

"We know, Red, we know," Tuthill said, "but one *did*."

They never did convince Red.

But the Southern 500 sure made believers out of everybody
else. That race was so important throughout the whole country
that every year after that, the car that won Darlington was the
one that all of the hot-rodders and speed nuts wanted. The

people who couldn't come to the race rushed to their newspapers the day after Labor Day to see who had won.

There were many good races at Darlington after that, but there was never an upset like that first one. Well, maybe I shouldn't say *upset*. Daddy wouldn't agree with me at all. Neither would Johnny Mantz, if he were still around. They both knew there would be a Plymouth in the winner's circle.

That's the way *real* racers think.

8

*We never stayed in a place where all
the rooms were hooked together.*

Who was it—Topsy?—who was supposed to grow so fast?
Whoever. That's how fast NASCAR was growing. I mean, it
didn't take any time at all for it to become the biggest sanc-
tioning body in the country—the world, for all I know. And
it was growing in all directions, man, it was spreading like
wildfire. There were races all over—up North, the Midwest,
everywhere. Daddy figured that if he was going to make a
success out of his profession, he had to take the race car wherever they were racing.

"If you're gonna make money," he said, "you gotta be there
with your hand out when they're passin' it around." It made
sense to me.

But, as hard as a lot of drivers tried in the early fifties, there
still wasn't a whole lot of money in racing. Daddy was winning
more than most, but it was still only about ten or twelve
thousand dollars a year. Back then, that was about as much
as a bank president was making. Well, a bank president in
our area, anyway. But it cost a lot in the way of expenses to
make that money. There wasn't much in sponsorships to offset
it either. Oh, you could pick up a few hundred here and there
by painting the name of a garage or something on the side of
your car, but that was about it. The rest you had to make the
hard way—you had to *earn* it.

Economic Principle Number One: To improve your profit margin, cut expenses.

Daddy figured that the best way to do it was to travel light. He could get by with a pit crew of one: me. I won't even waste space by telling you how I felt about that—you have to know by now. That responsibility probably caused me to grow up faster than anything in my life. From then on, I might have been young in years, but I sure wasn't in thought or action. I was always big for my age, so the new me fit right into the old body. I put all of the childhood things behind me: the wagon and bike races, all the games of kick-the-can, and the ol' swimmin' hole were little more than memories of the years when I was a kid. It was a short childhood, but it was a good one while it lasted. A lot of people have asked me if I ever felt cheated by having so short a childhood, and I always tell them the same thing: "You show me a kid who gets to do exactly what he loves most in the world—all the time—and I'll show you a happy kid."

That first summer I traveled alone with him was probably the best year of my life. We started in Pennsylvania and then worked our way farther north, to New York State. And the racetracks were better, too. Down home, like I told you, we were racing on little bitty tracks that didn't have any planning to them at all, but up North, there were bigger fairground tracks, and midget- and sprint-car tracks, and all of them had good, well-banked, wide tracks and big grandstands. There was a permanent feel to racing up there. The reason was simple: There were bigger cities, and bigger cities meant more people at the races.

Up there, racing had been around since the year one, so people were used to auto racing. Listen, there were people up there who had been race fans for generations. Down home, it was measured in months. A lot of the drivers from down home were running up North. The crowds loved it, because it was like the North-and-South deal all over again. They wanted to do it to us one more time. Man, I only wish the War between the States had been fought on a racetrack. You can believe it, our boys showed 'em—in cars, at least.

We had raced up North before, but never on a complete tour. It had always been: drag the car up there, race it, and come home. Most of the time, we didn't even spend the night in a bed, but now we were making a big deal out of it. I mean, we even stayed in tourist cabins and places like that.

Unless you did a lot of traveling in the fifties, you might not even remember what a tourist cabin was. Well, for your information, they were separate little cabins—not only a private room, but a private house. They always sat back in the trees and they all looked alike—tiny, white frame houses with one door and two windows. There was room to park your car beside the cabin. Every town had two or three different ones just outside the city limits. There were so few real motels back then that you almost never saw one of them, so we depended on the cabins. I mean, man, if we ever stayed in a place where all the rooms were hooked together, we were living high-on-the-hog.

But that didn't happen often. For one thing, cabins were not only a lot more plentiful, they were also a lot cheaper. I think they all had the same sign painter, just like they had the same cabin builder. The black-lettering-on-white-background sign was always lighted by a single light bulb. They had names like "The Green Parrot" or "HideAway" or "Fred's Tourist Court—Private Bath—Low Rates—AAA Approved."

Inside, there was a bed with a chenille bedspread that was once white, but was now a sort of off-brown, which had three or four cigarette holes burned in it. For the life of me, I don't know why they all didn't burn to the ground. There was also one straight-back chair, a combination nightstand and dresser, and two towels. The bathroom had a tile floor with a lot of broken tiles, a shower, and a shower curtain with a couple of torn-out eyelets. There was a small piece of paper taped to the inside of the front door that said, "Checkout time: 10 A.M.

Please turn off lights and leave key on dresser. Thank you. Fred."

There weren't many places to stay, period. And lots of times, we left a race and drove half the night before we found a bed. Many times Daddy stopped at place after place only to find that there weren't any vacancies. When it got real late, he just pulled off the road wherever he could get the two vehicles out of the way, and we slept in the car. He liked to stop at gas stations that were closed, because he knew they would wake him up the next morning when they opened, and we could gas up and get on our way early, so we could make the next race.

There never was any time to rest or to stop and see the sights. The next race might be hundreds of miles away, so it often took all the next day just to get there. If there was anything of interest along the way, I saw it at 60 or 70 mph. If the road was real good, I saw it at 90 mph. There were times when he towed the race car as fast as it would run on the track.

Maybe I should have been a hobo, I don't know, but I loved that kind of life. It wasn't easy, but to a former kid, it was about as close as I ever expected to get to heaven, or hoped to get, for that matter. I go back to my original statement— you know, the show-me-a-kid one. Well, here I was, staying at a different place every night, eating at a different place every meal, and helping with the race car day and night. What more could I ask?

Supper was always racetrack food—hot dogs and pop. For dessert, I had a Milky Way or a Clark bar. Fast-food places were about as rare as motels, so we usually ate at a diner— there were a lot of them up North. One in Oxford, Maine, even had a sign out front that said "Yes, we have grits." I felt at home.

We ate most of our dinners—lunch, as they call it in some places—in the diners or in little bitty, small-town restaurants. They were like the cabins: Every one was the same. There was a lunch counter with vinyl-covered chrome stools that spun around, some booths along one wall, and a few tables in the middle of the place. Behind the counter was where they fixed the food. The center of the whole cooking area was a great big griddle, where they made the best hamburgers in the world. Even today, I'd rather have a hamburger made on a grill like that than anything I can think of—except maybe Vienna sausage and crackers.

It was mostly a fun time, even when the race car broke. We looked up a Plymouth dealership, got whatever part we needed, and worked on the car out back of the dealership. They had jaks and hoists and all the things to make the job easier. If we were lucky, we worked out a deal to paint the name of the dealer on the side of the car for that race in exchange for the parts we needed. Racing was run on the barter system.

About the only name we didn't have on the car, at one time or another, was "Fred's Tourist Cabins."

When we raced close enough to home, we carried Chief and Mother along, and, even though I liked the idea of it just being Daddy and me, it was a pleasant change to have them with us.

But it was still tough for Chief and me to stay in the pits down South. The Tri-City Speedway in High Point is a good example: They had watered down the track before the race, as they always did, but this time they really got carried away with it. In fact, it was so muddy none of the drivers could see a thing through the chunks of mud on their windshield. Well, I was watching all of this and on the first caution flag, Daddy came in to get his windshield cleaned. I got what I could reach from the ground, and then I jumped up on the hood. I guess Daddy was watching what was going on out on the track, to see if they were ready to wave the green flag again, and he didn't see me up there. When they waved the green, he turned around and saw me. He motioned for me to hold on, gunned it, and took off for the track. I couldn't believe it: I was spread-eagled across the hood, holding on for dear life.

If he had missed getting out when the green went down, the whole field would have passed him up, so he made one lap around the dirt track and then he came back into the pits, with me sprawled across the hood. He got back out before too many cars passed him. The NASCAR guys couldn't believe it. *I* couldn't believe it. I jumped off the hood and started to run because I could see people coming at me from all directions—every one of them was madder than a wet hen. Man, they chased me clear out of the racetrack.

We left the next day to go back up North, and he never mentioned it. We were on the road again.

I knew all of the drivers on the NASCAR circuit; we were friends, but nobody had much time for personal things. Listen, Daddy and I didn't even talk much, except about what had to be done. He had a lot on his mind, I guess, but there were many times when we'd drive a hundred miles without saying a word to each other. We didn't have to make small talk—neither of us were any good at it, if you want to know the truth. When there was something that needed to be said, he said it, and he didn't beat around the bush. He said what he thought, good or bad.

Of all the other drivers, I thought Tim Flock was the best, because he was so smooth. He was a lot like Daddy. It didn't take me long at all to realize that getting out there on a racetrack and showboating it and whipping a car around didn't necessarily get the job done.

Tim always qualified well because not only was he smooth, he was consistent. He could drive around a track at the same lap-time, lap after lap, so that gave him an advantage: While some of the other drivers were turning a fast lap here and a slow lap there, Tim was moving away from most of them. He wasn't a show-off, like Curtis Turner or Joe Weatherly; he just ran, and when it was over he would wind up winning the race. He was smooth-acting, smooth-talking, and smooth-driving. I didn't know him too well; in fact, he didn't pay too much attention to me, but, next to Daddy, he was the closest thing

I had to a hero. Tim and Daddy ran for the checkered flag at the end of the race more than any other two drivers.

Tim and Daddy taught me *Racing Lesson Number Four*: It's not the fastest car that wins the race, it's the *quickest* one.

The whole Flock family was interesting. I've already mentioned the three racing brothers—Tim, Fonty, and Bob—and I've told you about Bob and his 'shine days, but there were others in the family, too, who were daredevils. I guess their daddy started the whole thing; he had been a tightrope walker, so the kids just followed in his footsteps. There was another brother who raced boats and a sister who was one of the first skydivers. And there was another sister, Ethyl—you're not going to believe this, but she was named after the gasoline additive—who drove race cars whenever she could get a ride.

It was a colorful family.

Tim had a monkey, whose name was Jocko Flocko. He had a racing suit made for Jocko, who actually rode with him in the race—until one day at Raleigh. Everything was going along just fine, Tim was leading the race, and Jocko was having a fine time, but another car spun into Tim and it knocked Jocko onto the floorboard, right over the exhaust pipe, where it was hotter'n blazes. Well, it burned Jocko and he got to running around inside the car, screeching like a barn owl. I mean, picture this deal: Here was a monkey going absolutely wild inside the race car. Tim had to come into the pits and give the monkey to one of his buddies. It was the end of Jocko's racing career.

Herb Thomas was another good driver, but he was sort of a cross between the hard-chargers like Curtis and the smooth ones like Daddy and Tim. If his car stayed together, he was plenty hard to beat. There weren't many races when Herb wasn't leading at one time or the other. If he dropped out before the end, he usually had the same thing to say: "I was leadin' when I went out, wasn't I?" And usually he was.

There were other good drivers: Bill Blair, Jimmy Lewallen,

Jim Paschal, Rex White, Bob Welborn, Jim Reed, Speedy Thompson—a lot of them. But I never asked any of the drivers any questions about driving a race car. You know, tips or anything like that. I figured if I was going to ask anybody, I'd ask Daddy, but I didn't even do that. I could tell what he was doing out there. I knew exactly what strategy he was using in every race, so there wasn't any need to ask. He probably wouldn't have told me anyway.

Daddy switched to Dodge in 1953 because they had a new V-8 engine with about twice the horsepower of the Plymouth, and he figured it might be nice to have as much horsepower as everybody else for a change. It sure would be different, I knew that.

He put a roll bar in the Dodge. Now, that might not sound like such a big deal, but he was the first one to use a roll bar. Everybody used army surplus seat belts and any kind of helmets they could find. There were even a few football helmets around NASCAR. Safety wasn't high on their priority list.

I gave up much of my solo crew-chief duties in 1953. There was a little more money available by then, so the whole family came along again. The big difference was that we went a lot farther away. I mean, we went to Ohio and Iowa and Nebraska, even to South Dakota. I was sure of one thing, I was going to make good grades in geography the next year, because I had been to a whole bunch of those places they had pictures of in the book.

I was surprised to find out that the tourist cabins were the same in the Midwest as they had been in the North. But traveling as a family made it even tougher to find a room. They usually didn't have one with two beds in it, so Chief and I had to sleep on the floor a lot of the time. Man, it got to be a big deal when we had a mattress under us.

We cooked out a lot of the time, and I looked at life as one big picnic, interrupted by races. I didn't know anything about it, but I always felt that we were living a sort of show business life.

While Chief and Daddy and I worked on the race car, Mother helped with the scoring at the track, and I'll tell you, they needed all the help they could get. I mean, in these days of electronic-this and computer-that, it's hard to believe that there was a time when they kept track of the cars on a racetrack with marbles in a cigar box. That's right, every car had an "official scorer," usually a friend of the driver, who was given a cigar box with exactly the number of marbles that there were laps. If the track wasn't really up-to-date, they used rocks— only the first-class ones used marbles.

The deal was, the scorer for each car would take a marble out of the box every time their car came around. That way, they knew exactly how many laps each car had made. They threw the marbles down on the ground and somebody picked them up and put them in a bucket. The next race, they divided them up again, and they were in business.

It was primitive, but it worked. At least, it worked until you got some guy who wanted to cheat. It was easy, all he had to do was yell, "There's a car gonna hit the wall over there!" or something like that, and when everybody tried to see if it was their car or not, he tossed one of his marbles in another guy's box. They had changed the system before Mother started, but it wasn't a whole lot better.

The short tracks and the many races took their toll on the race cars and they got to looking pretty ratty at times. We had to use a sledgehammer to pound out the dents, but the cars looked good from up in the grandstands, so that was all right.

On one trip to the Midwest, our car looked so bad by the time we left Nebraska that Daddy called the people at Dodge in Detroit and asked them if he could stop on the way back and pick up a new body. That way it would be ready for Darlington when we got home.

By the time we got to Detroit, they were ready. They had

taken extra care in stamping out the body and they were proud of it.

"There it is, Mr. Petty," the supervisor of the stamping line said. "There's not a flaw in it."

"It's nice," Daddy said. "You got a place where we can mount it on our car?"

They not only gave us a place, but they hauled the old body away, as quick as they could. I think they wanted to get it out of there before anybody saw it. Well, they just about died when we started knocking holes in the doors, so we could chain them shut. And when we started over the body with hammers and welding torches, strengthening this and beefing-up that, I thought the supervisor was going to cry.

But we got it all put back together, and we headed home.

It was still a lot nicer back in the South, as far as I was concerned. It wasn't any easier, just nicer. One night Daddy tore the car to pieces at Greensboro, so we towed it home and spent the whole next day pounding out the dents and replacing what needed to be replaced. Then we touched it up with a can of spray paint. He won the race at Roanoke, Virginia, on Friday night, and then came back to the track at Winston-Salem and won on Saturday night. The hard work was definitely paying off.

I guess I didn't have a normal sort of childhood: You know, the kind where your daddy comes home from work and you sit down to supper—the kind of life where you do the same things at the same time every day. But I'll bet I had more of a family life than most kids. We were together a lot; it might have been in a car or at a racetrack, but we were together. And everybody had the same occupation—racing. It was also our hobby and our vacations and our picnics and everything else. Fried chicken was our common bond.

During the rare times when we were home on Sundays, like during the winter when there weren't as many races, we visited, just like we did when I was real little. We always went to the Level Cross Methodist Church and then we made our rounds. So, you see, I didn't miss out on a family life because of racing; I had one because of it.

I know a lot of people who didn't have half the family life I did, and it wasn't because their daddys weren't race drivers.

The cars were getting faster and there was a good reason: Everybody was cheating. Don't get me wrong, I'm not putting anybody down. It was something that had been happening since the beginning of NASCAR; it just got more elaborate. As the drivers got more Grand National experience, they naturally wanted to go faster, and the right-off-the-showroom-floor deal just wasn't going to do it for them. It's another occupational hazard.

At first, the guys all took the engines apart and cleaned up everything. They matched parts and polished and made the engine as perfect as the original plans called for. It's called "blueprinting," and what it turns out is an engine that's just like it would be if it was hand-built, which it was, at that point.

The blueprinted engines developed maybe fifty more horsepower than a stock motor, but they were legal. Well, they may have been cheating a *little* on some of the engine parts, but not too much—at least not enough to get caught.

But faster speeds meant more mechanical problems, so, little by little, the guys—we did it too, I mean, we had to be competitive—cut their repair bills by replacing stock parts with heavy-duty parts. Technically, I guess, it was cheating, but I didn't look at it that way; we were not only making the cars faster, we were making them *safer*. And, since everybody was doing it, that made it right. I rest my case.

Most of the early problems had come from the suspensions, so the mechanics began to slip in heavier parts. First, they switched to heavy-duty shock absorbers, and then beefed-up wheels so they wouldn't break. But the stronger wheels transferred the strain to the hubs, which started breaking, so then it was heavier hubs and stouter spindles. All this caused tie-rod ends to break, and when they were replaced, the drag links let go. Part by part, they were building real race cars under those stock-looking body shells. It's an evolution that never stopped.

NASCAR had no choice but to ignore some of this, because the cars hadn't been safe in their original conditions. But they did insist on the motor being stock. They inspected the engine of every winning car, right down to the last nut and bolt.

Anytime you've got a deal where a bunch of guys are trying to outrun each other, you're going to find some of them who are willing to do it any way they can, and if you have to bend the rules a little, well, a man's gotta do what a man's gotta do.

Some of the best mechanics in the world were starting to turn up as a result of it. I'd be willing to bet you that some of the "wrenches" that have come out of NASCAR over the years are the best in the world. They might not have fancy degrees and big titles, like some of the bigwigs in Detroit, but they know more about what makes a motor run and how to make it go faster than anybody. They can't explain it in engineering terms, but a lot of those guys are true experts. Call them "shade-tree engineers" or whatever you want, but they are good.

I was studying everything they did. I already knew the basics of an automobile engine, but I was learning a lot more about the fine points with every race I went to. I had my eyes and ears open, and it was paying off for me. You see, I was doing a lot of the engine building for Daddy.

I'm not saying I cheated, but it sure didn't hurt to know what the *other* guys were doing.

9

The Chrysler I was driving squealed through the turn. "So that's how you do it," I said to myself.

"One hundred and ten percent." It could be on the Petty coat of arms. I mean, nobody had to tell me that was the deal it took to make it in life; all I had to do was keep my eyes open.

Daddy did tell me one time, "Richard, if you expect to make it in anything, you gotta put all you've got in it. I don't care if you're a clown or if you're sellin' pots and pans, you have to work harder than the next guy if you expect to be the best."

I never forgot it. He wasn't one for long speeches, so I figured I'd better file this one away.

I had seen the Petty philosophy in action all my life, because Daddy always worked hard, and then he saved his money. I guess it's why we had more than most of the other race driver's families. Almost all of the other drivers spent their money as fast as they made it; they partied and raised cain and, before they knew it, it was all gone, so they'd go back and race some more. And they'd spend that. But we were in a family business. It wasn't a sport to us. It might not have been a profitable business at first, but we did what we could to make it pay off. I mean, Mother not only packed lunch for us, but she made us save some back, just so we would have something to eat that evening if Daddy didn't win any money.

I'll tell you one thing, a lot of the other drivers went home hungry. It was a fact of life, if they didn't win, they didn't even have enough money for a hot dog on the way home. There were a lot of times when I saw drivers borrow a couple of bucks to buy enough gas to get home. It was a time of eating peanut butter sandwiches and sleeping in the car and holding the race car together with bailing wire for many of them.

By the time I was in high school, it looked like all of that was behind us. Racing was starting to make a pretty good profit for us. I could see the light at the end of the tunnel.

We were in good shape, so Daddy hired some other crew members; they became part of the family. Mother made them "wash up" before they ate, just like she always made us do.

"Cleanliness is next to godliness," she said.

Some of them didn't understand what it meant, but they washed up anyway. You did what Mother said—or you didn't eat. I wasn't even real sure what it meant, to tell you the truth, but I had been "washing up" for so long that it was a reflex action.

The new crew didn't change any of the family's responsibilities. Over the years, I had moved from washing the car to replacing parts to adjusting valves and anything else that needed to be "tuned." With the new organization, I was in charge of building engines. Chief had always moved right up behind me, taking over whatever job I vacated. Of course, we all did everything when push came to shove: like when Daddy blew an engine, all of us worked on building a new one.

I haven't talked much about my school days because, well, they were just about like everybody else's high school days and I figure that if I can't say something interesting, then I might as well stick to racing. The whole idea of this book is to tell you about the parts of my life that border on the unusual, and the high school period definitely wasn't unusual.

My high school days were as good as anyone's high school days, I guess. I went every day, did my homework when I was forced to, and I graduated. In between, I played every sport there was, and I even made all-conference as a guard on the Randleman High School football team. But even that didn't excite me too much. Don't get me wrong, I enjoyed sports, it's just that the cheer of the crowd never turned me on like it did a lot of the guys. I liked the playing part, but if the whole crowd had got up and left, I wouldn't even have noticed it. I would have been out there, trying just as hard to win as if the biggest crowd in the history of sports was there.

As far as my social life was concerned, well, it almost didn't exist, because I spent every spare moment working on race cars. Even during football or basketball or baseball season, I rushed home after practice, ate supper, and then went right out to work on the car—until Mother came out; I can hear her now: "Richard, it's *time*. Come on in." I can't say for sure, but I can guess that I might have been a better student if it hadn't been for race cars, but it's almost sure I would have been a better athlete. It's hard to say about either one. I know that I had a lot more enthusiasm for sports than I did for books.

It was during high school that we moved again. Granddaddy Toomes had passed away a year or so before, and when my grandmother died over the winter, Daddy bought the house I was born in. I knew it would be our last move, because all of us loved that place.

One of the first things we did was rebuild the reaper shed, so we would have a place to work on the race car. We had to put sides on the part of it that was open, so we got some rough-sawed lumber and we boarded up the whole thing. It had a dirt floor, so we worked on the dirt, but that fit right in—we worked on dirt and raced on dirt.

Chief and I had about the same kind of life. He was active in sports, and even though he still dragged one leg a little from the bout with polio, he was a good athlete. But, like me, he came right home after practice to help with the car. Our social lives revolved around an open-end wrench.

It took us about two months of working on the dirt floor before we all had enough of it. It was a mess. I mean, if you dropped a part, you always had to wash it off because it was too dirty to put in the car. Worse than that, there were times when I dropped a part and Chief stepped on it. We had to dig it out of the dirt. It just about drove us nuts. We decided to pour cement.

I'll never forget when Chief and I were mixing the cement in the big trough; I wanted to push him in it so much that I almost couldn't stand it, but I knew what Daddy would do to us. It didn't matter if both of us were about as big as he was, he would have knocked the tar out of us. Still, the temptation was great. But we got the job done without an incident, and we had a cement floor to work on. It was our first real shop.

That shop came at a very good time, because 1954 was a big year: Daddy won the Grand National Championship in a new Chrysler. He had been second a couple of times, but that year he got it all put together and he beat out Herb Thomas by about 300 points. Everywhere we went after that, they always introduced Daddy last: "And here he is, ladies and gentlemen, the *champion* of Grand National stock car racing, Lee Petty out of Randleman, North Carolina, driving the blue Number 42 Chrysler."

It's important to know when I first drove—I mean, on the street. Well, it wasn't actually the street, it was the hay field, where we also worked in the summertime. Everybody was busy doing one thing or the other and there wasn't anybody to drive the old '38 Ford truck through the field so they could throw the hay bales in.

"Richard," Uncle Bob said, "you wanna drive the truck?" What do you call that kind of question? "Rhetorical" or something like that? Whatever, he should have known you don't even have to waste your breath asking a kid a question like that. I was behind the wheel like a shot, and I had that truck moving.

I was five years old.

Of course, all I had to do was go real slow, and the "granny" gear—first gear, in case you never drove an old truck—did just fine. But I had to stand up on the seat and look out through the steering wheel, just so I could see to keep it straight.

From then on, I drove one thing or another all the time. Much later, I even sneaked the race car out a few times when Daddy was hauling something up to West Virginia or some place, and I drove it up and down the dirt roads around home. As a matter of fact, this may be the first he ever heard about it.

Daddy did have a 1952 Chrysler that he knew I was driving, though. It was our tow car, and I used to drive the daylights out of it on the back roads. I was getting close to driving age, so he figured it was all right. The cops knew I was driving without a license, but they didn't hassle me as long as I didn't get on the paved roads. I could drive as fast as I wanted to on the dirt. That was fine with me. I had always been happy on dirt.

We had a pretty good relationship with the cops anyway. They brought their police cruisers over to have us hop them up. The cops around our area had the fastest cars in the state, and we had a little bit of immunity—it was a good trade-off.

Anyway, I had been helping Daddy with the driving when we were towing the car for a long time, so I had plenty of experience. I could have towed the race car by myself, if it had been necessary. But none of that matters to a kid if he doesn't have a driver's license. I mean, the single most important thing to a boy when he's growing up is that little piece of paper that says "Driver's License." It ranks right up there with the Constitution and the Bill of Rights, and it's way ahead of your report card.

It's why, on the very day I was old enough to drive, legally, I was up early in the morning, dressed and ready to go. I shook Daddy awake.

"C'mon, Daddy," I said, "let's go."

"Okay, okay," he said. "Get the race car hooked up and I'll be right there."

"We ain't goin' racin'," I said.

"Well, why you gettin' me up then?" he said and rolled back over.

"It's my birthday," I said.

"Happy birthday," he said and rolled over again.

"Daddy, you gotta carry me over to get my driver's license."

"Hrrrumph," he said.

I could tell he didn't have nearly as much enthusiasm as I had, but I did get my license. Farm kids could get them just by saying that they had driven a farm truck. My life was complete.

It was only after I could drive on the main highway that Daddy gave me any driving tips. He didn't have to, I already knew all that from watching him, but it made him feel good, so I listened attentively. Well, I listened to everything he said. That's part of the deal I was saying before: In the South, kids listened to their parents out of respect—and out of the knowledge that if they didn't, they'd get their ears boxed.

But I will say that Daddy did want me to know how to drive good on the road, so that I wouldn't hurt myself. He even told all my high school buddies how to drive: at speed. I mean, he knew we were going to drive fast anyway, so he figured we might as well know how to do it right.

Two Driving Lessons (first and last): "Stay on the accelerator in a turn, that's the most important thing. It's when you jump off the gas and mash the brakes that you get in trouble. You have to power that car through a corner. Just back off the throttle a little when you're goin' in, and then tap the brakes just a little, so's to set the front end. Then get back on the gas. And always look way ahead, just to make sure what's up there. You gotta know what's comin' up all the time."

Everything Daddy told us was good advice, and Chief and Dale and Ronnie Hucks and a lot of my school buddies sat there with their mouths open, eating up everything he said. I did, too, even though I thought I knew it all. I'll bet all of us were better drivers because of it.

Being allowed to drive made a big difference in my life. I could hop in the car and run into Randleman or down to Asheboro or anyplace, and I was always driving over to Dale's house or to Ronnie's or somewhere.

I only wish I could have driven to school, because by the time practice was over, I had missed my bus and I had to thumb home. Mother didn't like that a whole lot. Come to think of it, neither did I. But I liked football a lot, so it was worth it. Besides, we had a pretty good team, and I found out early that winning sure beat losing in anything. We won twenty-six of the thirty games we played in my three years on the team. It was a pretty good record for a school that only had 250 students. I don't care what anybody says, I have to agree with what Vince Lombardi said: "Winning isn't the only thing, it's everything."

I think I liked the trips to the games almost as much as I liked the games. We went on a school bus, and we sang songs and carried on like we had when I was a little kid, except nobody took their lunch. We ate at the school hot-lunch room a couple of hours before we left, because the coach wanted to make sure we ate right. It was one of the few times in my life when I hung around with kids my own age or did something that didn't involve racing.

I was pretty big in high school—about 6 feet 3 inches and 200 pounds—so I didn't come up against too many boys bigger than I was, and when we were playing the sorriest team in the league one night, I took pity on them. It was a mistake. I was going downfield and I saw this little bitty fellow from the other team, so I figured I'd just let him go. I mean, he was *little*, I didn't want to hurt him. Well, as I went by him, he jumped up and hit me in the mouth with his elbow. It cut my lip open, and I had to sit out the rest of the game. There's a moral in there somewhere.

Dale was a halfback on the team and he was one of the best players we had. He was better than I was, to tell you the truth, and he was faster. I mean, you took that kid out of a wagon and off a bike, and he was pretty good. And Ronnie and Chief played on the team. All the kids I ran around with played every sport. You had to, otherwise there wasn't a thing to do around Randleman—except drive around.

I got to where I thought I was a pretty good driver, too. There wasn't a back road around that I hadn't driven at speed, so you can guess what popped in my head at this point. I went to Daddy and said, "Uh, Daddy, I was thinkin'. You know, I've had a lot of practice drivin' now, and I've been watchin' everything you've done on a racetrack, you know, and I, uh . . . well, I was wonderin' . . . you know, there's an extra car around now—the tow car—and . . ."

"No," he said.

"I haven't even *asked* you anything yet," I said.

"You don't have to," he said. "I know what it is, and the answer is *no*. You can't drive a race car. Wait 'til you're twenty-one. You'll have a lot more experience drivin' a car by then, and you'll have a lot more time to study what you're gonna do once you get on the racetrack. When you're twenty-one, you can race."

It was the end of the conversation. I went back to being a mechanic, and I really didn't think about it again. It was something that was to be filed away for another few years, and then I would just haul off and race.

Besides, there was always street racing.

When they're selling those record albums on television nowadays—you know, the "Hits of the Fifties" or whatever—they always show a bunch of guys and gals sitting around in cars at a drive-in, drinking milk shakes and eating hamburgers, and music is playing in the background, rock and roll music— well, I can relate to that, at least part of it. I never did get to listen much to the music, I never even learned to dance, because I was either playing ball or helping with the race car or racing on the road, but I sure can relate to the cars at the drive-in deal.

I used to drive down to the Circle-In at Randleman or on down to Tommy's Drive-In at Asheboro or to the Blue Mist, just east of Asheboro, and there were always a lot of cars there. Most of them were either hot cars or customized ones made to look like they were fast. We all knew which were the fast ones. You could just listen when they pulled in. The guys would gun the engines and they were loud, because they had Hollywood mufflers or cut-outs, so they sounded good. And when they backed off the gas, they'd pop and backfire.

There wasn't a whole lot you could do to a car in those days, at least, with the money most of the kids had, so they settled on as strong a car as they could afford in the first place, and then they hung a Smitty muffler on it or some deal like that, just to make it sound even hotter. That's why they revved them up as they pulled into the drive-in. It was to let everybody else know that they had arrived with their fire-breathing machine.

The only thing it did was start the b.s. You can picture it: Here comes this dude in his Ford V-8, cracking and popping, and immediately the cat in the Olds 88 says something like, "Anybody hurt in that wreck?" and the argument is on.

"Listen, buddy boy," the other cats says, "I can outrun that hunk of trash of yours *backward*."

"Yeah, but can you do it the way good drivers do it: you know, *forwards*?"

The race was on.

One of the first races I ever got in was with Clay Ruth, who had a really hot Olds. Well, I was in Daddy's '52 Chrysler, which wasn't exactly stock. The whole thing had started pretty much like the deal I just told you, and when it came to the challenge, we loaded up the two cars with boys and headed off to old Walker's Mill Road, down behind where Dale lived. There was a good, long, straight stretch up there.

When we got there, all the boys got out by the side of the

road to cut the weight down in the two cars. Also because they weren't crazy—it was one thing to go out and drive wide open, but to ride along while two other cats did it didn't show much grey matter. We had put a set of wire wheels on the car and it turned out that they weren't in tune. You know, you had to tighten all the spokes the same, otherwise the wheel wasn't true. Well, I found this out at about 95 mph. The car was shaking so bad that my teeth were clicking together. I could have backed off, but Clay would have beat me, so I kept my foot in it. Remember what Vince Lombardi said?

Clay had gotten me coming off the line, but I caught him about halfway down the straight and we ran side by side for what seemed like a long time. The Chrysler was shaking so bad that I had trouble keeping it on the road, but I began to ease ahead. The turn at the end of the straight was coming up quick, but I stayed right in it. Clay backed off. I tapped the brakes just a tad as I went into the turn, and I got back on the accelerator just as the Chrysler squealed through the curve.

"So *that's* how you do it," I said to myself.

The sound of those tires was one of the sweetest sounds I ever heard. I remembered how Daddy's tires sounded when I was standing beside the road and he was racing, and then I thought of what Otis Walker had said about his tires when the feds were chasing him: "Every tire sang a different tune."

It really *was* music to my ears. For the first time, I knew what he meant.

Right after that, we got a new Dodge, straight from Chrysler. It was supposed to be strictly stock, of course, but I always felt like maybe they "tweeked" it a little. You know, just made sure that everything was perfect on it. The only thing on it to show that it was anything out of the ordinary was a tachometer. Most of the guys had never even seen a "tach" before, so one day I was showing it to Ronnie and telling him how it worked.

"Well, I'll just bet you a hot dog that I can outrun you to the soda shop," he said.

"Are you out of your mind?" I said. "You mean to tell me that you think you can outrun this Dodge?"

"Yep," he said.

"Well, you're on, buddy," I said.

I figured he must be crazy. Ronnie had a '36 Ford coupe that was hopped up, but it wasn't hot enough to stay with that overhead valve V-8 Dodge.

But Ronnie had a plan.

There was a plowed field just before you got to the first ninety degree turn, so he took off through the dirt. It was enough of a short cut that he would have beat me easy. He told me later that he figured I would never take the new Dodge through that dirt, but he didn't know about Pettys and dirt, so I took off right after him. It looked like there was a tornado coming across the field. Dust was flying everywhere. I got in front of Ronnie and he couldn't see a thing, so he hit the farmer's plow that was sitting out in the middle of the field, out there where he thought it would be safe. Ronnie totaled it, but he didn't hurt the Chevy much.

By the time we got back to the main road, I was way in front, and the race was over for Ronnie.

"You know, Richard," he said as he was paying for my hot dog, "that's the first time I ever realized that you're gonna be a race driver too."

"When I'm twenty-one," I said. "In the meantime you wanna race back? For the Pepsi."

"I'll just buy it for you," he said. "It'll save us both a lot of time."

The drive-ins were there as a meeting place for street racers, as far as me and all my buddies were concerned. From there, we went to other places—racing places, like the long straight stretch of road over near Robbins or the road between Pittsboro and Liberty or the one over near Seagrove. There were a lot of good ones. There were usually just two cars racing, but a lot of times there were dozens of spectators, cheering us on.

We were racing one night over at Seagrove, in what might have been our last race. The other cat and I had gone down the road a couple of miles to where we had agreed to start, and, while we were gone, Dale and the other guys, who were waiting for us to come back, saw two sets of headlights coming the other way—side by side. It was another race, coming from the opposite direction at full speed. They ran out in the road and got them flagged down and off to the sides of the road, before we came over the slight rise. If they hadn't stopped them, there might have been the biggest four-car, head-on collision in history. And you might be reading a book about someone else right now.

After that, we did everything we could to make the races safe. I mean, we always cut off our headlights before we went over the top of a hill, just to make sure there wasn't something coming the other way, and we stationed guys at each end of the race course. It's still some kind of miracle that nobody got hurt.

When I graduated from high school I went to Daddy and told him that I wanted to buy a car of my own.

"Take the Dodge out back," he said.

It was exactly what I had hoped he would say.

It was a year-old Dodge that he had only used as a race car for a few races, so it would make me a good street car—my own street car. All I had to do was take out the roll bar, find the hubcaps, put headlights back in it, and I was in business. Oh, yes, I had to paint it. I figured the "42" on each side might be more than the cops could overlook. Besides, it did need a little body work anyway. I fixed it up and painted out everything that had made it look like a race car.

That fall, when football season started, I went to every game I could. I even went to practice a lot. Sounds like I really had school spirit, huh? Well, I'll have to be honest with you, there was a freshman cheerleader named Lynda Owens, you see, and she was as cute as a speckled pup. Man cannot live by racing alone.

You want to hear about school spirit? I volunteered to carry the cheerleaders to all the games. If that isn't human sacrifice, I don't know what is.

"I think it's nice Richard's still interested in his team," Mother said.

Daddy just looked at her. "Are you kiddin'?" he said. "He's got about as much interest in that football team as he does in *liver*. He's haulin' cheerleaders around."

That deal didn't fool him for a minute.

10

*I hit the water at about a hundred
miles an hour . . . and it slowed the
car down real quick.*

It's not that I hadn't been interested in girls before—I had—
I just hadn't taken the time to give them any sort of priority.
But, almost with the speed of light, there was something in
my life other than cars and sports: Lynda.

You have to keep in mind that I was new at this dating
game; even though I was a high school graduate, I didn't know
what to *do*. It was a lot tougher than building engines. So we
went to the drive-ins a lot—I didn't know anyplace else. And,
I want you to know, I didn't race—can you believe that?
Scratch that question.

We sat in my convertible and drank milk shakes and ate
hamburgers. And the guys all needled me unmercifully.

"Hey, Richard," they'd yell. "What's the matter? Won't
your sweetie let you race anymore? We dare you, Richard."
And then they'd all laugh like mad. Lynda was proud of me
because I resisted the dares; I was, too. In fact, now that I
think about it, I'm more surprised than proud.

The movie changed only about once a week in Randleman,
but we were always there for the new one, and we went to
Greensboro a couple of times a week, too. There were a lot
of theaters there, so, many times we went to two movies a
night. I could have gotten a job on the newspapers as a movie
reviewer.

On weekends, I still carried all the cheerleaders to the games.

119

When there wasn't a game, and in between movies and sports, I spent a lot of time at Lynda's house, playing gin rummy. I picked her up almost every night and we did something—even if it was just driving around. I've mentioned that before, but it's important to understand that people in small towns do drive around a lot. I mean, you don't go anywhere, you just drive around. Everybody does it.

I even took Lynda with me when I went to Winston-Salem or High Point or Greensboro to get race car parts. She waited in the car while I went in to get the parts, and more times than not I got to talking racing and, I swear, I forgot all about her out there in my car. She must have really liked me, because she never even got upset. I guess she understood how important racing was to me. She never once tried to change anything I did. For one thing, she was interested in racing. I guess that was almost mandatory if she was going to be involved with a Petty.

For the first time in my life, I liked being at home almost as much as I liked being at a track somewhere. But that didn't keep me from traveling. If anything, I was traveling more. In fact, it was about then that Daddy sent me on one of the biggest trips I had ever been on.

He raced up North one weekend and three days later, he had to run at Bay Meadows, which was just outside of Oakland. It gives you some idea how much the stock car deal had expanded. I mean, I'm talking Oakland, *California*.

He had some kind of deal with Chrysler that he had to handle in Detroit, so he told me to drive the race car to California. That's right, *drive* it to the West Coast. I don't have to tell you, it was all right with me.

The car sat up high because of the stiff springing; in addition to that, man, it was loud. We made a makeshift sort of street exhaust system by cutting an old Ford truck muffler in two and hanging half on each open pipe of the Dodge. It quieted it down a little. This way it only sounded like a semi. The way we raced it, it sounded like a fleet of semis.

I ran about 100 mph, clear across North Carolina, but I had to stop in Gaffney, South Carolina, because there was a big rainstorm. You see, the car didn't have windshield wipers, so I slid into a gas station and put some on. Race cars didn't have any more need for wipers than they did for mufflers.

From Gaffney, I did pretty well until I got to the other side of Dallas, Texas. Three police cars pulled me over—three. They made me get out of the car, and they spread-eagled me across the hood and frisked me.

The deal was, they thought I was hauling moonshine (I guess because of the high springs and all and the fact that the car just didn't look right). I sure didn't tell them it was a race car.

"Where you goin' kid?" one of them asked. He was looking in the car at the time. "And where's your backseat?"

It was looking more and more like a whiskey-running car.

"I'm goin' to California, officer," I said. "My older sister's sick, and I'm goin' there to take care of her." The seat? "Uh, I had to sell the backseat to get money for gas." It was the best I could do on short notice.

They didn't believe the story for a minute, but they let me go. I eased out of there as quiet as I could, and when I couldn't see them in the rearview mirror anymore, I nailed it. I was back up to a hundred in no time. Somewhere in the desert— I didn't even know where it was at the time, so I sure don't now—I came up on this sign that said simply "Arroyo."

"Wonder what that means?" I thought.

But I didn't have much time to wonder, because I found out real quick. I've never forgotten that word, even though it's only used out west—and maybe Mexico—I really don't know, but, as it turns out, an *arroyo* is a dry creek bed. They put the signs up because it not only means a dip in the road, it means that there might be water in it. It doesn't rain much in the desert (otherwise it wouldn't be a desert—how'd I get into this?), but, when it does, the water runs out of the hills like a dam broke and fills the arroyos. It had rained in the mountains.

There was about four feet of water in this one, and I hit it at about 100 mph. I couldn't see a thing for a few seconds. I mean, the car was completely engulfed in water and the spray must have been visible back home. It slowed the car down real quick, because hitting water is like running into a haystack. It's not as bad as a brick wall, but it's a whole lot worse than fog.

The car sputtered to a stop just past what I figured had to have been the Colorado River. I didn't even try to restart it. I knew there wasn't any use. There was water running out of everywhere. I let it drip-dry for a couple of minutes and then I got out and raised the hood. Everything was steaming in there.

I took off the distributor cap, dried off the points and everything in there, and then I dried the plug wires, one at a time. I took the air cleaner off to see if any water had gotten in the carburetor. It hadn't, so I figured I was all right. (I needed a bath anyway, so I wrote it off as the world's fastest shower.)

At the Arizona-California border, I had to stop for an agriculture check. I guess they don't want anybody hauling any fruit into California that was grown in Arizona. They have one on the other side, too, you know, the California-Arizona side, and those guys from Arizona aren't too crazy about having anything in their state that was grown in California—including Californians.

The trunk of a stock car is bolted down, and, naturally, that's exactly where they wanted to look. I had to get out and unbolt it, so they could inspect it. There wasn't anything inside but a big, old jack and some spare wheels and tires and Daddy's toolbox.

"Expectin' to break down?" the guy asked.

"No, sir," I said. "I'm goin' to California to open a garage." I was getting better. That almost made sense.

You may wonder what the importance of one race could be

to require all this fuss. Well, the NASCAR points were important. The more races you ran, the better chance you stood of winning the championship, that's basic math. Both Tim Flock and Buck Baker were ahead of Daddy in points, and he needed to get as many as he could. You see, by then, it meant several thousand dollars more to win the championship. There was a pretty big point fund, so everybody worked like mad to win it. Of course, it paid off on a sliding scale, all the way down to maybe tenth place, but Daddy wanted to be first again at the end of the season. I did, too.

He finished third in the race. I wondered if the trip was worth it. I was now thinking like a racer. I mean, I would have been excited about third at one time, but now it meant "you lose" to me.

The trip back was uneventful. That's the only word I can think to describe it. I drove 100 mph all the way back, except through towns, and then I cut it down to about 70, unless it was late at night.

I got all the way back to Harrisburg, North Carolina, before I got stopped. I guess the cop had been chasing me for about fifteen miles before he caught me. The only reason he did was I had to stop for gas. He came sliding into the station, and he got out of the car, all red-faced and huffing and puffing. I thought he was going to shoot me. I didn't see him when I went by at 100. I got a ticket.

I had driven all the way to California and back without a ticket. Well, to within seventy-five miles of home, anyway.

It was like blowing an engine on the last lap of a race—a 6,000-mile race. In spite of the brush with the Dallas cops and the dip in the arroyo and the ticket coming back, I still managed to make it in thirty-nine hours each way. It's a shame they didn't have that coast-to-coast race that came along in later years.

The following week, we ran at Darlington—two cars. Yep, we had expanded the operation. Marvin Panch drove the second car and ran third with it. In fact, he finished ahead of

Daddy, who blew a tire and fell way back in the latter stages of the race.

Right after the race, Uncle Julie hopped in Daddy's race car and I got in the one Marvin had driven and we took off for home. We were driving fast so that we could get home before it got dark, because we didn't have any headlights. I got stopped for speeding; don't ask me how Uncle Julie avoided it, I guess it was just my period for cops. Well, when the cop looked at the car, he went crazy. It didn't have any of the things the highway patrol had learned to love: you know, headlights, mufflers, windshield wipers, horn—none of those luxury items. In addition to the speeding ticket, he escorted me straight to a gas station to have all that stuff installed. It was very late when I got home and I could hardly wait to get to bed, but there had been a phone call. They wanted the car back at the track for inspection. Some idiot had protested the first three finishers. I had to get back in it and drive all the way back to Darlington. It may sound like ours was a shoestring operation, but we were more first class than most of the teams, I promise.

Carl Kiekhaefer had a lot of money. In fact, he may have been the first millionaire ever to come into NASCAR racing, at least that anybody knew about. You sure knew it about Carl, though, because of the kind of show he put on. He made his money building and selling Mercury outboard engines. There was "Mercury Outboards" painted all over the sides of his white trucks and white race cars.

When he came to NASCAR in 1955 it was like someone had booked Ringling Brothers and Barnum and Bailey. Nobody in racing ever saw anything like it. Keep in mind, up to this point, if a whole crew had on clean jeans and shirts that even remotely resembled each other, it was considered classy. And if a guy hauled his race car to the track on the back of a flatbed truck, well, man, everybody in the place talked about it, from the pits to the grandstands.

So when Kiekhaefer showed up with not only a whole fleet of the hot new Chrysler 300s, but box vans to carry them in, it was the biggest thing that had happened in the history of stock car racing. They even had a separate box van for parts and equipment—everything from spark plugs to spare engines.

The entire crew for every car had identical uniforms that were washed and starched for each race. Even his drivers had uniforms. This, too, was a first. Up to then, the drivers wore whatever they felt like wearing. Daddy, for instance, always wore a pair of cotton pants and a short-sleeve sport shirt. A lot of the guys wore jeans and T-shirts.

It got so that when the big Kiekhaefer trucks would roll in, some of the other teams would just about give up. It always made us more determined. Daddy was driving a Chrysler 300 too, and we might not have looked as impressive as all those guys running around in white, but we still weren't intimidated by them.

I'll have to admit that it was hard to ignore a deal like that.

One night it got so dusty that Kiekhaefer sent his guys down in the corners with flashlights—just inside the turns, so they wouldn't get run over. The guy was all heart. When they saw one of the big, white Chryslers coming, they'd turn the lights on, and, when he went on by, they'd turn them off. They were the only cars that could tell where the turns were.

Dust was a problem in those early races, and it wasn't always as easy to overcome as sending somebody off to the corner with a flashlight. It was so bad one night in Oklahoma City that Daddy came down the straightaway, stopped his car, got out, grabbed the red flag from the starter's rack, and actually stopped the race himself.

And another time, it was so dusty that nobody could see a thing. Everybody was just following everybody else. Well, Buck Baker was behind some guy who kept going slower and slower. Finally he stopped completely, and Buck ran into the back of him. Buck got out of his car and yelled:

"Why the hell did you stop?" ·

"Buck, I'm in the *pits*," the guy said.

The guy had decided to hang it up and Buck had followed him right up to his truck.

A lot of things happened to Buck. In one of those dusty races, he ran clear through the board fence one night, right out into the parking lot. He waited in his car and nobody came to check on him. He was mad as he could be when he walked back to the scoring stand.

"Why didn't nobody come and check on me?" he said. "Hell, I coulda been hurt."

They all looked at each other in amazement.

"We didn't even know you were out of the race, Buck," one of them said.

It was almost never peaches and cream. Rex White ran Daddy into the wall on purpose one night, and I was so mad I went after him when the race was over. I was only sixteen, but I was big for my age, and Rex was a little bitty man. I picked him up about a foot off the ground, and I was talking right into his face.

"Go ahead and hit me," he said. "You're bigger'n me."

Well, that tickled me. Here was this grown man—well, man, anyway—and he was saying "you're bigger'n me." I was ready to put him down when, all of a sudden, some guy came up behind me and hit Rex in the nose from over my left shoulder. It knocked him clear into the bushes. I guess it was one of Daddy's fans. I never did know who it was.

One of my favorite races of that season was in Winston-Salem. Tim and Fonty Flock were driving Kiekhaefer Chryslers and Daddy blew their doors off. Well, Kiekhaefer was so mad that he actually ran out on the track and tied the hood of Daddy's car down with a piece of wire.

"I'm protesting the race," he yelled.

He could do that, under the rules. So we had to take the car to a garage in town, so the NASCAR guys could inspect it. I was worried because I knew the carburetor wasn't exactly stock, but Daddy didn't show a bit of concern as we waited beside the car outside of the garage, while they got ready. We had carried Ronnie Hucks to the race with us, so Daddy said, "Ronnie, you just get under the car there, with your legs sticking out, and you stay there 'til I tell you to come out."

Daddy unwired the hood and was taking the carb off when one of the NASCAR guys stuck his head out and yelled, "Bring it on in, Lee."

"Just a minute, buddy," Daddy said, "we're drainin' the water out of the car and this kid don't know what he's doin'. We'll have it right in there."

The guy went back inside and Daddy switched the carburetor. And once we got the car inside, Daddy told Ronnie and me to change the rear end if we got a chance. Well, the first thing they did was take the carburetor off, the one Daddy had put on the car while it was outside—the legit one. They took it in the other room to check it against a stock carb they had laid out on the table in there. You see, the carburetor was the thing most of the driver's changed, so the first step in any inspection was to tear the carb apart and check everything. Daddy winked at me as he left the room with them.

The minute they were gone, Ronnie and I ran out to the truck and lugged that big heavy rear end in, changed it right on the spot and then got the one out of there that had been in the car during the race.

The car passed the inspection with flying colors.

"Weren't you scared they'd find out?" Ronnie said.

"Naw," I said, "we knew what they were gonna do. Besides, those Kiekhaefer cars had the same rear ends and carbs that Daddy's cars had. We'd'a just protested *them*."

Up until then, the Hudsons and Oldsmobiles had pretty much dominated NASCAR. Chrysler was now running a strong third. It was more than General Motors could stand, so they jumped into the racing scene with their Chevrolets and then their Pontiacs. This caused Ford to step up their program and, all of a sudden, there were factory people everywhere around racing.

The pot was really boiling.

I was going as far as I could go on the engines I was building, pushing the tolerances to the point where either NASCAR was going to step in and say "Whoa there, boy!" or the motors were going to start popping like roman candles. I worried about it—I mean, I didn't want to be the one responsible for Daddy dropping out of a race; but we had to be competitive, so I built them right on the edge, just a hair this side of a bomb.

I just about drove him crazy at the old Charlotte track one day. We pitted outside the track, right in front of the main grandstand, and a lot of the drivers took a short cut through the pits in the race. It gave them a better angle on the first turn, so here they would come, full bore, right through the pits and into the corner. There wasn't any rule against it, so it happened all the time.

Daddy wasn't doing it, because his car was handling well. But I was having to dodge the cars coming through the pits, so I could stay up near the fence and see what he was doing. I had to be in a good position to give him his pit signs.

About halfway through the race, it looked like his car was smoking, so I wrote "Engine?" on the pit board with chalk. It meant he was supposed to check his gauges, particularly his oil pressure.

Next time around, he gave me the "thumbs up," meaning everything was all right. But I could still see the smoke and I was afraid his engine was going to self-destruct. I held up another sign. He signaled back that it was okay.

That engine was smoking, I was sure of it. Another sign—this time he almost leaned out the window with his thumb in the air. It went on several more times.

Finally one of the other guys said, "Did you ever see anything like that? Man, that dirt's so hard, them cats is smokin' their tires. How 'bout that?" Well, it looked like it was coming from the exhaust pipe to me.

When Daddy got out of his car, he said, "You don't have writer's cramp, do you?" How did I know the smoke was coming from the dad-gum tires?

We went back to a Dodge in 1956, and then made the big switch to Oldsmobile the following year. It was the first time since we had been racing that there had been anything other than a Chrysler product in our garage. That is if you don't count Gilmer Goode's 1948 Buick Roadmaster.

The switch to Olds was a good one. Instead of buying cars, they gave them to us. The Petty name commanded some respect by then, and, with the factories into racing right up to their camshafts, there was one more high-cost item we could eliminate—buying the car. I would have been willing to bet, at that stage, that we would never have to sleep in the car again.

NASCAR had added convertible racing to their racing cards, so now we had two different kinds of race cars: a coupe and a convertible. And when we went to Daytona in 1957 to run the beach course, we carried three race cars: the two Oldsmobiles and a '36 Chevy coupe with an Olds engine to run in the modified deal.

It was an exciting time at the beach in those days. Anything could, and usually *did*, happen. Everybody raced up and down the beach and the streets with their race cars. Man, it was great. You've probably already figured out that I got to drive one of the race cars at night—on the street. I drove all over town, picking races with anybody who would run me. There were cars everywhere with no mufflers and with numbers on the sides of them. I was in seventh heaven.

The cops gave up trying to enforce any kind of speeding control. They had good reason to give up: They had tried it the year before, and the hot-rodders had taken over City Hall. They even turned over police cars. It was easier to just let everybody race.

There had been a tradition of skullduggery at the beach clear back to 1936, when Smokey Purser was flagged the winner of the first race, which was also a late-model event. After Smokey took the checkered flag, he just kept going, right up the beach. They found him later, trying frantically to get the modified parts off his car and the stock ones back on, so his car would pass inspection. They disqualified him. But he cast the die for future generations of Daytona racers.

Twenty-one years later, in 1957, they were still inspecting the cars at the armory, over near Smokey Yunick's "Best Damn Garage in Town." It was several miles from the track, and, after the cars were inspected, the guys drove them down to the race course. You could have stopped and changed cars on the way if you wanted to, and a lot of them did.

They should have called the whole thing the "Spirit of Smokey."

Nineteen fifty-seven started out to be a great year. Daddy ran well, the Oldsmobile was strong, and my motors held up good. By the time we got to Darlington, we were flying high. It came to an abrupt halt there.

Everything looked great before the race. Daddy had qualified eighth, and Bobby Myers, who was driving our second Oldsmobile, was second. He started in the front row.

The race got off to a fast start, with Bobby moving in and out of the lead in the first few laps. Daddy was moving up. But on lap 27, Bobby and Paul Goldsmith tangled and crashed. It was one of those grinding, heavy kind of crashes where the cars are flipping and coming apart. Everybody in the place was quiet.

Bobby's car rolled to the infield and lay there, smoking and steaming. It was totally destroyed. There was no movement inside.

Bobby was dead.

We never talked much about the crash.

11

"If she runs right, run 'er hard. If she don't, don't be afraid to back off."

—LEE PETTY

It was a day after my twenty-first birthday. I couldn't stand it any longer. I walked up to Daddy, who was working on one of the Oldsmobiles, and I said:

"I think I'd like to try driving—you know, on the track."

"Hand me a three-eighths box-end," he said.

I handed him the wrench. "I said . . ."

"I heard you," he answered. "Take the convertible over there," and he motioned with his right hand, the one that had the three-eighths box-end wrench in it, in the general direction of the '57 Olds rag-top race car that was sitting over in the corner of the shop.

It had been three years since I had mentioned my racing career, and it was handled as casually this time as it had been before. I can't say that in the years since I had first brought up the subject that I had this burning desire to race, I really hadn't. I had accepted what he told me, and let it go at that. Now I was twenty-one, and it was time to see if I really did want to be a race driver. If it turned out that I was happier as a mechanic, then that's what I'd do.

None of us ever got too emotional about anything. It might make it more interesting reading if I said, "*I stood there with tears running down my cheeks, and in the misty, half-dawn light of the shop, I could see the gleaming Oldsmobile convertible beckoning to me. . . .*"

But it didn't happen that way.

The Olds was sitting over there, covered with about an inch of dust because it hadn't been raced since the end of last season. I walked over to it, raised the hood, and I said, "I reckon I better jerk the motor out of this rascal and rebuild the dadgum thing."

"That's where *I'd* start," he said.

I spent the next three days getting the car ready. I used every trick I had learned over the years till there wasn't any question in my mind—the car was ready. As far as I was concerned, I was as ready as I was ever going to be. Daddy checked on me, from time to time. Oh, he tried to conceal it, but he was checking. He'd stop and talk to me, which he never did before, and as he talked he was looking right past me to what I was doing at the time. He was just making sure that what I was doing was right.

This might be a good place to bring up something that's always sort of bugged me.

There hasn't been much that anybody has ever said over the years that I've even given a second thought to—good things or bad things, and there's been some of each—but a lot of the other drivers, including some of the ones I started driving with, have said, "Well, it's no wonder Richard Petty's broken all those records. Why wouldn't he? He was handed everything on a *silver platter*: ready-to-win race car, money, everything." Now, I don't want to protest too much, like that Shakespeare fellow said, but take a look at the deal when I was starting to race: They're right, Daddy *did* give me a race car to start with. Well, actually he didn't *give* it to me, he let me drive the second car for Petty Engineering—a car I had built. As far as the money was concerned, anybody that knows Daddy knows that he doesn't give anything away—you have to work for every dime you get from him. So, you see, I wasn't handed anything on a silver platter—pewter maybe, but not silver—and, after all, pewter's always been called "the poor man's silver."

This was a perfect place to get this off my chest.

So, as they say on television, "When we left our young hero . . . " he was rebuilding a race car. Well, I was, and when it was all finished and ready to race, I picked a number for it: forty-three. Why not? It came right after forty-two.

It was right then that one of racing's most famous car colors was invented. We had a gallon of white paint and a gallon of blue, so we mixed them together and "Petty Blue" was born. It was about as glamorous a beginning as the number thing, but every Petty race car after that was painted the same color. We have it copyrighted.

Along the way, somewhere between the painting and the lettering, I hired Dale as my crew chief. It was a logical choice, since he had been in on all my racing, from wagon to street. Chief would work on Daddy's car and Dale would work on mine. It was still a family deal.

The car was ready in plenty of time for the race at Columbia.

We were all hooked up and ready to go. There was Dale and Red Mylar, who had been around NASCAR as long as the rest of us and was now working for Petty Engineering, and me—you know, the race driver. Daddy and Chief were going to race the hardtop in Asheville. They were parked behind us in the drive, all set to pull out when we did. I was about to get in the tow car when Daddy walked over to me. He put his elbow on my shoulder and he leaned close and gave me about the only piece of advice since I first started driving a car.

"Richard," he said, "lemme tell you something: If she runs right, run 'er hard. If she don't, don't be afraid to back off. You won't win 'em all, anyway." There's one thing for sure, you won't waste a lot of time reading page after page of heart-to-heart talks between Daddy and me.

I had made the trip to Columbia a dozen times—maybe two dozen—and, as much as I'd like to say this deal was different, I can't. It was like all the rest, except Daddy wasn't there. I wasn't all uptight and nervous or anything like that; in fact, it was just the opposite. I was as relaxed as I had been on any other trip. Dale was a basket case.

"You sure you know what to do in the race, Richard?" he asked, about twenty times.

"Sure, Dale," I said, "you go down to the corner and turn left."

"Very funny," he said. "You know what I mean: stayin' out of trouble and all that. Do you know what I mean?"

Well, one thing Daddy *did* tell me once was, "If you wanna be sure you're gonna stay out of trouble, don't unhook the race car. Go up in the stands and watch the race, and then tow it home."

"Yeah," I told Dale. "If you wanna stay out of trouble, don't unhook . . . "

"I know, I know," he said, "I was there when your Daddy said it. I just hope you know what you're doin', that's all." I thought I was going to have to stop to get him a tranquilizer.

Columbia was one of the best tracks in the South and it was one of the worst—it all depended on who you talked to. There's no question that it was fast, because it was mostly sand and white clay. You see, white clay is an entirely different deal than the red clay we had in the Piedmont and most of the other regions of the South.

They called white clay "bull tallow," and, I'll tell you, it got as hard as cement. The tires would squeal on it, that's how hard it was. But you couldn't slide on it as much as you could on red clay, and that made it hard to drive for a lot of people. Naturally, you could slide some—you had to or you couldn't get through the corners fast—but the tires got a bite in that stuff, and it wasn't like the red clay, where you thought you were never going to *stop* sliding. There were drivers who were power slide experts, guys like Buck Baker and Joe Weatherly, and they didn't like the tracks down there in the Pee Dee River region of South Carolina at all.

I didn't know, because I hadn't really driven either kind of track—that is, if you don't count the hundreds of miles of back-road driving I had done on the red clay roads around home.

But Columbia was a white clay track. It was a half mile, or maybe six-tenths—it all depended on how the guy who graded it took the turns. Since it was almost totally flat, he could grade it a little wider if he felt like it. It changed with almost every race.

The pits were inside the track at Columbia, so we hauled the race car in there and unhooked it, and then we went over everything for the umpteenth time. I didn't want some dang-fool thing we'd forgot to do to be responsible for knocking me out of my first race. When we were satisfied the car was ready, I got the helmet I had bought at the hot-rod shop in Greensboro out of the truck, and I climbed in the car.

"Are you sure . . . " Dale started.

I touched my forehead, just in front of the leading edge of the helmet and then I snapped the forefinger in his direction. " 'Bye," I said. "Y'all wait around for me, now, ya heah?"

I fired up the Olds and got ready to take it to the track for some practice laps before qualifying.

Driving a race car is not like learning to play golf or something where you have to learn to hold the club the same way everybody else does to get the job done. You don't have to hold the steering wheel a certain way, and you don't have to bother about how somebody else sits in the race car or what groove he runs in out there or anything like that.

I had watched guys like Joe Weatherly, Curtis Turner, and Tiny Lund throwing dirt up into the stands, and then I'd seen Daddy come by and pass them on the inside and go on. I remembered so many times hearing the fans hollering for the flashy cats, and then seeing those same guys run second or third, so I had a pretty good idea how I wanted to drive.

I fastened the seat belt that laid in the seat beside me and I dumped the convertible in first and headed out of the pits and on to the track in turn 3. There were several other cars on the track, so I stayed down low for a couple of laps, until the oil in my motor was heated up. When I was sure the car was ready, I pushed the gas pedal down pretty hard and I felt the rear end kick out a little. The tires spun, and then they got a bite and the car shot off for turn 1. I went up high, near the fence coming out of turn 2 and I nailed it going down the back straightaway. Just before I got to turn 3, I jerked the steering wheel to the left and punched the accelerator. The car crossed up some, but not as much as I had expected. I was heading straight for the board fence in turn 4. I had to back off.

I made several more laps and came back into the pits.

"Looks like maybe we need to change the front sway bar," Red Mylar said. "I think it could use a heavier one."

I honestly can't say that I would have known to do that, you know, just from the feel of the car, but I probably would have known it if I had been in the pits watching, like Red and Dale were. So I helped them change it. The car did feel better when I went back out. It was good enough to put me right in the middle of the pack. I qualified thirteenth, which I wasn't ashamed of. I mean, most of those cats behind me had been racing for years.

When the starter dropped the green flag, all hell broke loose. Cars passed me on both sides; one hit me from behind and a car got sideways in front of me. I tried to steer around it, but there were cars so close to me I couldn't. I slid into it, but I got by.

I was running pretty good—at first. Maybe I got a little too much confidence, because on about the fourth lap, I went into turn 1 pretty fast. The car slid up against the guard rail, and I could feel a dull thud. It was rough on the sheet metal. I got it down from the fence and stood on it. I brushed the wall in turn 3. Man, I was going to have to rebuild the car when I got home, but it was worth it—I was having *fun*. I hit the fence with the front of the car once, but the big bumpers on the Olds bounced me back on the track. It was like I was playing a pinball machine, but I was the ball.

I'll bet I had seen a hundred races from the pits, but the

view from the driver's seat was a lot different. For one thing, when you're in the pits (or the grandstands, for that matter) you see everything. In the race car, you have to keep your eyes on the track right in front of you so much that it's like you're not even in a race—at least, not in a race with a whole bunch of cars. On a short track like I was on, you're only concerned with what's directly in front of you and right behind you and on either side. You're in your own tiny bubble of a world. It's almost like the track is revolving and you're standing still.

I decided that I had to find me a "rabbit," someone who knew what he was doing, so I could figure out what the best way around the track was. Little Joe Weatherly came by and crossed up his Ford right in front of me, so I crossed up the Olds. Little Joe went into turn 1 low, so I went into turn 1 low. Then Little Joe ran right through the board fence, but I thought, "I don't think that's the groove I want," so I backed off and looked for another rabbit.

Little Joe had blown a tire when he went into the corner and it got him running sideways, and then backward, and then he was gone. I saw exactly what had happened. It was a whole other ball game from out there. In the pits it looked like there was time to correct for things like that, but I realized that it all happens very quick.

At about the halfway point, Johnny Allen blew a tire coming off turn 4 and the car not only went through the fence, it went clear up under the grandstands. I thought for a second that everything was going to come tumbling down. Boards were flying everywhere. I put my arms up in front of my face. It was a reflex action. I guess Little Joe was standing in the pits, so he ran over to where Dale was.

"Your boy needs relief, he's peckin' on his hat," he said. "When he comes in, I'll take over."

I didn't realize what it looked like to the guys in the pits, but when you touch your helmet, it's a signal that you want somebody else to take over. Little Joe got his helmet on. He was ready. You see, when a race driver gets his mind set on racing, he feels cheated if he doesn't get to finish a race. That's why drivers usually stay around the track, even after their car goes out. They never give up hope of winning the race—or, at least, of finishing it—it doesn't matter whose car it's in.

I didn't come in. Little Joe took his helmet off.

Later on, I was getting so hot that the sweat was running down in my eyes, so I was trying to wipe my head.

"Look," Little Joe said, "he's doin' it again." He put his helmet on. I stayed out there. It happened about three or four times, and Little Joe finally just went home. Helmets are hard to get off—it hurts. "Damn kid don't know what he wants," he muttered as he left.

When the race was over, I was in sixth place. Fireball Roberts won it and Bob Welborn was second. It wasn't a bad finish for my first race, but I have to admit, I didn't outrun anybody, I just out*lasted* them. I had stayed out of trouble pretty much, and I had been able to run the entire 200 laps without crashing— Bad. The rear bumper was completely off and the right side was ground down a little, but the car wasn't in that bad a shape, considering the fact that I had just taken my first race-driving lesson in it.

Dale slapped me on the back and yelled, "That was good, buddy."

I asked about Little Joe. "I saw him over here with his helmet on, where'd he go?"

"His ears got sore, and he went home," Dale said.

We hooked up the car and took off on the 150-mile trip home. I had gotten my first taste of driving. Do you know, I wasn't sure if I wanted to do this or not. I knew one thing: It didn't scare me. But, on the other hand, it didn't turn me on as much as I thought it would. Maybe if I had won . . .

All the way home I kept thinking about how much harder it was to drive a race car than I had thought it would be. And I realized how much better the good drivers like Daddy and Tim Flock really were. They did everything so smooth and so natural that you didn't even notice them until the race was over and you saw them down there taking the trophy from the track promoter and getting kissed by some lumpy girl in a bathing suit with a ribbon running from one shoulder to her other hip.

And it was easier for me to see why some of the cats looked so flashy: They just went into the corner and *threw* the car—it didn't matter if there was anybody in their way or not. Most of them depended on the other guy getting out of the way, and if he didn't, they wrecked. That wasn't good driving. You see, I *knew* what good driving was, even if I didn't have it down pat yet.

I thought, "Man, if I could just go out there and practice every day, like I did with the passenger car before I got my driver's license, I could master it in no time." But I realized that you didn't do it that way. You served your apprenticeship by learning on the track. It was on-the-job training. Well, I sure wasn't going to quit until I could run with some of those other cats. I mean, I might not have made up my mind yet to make it a lifetime career, but I sure was going to give it more of a try than just one race.

We took the car home and got it ready to race the following week in Winston-Salem. There was a race in Toronto, Canada, the week after that.

I wasn't a brave race car driver. I mean, I didn't do any more sliding than I had to. That first year, I ran behind Curtis and Little Joe and Possum Jones and Bob Welborn as often as I could, which wasn't much at first. I'd qualify in about the middle of the pack, and then, when the race would start, those cats would just fly off and leave me, so when they lapped me the first time, well, man, I'd just fall in behind and run in their groove. I got so I could stay with them for three or four laps before they ran off from me again. Then the next race, I could stay with them for maybe six or eight laps, and then ten or fifteen.

I'd run down the straightaway, and I'd pitch it like they did, and then get back on the gas when they did. Pretty soon, I had learned enough that they didn't lap me any more. I learned exactly how each one of them drove the dirt, and pretty soon I could see how I could improve on some of it.

You could take care of your equipment, even on dirt, where you had to go into the corners sideways. A lot of drivers did, and you hardly ever saw them break any wheels or axles or anything, so it didn't take me long to start driving the same way. For one thing, it meant there wouldn't be as much to fix the next day. If I turned the car over, I had to beat the roof out, and if I broke anything, I had to weld it. I had an extra incentive to take care of the car. I mean, most of those other cats were driving cars that belonged to someone else. They didn't have to fix them.

I didn't stroke it which means taking it easy on the car, but I did try to stay out of trouble as much as I could. The good drivers had less wrecks; in the long run, they tore up less equipment. And there were drivers who looked so smooth, right up to a certain point—Johnny Allen was a good example. I mean, he looked like a million bucks out there, just as smooth as silk, and then he'd make some stupid mistake and tear the car all to pieces. Well, I guess you couldn't say "stupid," it was more that he lost concentration, I suppose. In this sport, you have to keep your mind on what you're doing every second. It's not what you'd call a forgiving sport.

Johnny wasn't the only one. I'd think this cat or that cat was gettin' the job done, and then, all of a sudden, there would be a caution flag, and I'd come by, and there would be his car, upside down. The guy just ran out of brains, that's all.

Herb Thomas was another story. He actually looked crude out there, but, I'll tell you, he ran that car. There's no question in my mind, Herb would have been one of the greats of NAS-CAR if he had stayed around, but he got hurt pretty bad in 1958 and he quit. As it was, he won two championships and finished second several times, but a lot of people have forgotten about him, because he wasn't around long.

Herb was a tough competitor. Not all race drivers are tough—and I'm not talking about *rough*: There's a difference. A *tough* driver is a winner, for one thing. He doesn't necessarily have to be rough, but he'll do anything to win. Junior was tough, and so was Buck Baker. They could win with any kind of car.

Daddy was tough, probably the toughest I've ever seen. If he could win without denting up your car, he'd do it; if it took beating on you, he'd do that too. But he only did it if it was necessary. Junior would do it, just because he liked to. Curtis did it because it looked good. And, you know, when you get right down to it, Curtis was more showoff than he was race driver.

On the whole, though, I think the drivers back then were a lot tougher than they ever were afterward.

It was my fourth or fifth race before Daddy saw me drive.

"You're goin' in a little too low," he said. I already knew it.

He told me a few things like that from time to time, but I had usually already figured them out for myself. And, in all fairness to Daddy, I'll have to say that you can't tell anybody else how to drive, anymore than you can tell a baby how to walk. Everyone has his own style of driving—he has his own style of walking, for that matter—and he has his own abilities and limitations, and he has to discover what they are, all by himself. You can tell someone else how you drive *your* car, but it's about useless to tell him how to drive *his* car.

No matter how much ability a guy has, it's a slow learning process before he gets to the point where he can really use it. Experience eventually takes over and you start reacting the right way without having to think things through. I mean, there isn't a whole lot of time to think out there, so the cat who thinks the best and the fastest is the one that wins the most races.

There wasn't any one particular driver I patterned myself after. What I tried to develop was smoothness. I knew you couldn't attack the car; you had to be a part of it. And another thing, I never did feel that I had to prove anything to anybody (you know, like I was the son of Lee Petty or anything like that). In fact it was just the opposite: If I made it in racing, I wanted to do it on my own. I wanted to develop a style all my own. I knew that attitude and confidence were important, and I had both: *attitude* from having watched so many great drivers and *confidence* from having built the race car myself.

I started to find the best groove: the one where I could run fastest. If some other cat was running faster than I was, I figured he had a better groove than I did, so I took a look at where he was running. For a long time, racing was a matter of compromise for me—and of trial and error.

I'll tell you one important thing, right here: Daddy didn't give me any special consideration on the racetrack. I was just another car to him, and he would just as soon beat me as he would a total stranger. But he was a real racer, and that's the way they think. I know, I keep saying that, but I can't repeat it too often. I'll give you an example of something that happened after I had several races under my belt:

I was probably doing better than I ever had. I was in third or fourth spot, and it was late in the race. Cotton Owens was leading and Daddy was chasing him. They both came up to lap me and Cotton knew I was a rookie, so he backed off to give me time to get through the corner. He knew he could pass me coming out of the turn. Well, this was the chance Daddy had been waiting for. When Cotton backed off, Daddy went charging right by him. The only trouble was, here I was, right in Daddy's path. He hit me and knocked me into the fence. The impact tore the bumper clean off my car. Daddy won the race.

I didn't say anything after the race, but it made me mad. I

mean, all I was trying to do was stay out of the way, and he came barreling in there and *wham!* he knocked me into the boards. It wasn't easy fixing up those cars; he knew that. But that was how Daddy drove.

We didn't drive too many races together for a while, and it may have been just as well. I couldn't beat Daddy and for some reason, I hated to lose to him more than to anybody else.

Many of those old tracks were dangerous, particularly the ones with wooden fences. I would much rather have no fence at all than have to run a track with a board fence, because that kind of fence will pull you right into it. The boards give just enough that the car hits a post, and then more fence comes out, then more posts, then the first thing you know, your car is torn to pieces.

It happened to Fireball one night, and his car was wiped out, so he was walking back to the pits. A reporter ran up to him and said, "What happened out there Fireball?"

Well, those guys ask questions like that all the time. Most of the time the drivers answer the dumb questions. Sometimes they don't. After you've crashed is definitely not the time you want to be interviewed.

Fireball glared at the guy and he said, "I crashed. It *is* possible to crash out there, you know."

A lot of those guys were funny. We were racing at Savannah one night and Junior Johnson brought his race car in the pits and said, "Man, it's so dusty out there that if you threw a bucket up in the air, it wouldn't even come down."

To some of them—like Curtis—racing was one big party. I mean, if he won, it was okay, but if he lost, that was okay, too. It didn't make one bit of difference to him if there were any spectators out there at all; he liked driving so much that he would have done it no matter what. He just enjoyed being master of that car for whatever time it lasted. I'll tell you, he beat a race car to *death*. He was one of a kind.

Junior looked at it almost the same way, but his ultimate goal was winning. He drove the same way as Curtis, but there was a good reason for it in his mind: He felt like that was the way he had to drive to win the race. It may be that Curtis and Junior drove that way because they both came to NASCAR straight from the whiskey-running trade. Little Joe was halfway in between Curtis and Junior: He loved the thrill of driving, but he thought winning was better than losing.

I drove nine races in 1958 and won a total of $760. That just about paid for the gas and the hot dogs—not even the pop. It made me wonder if it was worth it. I mean, I really did like driving the car, but I had only finished one race in the top ten, so I thought maybe I wasn't cut out for it. Maybe I was meant to be a mechanic, and I should stick to what I had started out to be.

After all, driving was hard, hot, dirty work, and, on top of that, it was dangerous. We all knew that, right from the beginning. We had seen bad wrecks and people get hurt and worse. We had seen it close up, like Darlington. I thought about Bobby's death when I tried to make up my mind, and suddenly I realized that I had to make the decision because of me, not because of what had happened to somebody else.

"Whatta'ya think, boy?" Daddy asked. "You gonna try it again next year?"

"I reckon so," I said.

"It's up to you," he said. "If you do, do you wanna stick to the salary you been gettin', or do you want a percentage of your winnings?"

I thought for a minute. By running all the races the next season, I should make a pretty good amount of money, but it was a family business, so I decided to stick to my salary, and put my winnings back into the business.

If you want to know the truth, it wasn't the "family business" half as much as it was "good economics" that made up my mind. I hadn't made all that much in racing, and

Dale Inman guides the world's single most successful race car, the 1967 Plymouth, onto the trailer, in the days before cars were transported on elaborate 18-wheel rigs.

The famous last-lap crash of the 1976 Daytona 500: My car crashes into the wall (*left*); David Pearson's racer (*right*) spins off the concrete and heads for the infield. Pearson limped across the finish line to win, as I desperately tried to restart my engine.

Chrysler's racing boss, the late Ronnie Householder (*left*), and I hold the winner's trophy for the 1964 Daytona 500. Daddy holds my 1964 NASCAR championship trophy.

A graphic illustration of how many men it takes to win a Grand National race, as my entire crew hops on the bandwagon on the way to Victory Lane.

Lynda and Rebecca join me in Victory Lane at Rockingham in 1974.

SCHOOL DAYS 1952-53

1945-46

Two school photos.

The things the press says have made me famous: my smile and the ever-present sunglasses.

At home with the children, 1967.

Racing has always kept me away from home a lot, but when I am at home I'm with my family, as here in 1967.

Me looking over my 1960 Plymouth race car.

A bearded Maurice ("Chief") Petty talks with me during the race on the two-way radio.

Grand National stockers frantically pit under the caution flag. My car is in the front.

My spectacular 1970 crash at Darlington, in which I dislocated my shoulder.

The rigors of racing, as seen in my face and the grime of spent tire rubber on my uniform following one of my record-breaking twenty-seven victories in 1967.

I knew a percentage of almost nothing wasn't going to get the job done. A base pay made more sense. I've always said it was for the "family." It sounded real good in interviews.

It must have worked; Daddy gave me a raise.

12

When you're leadin', you feel like you own the track.

The towns flashed past my eyes: Columbia, Spartanburg, Greenville, Hillsboro, Charlotte, Wilson, Atlanta, Savannah, Valdosta, Wilkesboro. And with every race, I picked up a little more knowledge. With some, I picked up a lot.

We went into the North. In fact, it was at Fonda, New York, one night when the pace car took us on the strangest deal of my entire racing career. The caution flag came out because there was a wreck that should have made the *Guinness Book of World Records*. There must have been twenty cars involved, so they brought out the pace car to lead what was left of the field around the wreck on the back straight, until they got the mess cleared up. Bob Latford, who was doing public relations for NASCAR, was driving the pace car so he took us around the back straightaway and down off the track, onto a road that ran right beside the track. We went out the gate. He had the only car with headlights, so we all had to stay up as close as possible so we could see.

I could swear I saw a tombstone. "There's another one," I said out loud. I don't know who I was talking to, but it was a sight you don't see too often in a race. At least, it's one you don't *want* to see too often. There were tombstones everywhere and we were driving around them and between them, everywhere, at about 50 mph. We were in a cemetery.

It turns out that it was the only way to get around the wreck in the back straightaway. We made about five laps through the graveyard before we could get back on the racetrack.

In spite of things like driving around tombstones, some of the tracks were starting to improve; they even paved some of them. I noticed something right quick about running on asphalt: Smoothness was even more important than it was on dirt because we went faster, so I worked hard on getting my technique down as smooth as I could.

Columbia was an unusual track; we ran asphalt track tires there at times because the white clay got so hard. But you really didn't know what to run until you got there. We had to take two sets of tires—one for dirt and one for asphalt.

Most of the tracks, of course, we could predict from race to race. At Hillsboro, for instance, we could have used a tank, because you couldn't stick to anything. They didn't run enough races there to keep it up, so it got to looking like a plowed field by the end of the race. Spartanburg was smooth one race and rough the next. It sure kept things interesting; you never knew what to expect.

At Nashville one time they had dug out rough spots in the pavement to repair them, but nobody remembered to call the guy with the asphalt truck, so they went out back and shoveled all the old stuff back in a truck and dumped it back in the holes. By about the tenth lap, the track was full of tank traps.

It took talent to drive them all, because the tracks were so different. Spartanburg, for instance, was a sideways racetrack: You had the car cocked just about all the way around. You'd no more than get it straightened out coming out of turns 2 and 4 when you'd have to get her sideways again for turns 1 and 3. You just ran down the straight, threw the car at the corner, waited for it to catch, and then you got back on the gas. You let it run up against the curbing where it was still wet from the prerace watering-down. Greenville was the same way. Halfway down the straight, you cocked the car and slid it in the corner, and then you got on it just before it hit the fence.

When the track got rough, you had to change grooves. You couldn't always run where you wanted to, because there might not be a track there by midway through the race. So you'd have to look around and find a place where you could run, and where the car would last for 200 laps. It helped to be around at the end of the race.

I ran some tracks, where you started out in, say, a low groove, and before you knew it, the cars threw up enough dirt to build up a big mound in the middle of the track, maybe two feet high. You couldn't crossover or the dirt wall would flip you, so you had to decide before you went into the corner, which groove you were going to take.

There was always something happening. At Wilson, North Carolina, one night, it got so cold that people built fires under the grandstands to keep warm. They caught the wooden stands on fire and they ended up burning clear down. They had to stop the race because the town's fire truck was in the infield.

I was running at Myrtle Beach, South Carolina, one night when my throttle stuck. We have an on/off switch on race cars, so I flipped it off, but by then all I could see was dirt. I mean, there was nothing but tan when I looked out the windshield. The car was already on its nose. It flipped end-over-end about three times, and the last flip carried it right out into the swamp. It landed on its wheels in a big splash of water, then everything got dead quiet. All of a sudden, I heard another splash; not as big as a race car, but bigger than a possum. And then I heard another one. I thought, "Oh, lord, alligators."

I got out of the car real quick and climbed up on top of it. I could imagine water moccasins and gators and everything in there. I thought, "I don't need none of this." I survived the crash and I sure didn't want to get eaten up in the swamps. I stayed right there until they got me out with a wrecker and a long tow line.

You may think I'm goin' on a little too much, but I'm just picking out some examples. There was something different every night—I promise. But it must not have bothered me, because

I sure stuck with it. If you want to know the truth, I sort of liked the crazy part of it. If there hadn't been some wild deals happening, driving a race car could have gotten boring. It didn't, I'll guarantee you.

No matter what happened, the Pettys stuck together. I was running the old track at Asheville, and I had run off and left everybody. It looked like I had it won, but a wheel bearing went out and I almost had to come to a stop. I was through. Well, when Ned Jarrett caught me, he ran right through me instead of waiting until I pulled off. He knocked me into the wall and ripped my car up.

When he stopped to get the checkered flag, I jumped out of my car and went over and reached through the window and got him by the shirt. I was just getting ready to punch him when I heard a big commotion. I turned around to see Dale and Chief beating the tar out of one of Ned's crew. It turns out he was coming up behind me with a knife.

He never tried that again. And I don't believe Ned ever ran me into the wall again, either.

I know, I keep talking about dust, too, but it was our worst problem, in one form or another. When a race started, there was always mud, because they had just watered the track down. You'd have to reach outside the car and try to wipe it off the windshield. Then by the time you'd run fifty laps, it got so dusty you couldn't see a thing. There was as much dust on the inside of the windshield as there was the outside, so you had to wipe off on both sides.

You finally just had to take your goggles off, because the dust would get on the inside, and you'd sweat and that turned it to mud. My eyes were as red as the clay for two days after a race.

One night, I was following Herman Beam down low because I couldn't see to pass. Herman went so slow that everybody called him "Turtle," so I figured it would be safer following him than getting run over in the groove. When I thought it was safe, I pulled out to the right to pass and get back in the thick of things. I didn't know how low we were. I hit a light pole. Herman was driving in the infield. Man, we weren't even *on* the racetrack.

When I started driving, nobody knew much about setting up a race car. Today, everybody fine-tunes cars with computers, but back then, we went to the track, unloaded the car, ran eight or ten laps, and qualified. If it wasn't right when it came off that trailer, forget it. If a car didn't handle right, you stayed out there and you *made* it handle. There wasn't any such thing as making an adjustment to the car during the race. If you started out wrong, you stayed wrong.

If something broke, it broke. You could take it easy on a car, but only up to a point. After all, you were out there to win, not to bring your car home in one piece. The race driver's motto in those days was, "I had to borrow money to get here, I'll borrow money to get home."

Early in 1959, Daddy decided to go back to Plymouth. Olds had pulled out of racing and we were having trouble getting enough parts to run both cars, so I stayed with Olds just to use up the parts we already had. We may have coined the phrase "Waste not, want not."

The day of the race at Lakewood in Atlanta, everything seemed to come together for me. There had been a lot of crashes and broken cars, and I suddenly found myself in the lead. Keep in mind, that on a short track, you're not just out there in front, all by yourself. There are cars all the way around the track and you're passing just as many if you're running first or fifth. There's never a break in traffic on a short track.

It didn't matter. I felt entirely different. Everything may have looked the same from first place, but it sure wasn't. You get a feeling when you're leading that you don't have any other time. I don't know, it's kind of like you *own* the track. You also get to wondering what's going to happen next. Will you be able to stay out of trouble long enough to actually win, or will somebody knock you out the next lap? Those things go through your mind. Even though it was the only time I had ever been in that position, it never changed after that. I had the same feelings every time.

Well, I did stay out of everybody else's way, and they waved the checkered flag at me when I came across the finish line. It had taken parts of two seasons, but I finally got to find out what it feels like to win a race—in a race car. It was a warm feeling, like you get when you're opening Christmas presents. I took the car straight to the winner's circle area, and I looked around for Daddy, expecting to see him come walking up any minute. But for some reason, he had stayed out on the track for another lap.

I was sorry he wasn't going to be there to see me get the trophy, but I guessed he could see the thing later. I hadn't any more than gotten it in my hands when one of the NASCAR guys came up and said, "Hold it a minute, Richard. There's been a protest. Wait here."

"What could have gone wrong?" I wondered. I was sure I hadn't done anything wrong. I wondered and waited for what seemed like hours (actually it was only minutes). The guy came back.

"We're awful sorry, Richard," he said. It was the same kind of thing Daddy used to say to me before he whipped me. "But there's been a mistake. We actually waved the checkered flag a lap too soon. But don't feel too bad, it's all in the family. Your Daddy's won the race." He took the trophy and started to leave.

"Hey," I called after him, "who protested?"

He looked at me kind of sheepishlike. "Why, your Daddy did," he said. I learned the meaning of "bittersweet" that day in Atlanta.

There was a good reason for it—I guess. All of the factories had pulled out of racing, and that left everybody with a year-old—or older—car, so NASCAR had tried to encourage everybody to get new cars. They had offered a $500 bonus to anyone who won in a new car.

"I had the new one, son," Daddy said. "It made us more money. Besides, you've got lots of time to win races. We're in it to make money, you know."

"I know," I said.

He was in a battle with Cotton Owens for the championship and he needed all the points he could get. There was every reason for him to protest the race, but a lot of people didn't understand. "Don't you feel bad, Lee, you know, about Richard not winnin'?" one guy asked.

"I reckon not," he said. "When he wins he can have it, but he ain't gonna have it given to him." I wonder where those guys were then who said I had everything handed to me on a silver platter.

Over the years, I'll bet I've had to answer questions about that story more than any other one, and I've always said the same thing: "It was a family business, and it was better business for him to win than it was for me." I've never told anyone how I felt that day. But I told you I was going to peel back the outer layer and show you the *inside*, so here's how I felt when I walked back to the pits without the trophy: I had heard a thousand times that "you have to earn everything you get." And I believed that, but I didn't think it would have hurt to give just a little bit—say, one lap.

I got over the feeling the next time I got in a race car, because that's one of the good things about it all—there's always another race, and racers heal quick. When you fire up that engine again, the past is all gone, and you have only one thought: What's going to happen in the next 200 laps or so?

Daddy knew that a whole lot better than I did. It was a hard way to learn it, but I never let one race worry me again. It's the next race that counts, no matter whether you've won this one or lost it. I never again expected anyone to give me anything—not one lap or one foot. If I did that,

I wouldn't be much of a race driver myself. It's probably written somewhere.

That year at Charlotte, Junior was leading the race and he was trying to keep Daddy from passing; he was using up as much of the track as he could, so Daddy just ran into the back of him. It bent Junior's rear fender into the tire and it blew, sending him into the fence. Junior got into the pits, and while his crew was changing the tire, he grabbed a Coke bottle. He got the car running and charged back out onto the track to get Daddy.

Junior ran Daddy into the infield and both of them came flying out of their cars. The fight was on, so Chief and I ran over there as quick as we could. Junior was swinging the pop bottle but Daddy punched him anyway. The most awful fight you ever saw went on for about five minutes. They finally had to get the Charlotte chief of police to break it up.

"What'd you stop us for?" Daddy asked.

"Yeah," Junior said, "we wasn't hurtin' anything."

They weren't. They were settling it themselves. They didn't need NASCAR or anybody. But we were right there to lend a hand if Daddy needed it.

There were times when one of us did have to help. Or, at least, we thought we did. Like the time when I was a kid and Daddy and Tiny Lund got into it. Daddy had beaten Tiny, but Tiny protested. That got them to arguing, and then the fight started. Anybody who tackled Tiny needed some help, because Tiny was about as big as the state of New Jersey. That didn't matter to Daddy. He punched Tiny in the eye. Tiny didn't even flinch. That was a bad sign. He swung at Daddy but missed, and Daddy wrestled him to the ground.

Speedy Thompson tried to separate them, but he couldn't do it, so Chief and I jumped on Tiny. And then Mother started hitting Tiny over the head with her pocketbook. It was like a scene from a Laurel and Hardy movie.

Tiny gave up. "When you beat a Petty, you have to beat the whole damn family," he said as he walked away, rubbing his head.

Racing seasons weren't as long back then as they are today. We were finished up by September, so we always spent the fall and winter months at home, working to get the new cars ready for the next season. Now, I don't want you to think that my social life had gone away, just because I had started driving race cars. It hadn't.

Over a period of a couple of years, Lynda and I had seen about six hundred more movies. We were getting tired of movies. If you want to know the truth, we had both decided that it might be a whole lot simpler to quit trying so hard to find things to do and places to go. It might make life a whole lot simpler, we figured, if we just stayed home, and made things more permanent. So we got married.

We moved in with Mother and Daddy. It seems like that old house was where everybody moved when they started a new life. It was where you lived while you were waiting to move somewhere else. So that's exactly what we did. We lived there until I could save enough money to buy a house trailer. When I had the money, we picked one out, and then we put it out behind the house. It was a perfect spot. I only had a hundred-yard commute to work.

It was a good life. For the first time, I had something other than racing that I could count on. I had lost out on just about all of my social life through high school because of racing, but Lynda made up for everything I had missed. Coming home was a special time of the day for me. We relaxed and talked and watched television. It worked out fine, because I was too tired most of the time to get cleaned up and go out, so I probably still wouldn't have had much of a social life if we hadn't gotten married. It was there when I got home, because she was both my wife and my best friend.

You know, if I hadn't gotten married when I did, I probably never would have, because racing became more involved every season after that, and I had less and less time of my own. I'm glad she came along in my life when she did.

There's no doubt in my mind that the Daytona International Speedway made more of an impact on my racing life than anything that ever happened. It opened in 1959, which couldn't have been more perfect for my career, because it brought in the era of the superspeedway. The fact that it came when it did was what was so important to me.

At Daytona—and at the other superspeedways that followed—I had as much of a chance as anybody, because I had as much experience as anybody. On the short tracks, I was at a real disadvantage, because most of the drivers I had been driving against had been driving those tracks about as long as there had been tracks there. They didn't have to learn the tracks and how to drive them. They found that out while I was still in knickers; I *did* wear knickers, but don't you tell anybody.

But, back to Daytona: It turns out that I might even have had an advantage. I didn't have any bad habits to unlearn. The other guys had to unlearn a lot of things because this track was unlike anything anybody had seen before.

In case you don't know, the Daytona track is a big one— two and a half miles long with high-banking turns. It looks like there should be snow on top of them. Bill France built it, and he took the Darlington idea and went one step farther with it. What he built was the best racing facility in the world at the time. It's not too far behind right now.

Everybody predicted that speeds on that track would be phenomenal. But even before we got there, the speed had taken its toll. Marshall Teague, who was from Daytona and who had been one of the earliest NASCAR heroes in a Hudson Hornet, was testing a car that Chapman Root had built for Indianapolis.

He got the car up to 160 mph when something happened. Nobody will ever know what, but the car started flipping. There wasn't anything left of the little roadster when it was over, and Daytona's own hero had been killed instantly.

It's a shame Marshall never got to actually race there. He would have been good.

Daytona looked even bigger the first time I saw it than it does today. There weren't as many buildings or grandstands, and the track just sat out there and looked about as big as Kansas City. It was all out in the open. It looked awesome.

There was a driver's meeting before anybody was allowed to get on the track. Bill France said, "All right, boys, none of you has ever been on a track like this before, so I want you to run a lot of laps, down low, slow, before you even try to get up on the high banks. Just run down there above the apron till you get used to it. Got it?"

"Sure, Bill," we all said. And then we got in our cars and ran wide open, right up on the banks. Telling a race driver not to run fast is like telling a kid to stay out of the cookie jar—or not to think about an elephant. It's about as dumb as having to drive 55 miles an hour on the highway.

I'll try to tell you how it felt to drive that fast at Daytona: For one thing, it didn't seem that much faster than driving at Darlington. The track was so much wider that there were two or three grooves, so you didn't have to slow up hardly at all in the corners. But being up on the banks was a different sensation. I mean, those banks were so steep that you could look out your side window and you were looking straight down. It was like banking an airplane. Little Joe Weatherly said he was afraid he was going to fall out of his car.

The first few laps seemed to take forever, because the track was so long. I thought I would never get back around to where the main grandstands were on the front straightaway. But after a few laps, I began to adapt to it. It scared the daylights out of some of the drivers, but I think they let it buffalo them before they even got out on it. Others took to it like a duck to water. I was one of those who liked it.

Maybe I liked it so much because I felt like a pioneer. At Daytona, I wasn't just some kid who came along to run with the older guys. We all started together. Daddy didn't like it a whole lot and Buck Baker said he hated it. Listen, Glen Wood quit racing because of it and because of the superspeedways that followed it.

My attitude was this: "Here's a big, old track with plenty of room. I believe I'll run up here." And I did—right then, I formed a habit of running up high. To be honest with you, I found out that if I ran up high on the banks and came charging down off them, I could go faster. It was sort of like racing downhill with the wagons and bikes. Besides, my car didn't have as much horsepower as a lot of those other cats, so I needed the momentum of the Daytona "hills" to be competitive.

I wasn't trying to be flashy; I just couldn't keep up otherwise. And the name of the game definitely is keeping up. I also found out that it let the car run more free. It seemed to be easier on the car and on the tires to run that kind of groove. And it was easier on me. I mean, if you just go down there and turn a hard left, it bogs the car down and makes you tired after a while. If you turn easier, like driving up high and angling down off the banks, the rolling friction doesn't slow the car down as much.

In addition to that, I figured that if I hit the wall, there was a much better chance that I would do it sideways. When you're down low, there's always more of a chance of hitting it head-on. Those are the bad crashes. I liked my high groove, and everything that went with it. It gave me my own racing philosophy.

The year before, Paul Goldsmith had the fastest qualifying time in the last of the beach races. He averaged 140 mph in his Pontiac in a straightaway run down the paved section of the beach course. To give you some idea how fast the new speedway was, Cotton Owens won the pole position for the first Daytona 500 with a speed of 143 mph, which was his average speed around the track.

Fifty-nine cars started the 500-mile race and, I will have to admit, it was thrilling. It wasn't a thing like any other race I had ever been in. I mean, race drivers always try to get the edge on the starter and the rest of the pack. You always know about when he's going to wave the green flag to tell you to stand on it, so you try to anticipate exactly when he's going to do it. You try to watch for his arm going up with the flag, and then you stand on it a fraction of a second before he waves it. That gives you a tremendous advantage over the guys in front of you, and if you do it just right, you can pass several cars and nobody even notices what you've done. Except, of course, the cars you've just passed while they were waiting for the flag to come down.

Well, I was way back in the pack, so I felt it was important to get up front as soon as possible. The only problem was, the starter was so far away that I could barely see him, so I couldn't tell when to punch it. The only way I knew was when about six cars went past *me*. I mashed the gas pedal to the floor and held it there. With all the other cars on the track, there was a much greater sensation of speed than there had been in practice or qualifying. I was going past some of them real fast, and some were going by me. It was like rush-hour traffic. But the biggest difference was when I got to the corner.

The normal deal in going through a corner is to decide which part of the track you're going to drive and then see if there's anybody there already. At Daytona you could just pick your spot and power right in there. If there was some other cat going in at the same time, he just took another groove and the two of you went in, side by side—even three could do it. There wasn't another track like it.

Bob Welborn and Tom Pistone and Little Joe Weatherly

fought like mad for the lead for the first twenty laps or so, and then Fireball Roberts took over. After that, a whole bunch of people shared the lead for a little while, but, late in the race, Daddy took over. For somebody who wasn't all that excited about the new track, he sure was doing pretty good.

I had gone out of the race with mechanical problems, so I had a good chance to watch the show—and some show it was. If Bill France had written a script for it, it couldn't have been a better race. Johnny Beauchamp and Daddy seesawed back and forth for the rest of the race. Johnny would lead one lap and Daddy would lead the next, and, at the finish, they were neck and neck at the checkered flag. Nobody could tell who won. At first they said Johnny had won, and then they said, "No, it's too close to call. Send this film out to be developed and we'll let the photograph tell the story."

Well, they must have sent it out to the corner drugstore, because it took them three days to decide who won. Bill France finally made an announcement: "Well, fellas," he said, "it took us a long time, but we agree. The winner of the Daytona 500 is Lee Petty."

You know, it was the only race I had ever run where I didn't feel too bad about not winning, because I felt like I did as good a job as most of those other cats, and I knew that I could come back there and win a race. Somehow, I felt this was going to be my track.

I had discovered something at Daytona that was the strangest sensation I had ever run across. I didn't realize what it was at first, and I didn't tell anybody—not even Daddy. You see, there was a phenomenon happening out there that made my car run faster. That's not something you share with anybody, not even your daddy.

They had two hundred-mile qualifying races, and I noticed it first in those, when I was running off the banks to keep up with the pack. Every once in a while, I would go whizzing by them as if they were just sitting still, and then, a little later, the whole pack I had just blown off would come flying by me. I said, "Man, there's something goin' on here. I don't understand it, but I sure do like it."

It was almost like finding extra horsepower. I started experimenting. I seemed to be running faster when I was passing somebody—there was a surge of power, something that made the car go faster when I pulled out. It was like a slingshot.

It worked so well for me that I got all the way up to fourth place in the qualifying race. There were five laps to go. I stayed right in the position I was in. I knew something those other cats didn't, and I was going to save it until the last lap. When the white flag went out, everybody started to get in position for the dash to the checkered flag. The cars in front of me went into turn 1 down low, and I got up high and dove down, right behind them when we came out of turn 2. I fell in behind Shorty Rollins, ready to make my move.

When we started down the back straightaway, I pulled the slingshot trick. I shot past Shorty into the lead. I was really proud of myself. Here I was about to win the first race ever run at the new Daytona Speedway—I thought.

I had done exactly the right thing. The only problem was that I had done it too soon. Two turns too soon. When we got to turn 3, the cars I had just passed went right on by me. Shorty won the race.

But I had discovered "drafting." At least, that's what we call it today. I still didn't say anything about it, but I watched Daddy and Johnny Beauchamp do it in the 500, when I was standing in the pits. In fact, I could see a lot of the drivers doing it. I wondered if they had figured it out yet. I knew it was only a matter of time until they did, but at the moment, I felt like I was the only one who really understood it.

Of course, I didn't understand why it worked, I just knew how. And I was right about one other thing: By the next race, almost everybody had figured it out, and even the newspapers were talking about the new drafting sensation at Daytona.

There's a certain amount of it at every track, but it was

more noticeable at Daytona because we were going so much faster there, and there were so many places where we were running wide open in clean, undisturbed air. It wasn't like the short track where every foot of the way was in traffic.

Here's what was happening: There's a bubble of air moving over the race car—it's there when anything moves through the air. They study things like that in physics classes all over. Well, it's kind of teardrop-shaped, they say. You can't see it, of course, unless you're in California, where you can see the air. If another car pulls up real close behind you, say, a foot or two from your back bumper, he slips into your bubble and yours and his combine into one longer, more streamlined bubble. It makes both cars go faster, and run freer. You even get better gas mileage.

When the car behind breaks out of the draft, the effect he gets really is like a slingshot. That's what we call it now: drafting or "slingshotting." After that first Daytona, everybody started doing it. But it took a while before I got used to looking up in the rearview mirror and seeing nothing but race car. I mean, here was this dude in my backseat—at 150 mph. But then I was in somebody else's backseat, too.

By the time I got to Columbia again, I felt like a veteran. I guess the way I learned to drive—you know, the baptism-under-fire deal—forced me to pick up everything fast. I felt good about my driving. It's a whole lot like jumping into water that's over your head: If you're ever going to learn to swim, you do it real quick. Well, when you've got about thirty other cats aiming right at you in a race car, you learn to get out of their way. If you can do it by outrunning them, that's all the better. And it's a whole lot easier on the car.

I was determined to do it the right way at Columbia. I didn't want to establish a reputation of being a loser, and two races in a row there would have done it, in my mind. It was a convertible race and Daddy was off racing somewhere else, I don't remember; all I know is that he wasn't there. It was a good night. I qualified up near the front, and, in the practice that followed, my car felt better than it ever had. The Olds was sticking just the way I wanted it to. I'm not much for premonitions, but I was sure this was going to be my night.

I managed to stay up near the front of the pack all night. There must have been half a dozen times when somebody spun right in front of me, but I was able to avoid them and stay in good shape. With ten laps of the 200-lapper left, I had managed to get up to second place. The Olds was still running great, but I couldn't get past Jack Smith.

When I saw the white flag, I knew I *had* to get past him, no matter what. I didn't have drafting to work with because it doesn't work on a half-mile dirt track, so I knew I had to manhandle the Olds into the lead. There wasn't enough time or track to do it with strategy. When we went into turn #3, I stayed on the gas longer than I had before. Jack slid wide because I guess he saw me out of the corner of his eye, and he was hoping I wouldn't hit him. But our cars touched; his bounced into the fence. I mashed the gas pedal and took the lead. It was all over. I could see the starter with the checkered flag held over his head. When it came down it was almost like it was in slow motion.

This time there wasn't any protest.

I had won my first race. But I still kept looking around after they gave me the trophy, just to make sure there wasn't somebody coming to take it away from me.

The whole deal felt good.

One other thing: I was named "Rookie of the Year" by NASCAR. They told me it was the second-best deal to winning the championship. It was an honor. But it would have been better if they hadn't said "second best."

13

The sound of the crash was like distant thunder, rolling across the track.

One of the nice deals that comes with being a new father is that you immediately get to start mapping out your kid's life. I mean, his eyes are barely open, and he's still sort of purple, and you're telling people what he's going to be when he grows up. Well, one of the few deals I didn't have Kyle doing "when he gets big" was driving a race car. As much as a third-generation racing Petty appealed to the press, it still wasn't high on my list of professions for my son. The truth is, I thought he might be better off doing something else—anything else. I figured there had to be a better way to make a living.

There's a country music song today that's called "Mamas, Don't Let Your Babies Grow Up to Be Cowboys." Well, back then, it would have been "Mamas, Don't Let Your Babies Grow Up to Be Race Drivers." Being a race driver wasn't the most respected profession at that time.

Besides, he was obviously going to do something very important and would no doubt wind up with his picture on a postage stamp. I was as proud of my new son as any father had ever been and so was Lynda.

But I will admit, there were times when I wondered if a NASCAR guard would be running him out of the pits in ten or twelve years. I was sure of one thing: Just as soon as he was old enough, I expected Lynda to start carrying him to the races with us. I wanted the same kind of life for my family that I had when I was a kid. I know what I said, but it wouldn't hurt to have him around racing, would it? It was a way I could spend more time with my new family and still get my job done.

I'll have to tell you, I was starting to enjoy my work more. They had stopped running the convertible class, because there weren't enough good drivers to make it interesting for the fans in two classes. It had been sort of a joke anyway; I mean, we had one top and two cars, and we put the top on whichever one was going to run in the hardtop race. There really wasn't any other difference in the cars.

I got a new Plymouth like Daddy's. And I promptly got started by winning my first hardtop race at the old Charlotte fairgrounds. I outran Rex White at the checkered flag. Daddy, whose car had broken during the race, had jumped in Doug Yates' car and finished third.

It turned out to be an outstanding year for me, considering the fact that it was only my second full year in racing. The experience I had gotten the year before had really started to pay off, and the new car seemed to be the crowning touch. Until I got the new car, I hadn't realized how hard I had been driving just to keep up in the Olds. Who knows, I might have won more races the year before if I had the Plymouth then.

It's really hard to look back at those days and say for certain, but we all sure had the impression that some of the guys in NASCAR did everything they could to help the drivers they liked. I've never been able to understand it, but they never did seem to like Daddy. I mean, here was a man who had been around from the start and had stuck with them through thick and thin, but they always seemed to favor the other guy— no matter who it was—in any kind of dispute. I was new and they weren't too wild about me. I guess the fact that the Pettys were so independent didn't help a whole lot. We all said exactly what we thought, without mincing any words, while a lot of those other cats brownnosed them to death. Maybe it was a combination of all of that.

Whatever it was, we weren't too popular. If they wanted to

play their favorites, I wasn't going to let it upset me. Well, I *thought* I wasn't. I found out different in the first World 600 at Charlotte.

You remember I said that Daytona opened a new era in racing? Well, it did. Both Atlanta and Charlotte opened high-banked, mile-and-a-half tracks in 1960, and it couldn't have made me happier. It firmly convinced me that I had come along at exactly the right time. I was in on the birth of the new life of NASCAR—the superlong, superfast racetrack—the superspeedway.

But when we showed up at Charlotte for the World 600, the "600" stood for 600 miles, the world's longest stock car race, it started an open feud between the Pettys and NASCAR that has lasted in one stage or another to this day.

Here's what started it: There was a grass strip just before you got to the pit road, and some of the drivers had used it as a short cut a few times during practice and qualifying, so before the race, they told all of us that anyone caught driving across the grass strip to get into the pits would be disqualified. We accepted that.

We had three cars in that race. Bobby Johns was driving Number 41. Well, during the race, Daddy blew a tire coming into the dog-leg in the front straightaway and his car spun down through the grass. He didn't hit a thing, so he dumped it into first and took off through the grass, heading for the pits for a new tire. He was back in the race in no time.

About halfway through the race, someone hit me coming out of turn 4, and I spun down through the grass and went into the pits, since I was handy. Well, we drove like mad and made up a lot of the time. As a matter of fact, we were real happy about the outcome of the race. Bobby Johns finished third, I was fourth, and Daddy was fifth. It was a great showing for the team; it meant that we were going to take home a pile of money.

Daddy and I lined up at the payoff window after they had announced that they were ready to pass out the winnings. It must have been seven o'clock at night, and we were tired. It had been the longest race we had ever run, and we had probably worked harder than we ever had; but it was worth it. Our part of the payoff should have been several thousand dollars.

When we got to the window, the guy said, "Well, y'all don't get any money. You two were disqualified."

I won't even tell you what Daddy said, because there might be some kids or preachers who'll get ahold of this book, and it just wouldn't do. I will say, that we argued for a long time, but those guys just wouldn't give in.

They had disqualified us because we went into the pits from the grass.

"But we didn't drive down there, we spun down there," I said.

"It don't matter," he said. "We tol' you 'bout it. And you done it."

You see, the NASCAR guys knew they were going to disqualify us at the time the spins happened, but they let us stay out there and risk our lives and spend a lot of money on tires and gas, just to make their race look better. We had a pretty good following by then, so I guess they wanted to keep our fans at the race, so they would buy hot dogs and pop or whatever.

Daddy and Rex White were in a battle for the point standings, so I think that had something to do with it, too. Rex was their fair-haired boy. It was obvious we weren't. I heard later that Rex was the one who complained about it, and I wasn't surprised. I think a lot of the drivers were jealous.

They disqualified Junior Johnson too for doing about the same deal. It made us feel even more like those guys were playing favorites, because Junior was in our boat. He wasn't very high on their hit parade either.

I told you this wasn't going to be a race-by-race account of my life and that we would spend a lot more time with the early days—the "growing pain" years. But they weren't all bad; in fact, they were almost all good—almost. For instance, I think it was that Charlotte race that first awakened the public to how important pit crews had become. Before the superspeedway, there wasn't even much need for a crew. If you had to come into the pits, it usually meant you were out of the race anyway, so there wasn't any great need for a speedy crew. And if we had a crew at all, it was usually some friends who went along because they wanted to be part of the race. So it was a casual sort of deal, at best.

We usually had a full crew, but at Charlotte we had only one crew for all three cars, and they probably worked harder than any crew ever had. There were a lot of blown tires and broken windshields and problems of all sort, and, with three cars, there was one of them in the pits almost all the time. After those guys went over the pit wall the first time to take care of one of our cars, I don't think they ever went back to the other side. When the race was over, they were sprawled out in the pits. A couple of them never even went to *see* a race again, let alone work in the pits.

But it wasn't our crew that everybody noticed, it was the Wood brothers. They were the first to have a really professional pit crew. They had practiced more than most of the drivers, and people went away from the race realizing for the first time that a pit crew could easily make the difference between winning and losing. The Wood brothers became an almost-instant legend.

The new Atlanta track was even harder on tires than Charlotte had been. It had long, sweeping turns and it ground the tires down in no time at all. Neither of us did well at Atlanta that year. It wasn't because of tires; it was just one of those years.

The superspeedway era brought more race fans out, and as more fans came, the factories got more and more interested. Racing was just starting into its heyday. Executives from Detroit started coming to all the races.

I won three races and $35,000 with the Plymouth in 1960

and I was runner-up to Rex White for the championship. Daddy finished sixth. I'm glad we're at this point, because it was an important period for me; it was the first time that I realized that my life story, if I ever got around to writing it, wasn't going to be a "rags-to-rags" story.

It was hard for a lot of the old-timers in racing to imagine that my season had been more successful than Daddy's. If you want to know the truth, it was hard for *me* to imagine. And to confuse matters even more, it was the year that Maurice tried his hand at racing. A lot of people don't remember that, but he did try it, and I'll tell you, it's a shame he didn't continue, because he may have had more talent for it than I had. But I guess he didn't have the desire. And it takes a heap of that, if you're going to be successful. Talent alone won't do it.

Chief had some physical problems, because of his early illness; it affected his eyesight so that he had to cock his head sideways to see real good. That gave him problems in the race car. But it was unusual, to say the least, while he was out there—there were three Petty Blue Plymouths on the track at the same time—41, 42, and 43.

One of the track announcers said one time, "And here's half the population of Level Cross, North Carolina, ladies and gentlemen, the racing Petty family—Lee Petty, Richard Petty, and Maurice Petty."

We thought it sounded good.

The end of his racing career came at Columbia one night— exactly the place where mine had started. All three of us were running pretty good, but Chief tangled with another car coming out of the second corner and it sent his car into the fence. The right-front corner dug in the dirt at just the right angle to send the car sailing over the guardrail. His car bounced one time on its top and then rolled a couple of times. Man, it totaled it.

When the caution flag came out, I could see the car lying down there, where it had come to rest on its side. I couldn't see if Chief was all right or not, but by the next time we came around, he was out of the car. I could tell by the look on his face that his racing career was over.

After the race, he was in the pits, waiting for us.

"Do y'all really get a kick out of this?" he asked.

Daddy laughed out loud. "I got a feelin', Richard, we're gonna have our mechanic back," he said.

"You're damn right you are," Chief said. "Listen, a man could get *hurt* out there."

Nineteen sixty-one *started* bad. Goodyear had made its debut into racing a year or so before, and they were working like mad to catch up with Firestone, who had been around for a long time. I'll have to say Goodyear was doing a good job, considering the fact that they were such newcomers. I knew how they felt.

The only problem was that their engineers didn't have much to compare their efforts to. I mean, they didn't have the racing heritage that Firestone did, so they had to depend on some of the drivers giving, or probably selling, them their old Firestones, so they could study the tire compound and try to improve on it.

Goodyear asked me to test tires for them in Atlanta at the new speedway and I jumped at the chance. Not only did they offer to pay me a bunch of money, it would give me some experience on the new track that none of the other drivers would have.

Our dealing with Goodyear went all the way back to 1957. Daddy was one of the first drivers ever to test for them. He and Jimmy Lewallen and Tiny Lund had gone to Hollywood, Florida, to a short track down there to try out their first batch of racing tires, but they hadn't had a whole lot of success. Jim Reed had won the 1959 Southern 500 at Darlington and Daddy had won at Daytona on a set of Goodyears, but those were by far their best efforts.

Our cars were always ready to race when they were rolled off the truck, so that's why they contracted me to drive for them. They knew they wouldn't have to sit around and wait, like they would with a lot of guys, while they worked on the race car to get it ready. For some reason, there was always a lot of tinkering with most of the other cars.

I got right in the car and said, "Let's go, boys."

The first set of tires were pretty good, but they weren't anything unusual. I told the engineers, "They're okay, fellas, but they're nothin' to write home about."

"Don't worry," said Jim Loulan, who was the head honcho of race tire engineering, "we've got a set of supersticky ones we want you to try. Those were the same as last year's Firestones. We just wanted you to have something to compare the goodies with."

"Where'd you get the Firestone compound?" I asked.

"It came to me in a dream," Jim said.

I waited while they bolted on the new wheels with the supersecret tires. When I went out, I couldn't believe those tires. Man, they would stick anywhere. I could have driven up the side of the timing stand. I came in after ten laps, just like they had told me to, so they could check the temperature of the tread surface to see if there was too much heat buildup—that's what causes most blowouts—heat.

"Temperature's good," said Ed Alexander, one of the engineers.

I had been looking at the tires myself. They were the greatest tires I had ever been on, but they were completely bald. Nobody said anything about that.

"Okay, Richard," Jim said, "we need another ten laps."

"Listen, have you guys bothered to look at anything other than your temperature gauges?" I asked. "I mean, those tires are as smooth as a baby's butt. They won't make ten more laps."

"Aw, sure they will," Ed said. "You leave that up to us. They'll make it, trust us."

I was supposed to trust the new tire kid on the block.

"Oh, well," I thought, "I'm gettin' paid for it."

The tires felt even better than they had before. I couldn't understand that, particularly since they were smooth. I had the Plymouth sailing—five laps, six, seven, eight, end of test.

I felt the jerk of the steering wheel that every race driver knows too well. A millisecond later, I heard the explosion. The right-front tire had blown. The car wrenched sideways and I heard the right-rear blow. And then I felt the crash. The car hit the wall broadside and spun down across the track and into the infield. Then it shot back up across the track and hit the wall head-on—that's when it hurts. It's a dull pain, like when somebody hits you in football, but then it hurts only in one place. When you hit hard in a race car, it hurts all over. Your teeth hurt, your eyes hurt, you feel like you've been stuffed into the glove compartment.

The car was totaled. I was bruised but all right.

If the tires had lasted two more laps, I could have gone home and relaxed before we had to leave for Daytona. As it was, I had to go home, where we all worked day and night to get another car built for me for Daytona. Goodyear paid all the bills, of course, and they felt real bad about it.

It was a good time to bring my old high school buddy, Ronnie Hucks, into the picture. He had come back from the service, but it hadn't been a happy homecoming. He had developed cancer in his thigh and they had to amputate his leg. I hadn't seen him since he got back, but I heard that he had an artificial leg, and that he was feeling pretty dejected, so I called him and asked him to go to the Randleman football game with me. He told me that he'd learned to drive an automatic transmission car, and that he'd meet me there. I figured he wanted to do something for himself, so I said, "I'll meet you in the grandstands."

I didn't know how I was going to handle it when I saw him, but when I got there, any question I had was gone. Everybody who knew us from our high school football days were sitting around Ronnie, but they were acting strange—like they pitied him. I could tell that it made him feel even worse. Nobody said a word about his leg, which made it even more uncomfortable for him. I knew somebody had to say something about it. I mean, it was pretty obvious.

"Boy, them cats sure cut that thing off *short*, didn't they," I said.

Ronnie slapped his good leg and laughed like mad. He said, "Thanks, Richard. If somebody hadn't said something about it pretty soon, I was gonna go home."

From then on, Ronnie helped us around the shop with odd jobs, and he started going to the races to keep records for us— you know, how many laps before we pitted and what broke and how long the pit stops took, that kind of stuff. It really helped us, because we needed to know if we were messing up in the pits or out on the track or whatever. Racing was starting to get more complicated, but we had our own statistician. He's still with me.

We got to Daytona early in 1961; most of the other cars weren't even there yet, but we had high hopes. We wanted plenty of time to make sure everything was perfect, and we needed time to figure out how we were going to stay a step ahead of NAS-CAR.

Both Plymouths were running even better than we had hoped for. A lot of the credit went to Chief, who, by then, was setting up the chassis real good. And the engines I had built felt strong—I hadn't felt that good about a car, ever.

The first real test we had was in the hundred-mile qualifying races. I was scheduled for the first one and Daddy for the second. You have to understand that a hundred-mile race is a whole lot different than a 500-mile one—other than the obvious fact that it's over with quicker. But that's the key; it's over quick, so you don't have time for a whole bunch of strategy. The idea is to run as fast as you can, all the way, so every race driver does the same thing: When the starter waves the green flag, he mashes the gas pedal down, to about the front bumper, and he holds it there until the race is over or the car breaks— or somebody runs over him—or vice versa.

They have the qualifying races because the fans love them. It makes a whole lot more money for the speedway. The fact that it gives every driver one more chance to crash up his machinery before the 500 never enters anybody's mind. It's racing, so we do it. Listen, if they told race drivers they had to run 500 miles *backward*, they'd try it.

I got a good start in the race. I was back about five or six cars, in a perfect position to see what was going on before I made my move for the front. Fireball Roberts and Junior Johnson moved their Pontiacs out front real quick. Marvin Panch was right in front of me in another Pontiac, so I figured I would see how my Plymouth was going to do. I wasn't too happy with what I found out. I couldn't get past him. Not only that, the General Motors cars were fast enough that I couldn't even get up close enough to draft them.

I was able to stay in contention, but it was only by driving my high-groove, down-off-the-banks style. With one lap to go, Fireball whizzed by me, with Junior right in his draft. I tried once more to grab their draft and make a three-car train out of it. I got up as close as I could, but I couldn't feel the effect of the draft—you really can tell.

We went into the first corner wide open. Suddenly I could see the entire right side of Junior's white car. My whole field of vision was filled with the side of his car. Smoke was erupting from all four of his tires, and I could see him trying to gather it up. I turned to the left a little, hoping to miss him. He was still there. I turned a little more. It wasn't enough. I moved the wheel as far as I felt I could, trying to walk that narrow line between missing him and spinning my own car—believe me, at 150 mph, the line is a very fine one.

I slipped off the tightrope. My car went into a slide.

Junior's car smashed into the wall and rebounded straight

for my sliding Plymouth. Just as I spun into the grass, Junior's car hit me in the right-rear quarter panel. The impact sent my car back across the track, heading straight for the guardrail that runs all the way around the track.

I felt the impact and I thought, "I hope the car stays up here against the wall." I didn't want to be bounced back down into the middle of the rest of the traffic, and hit by a dozen other cars. But I didn't have to worry. I felt the race car start rising up. It rode right up the wall and seemed to run along on top of it for a long time. I could feel the undercarriage being ripped away.

And then I went on over and started my free fall.

It only stands to reason that if the banks are four stories high on the inside of a turn, then it's four stories down on the outside of the track. That's what it is at Daytona—it's the same height as a four-story building. It definitely is not the place to drive a race car off.

Everything was real quiet for a few seconds. I thought, "Oh, boy." I knew it was going to be bad, so I let go of the wheel and took a big breath. And I held it.

I remember the noise as much as I remember the sharp pain that shot through my body. I had felt the pain before—maybe not as bad, but I had felt it. But the noise was like an explosion, and it kept echoing again and again. It was almost like it was bouncing from side to side and from end to end inside the car—a hollow, drumlike sound. It went away, and then there were little sounds—crackling, popping, tinkling noises. I guess it was the car breathing its last breath.

I sat inside the tangled mess of dead race car (the one I had been so pleased with a day before), and I looked at the roll cage. I remembered welding all that steel pipe, and I thought of how Chief and I had put the whole car together. I guess I was stunned, because it wasn't the time to think about building the car, it was time to get out of it.

I unhooked my shoulder harness, pulled myself up through

the opening where the windshield had been, and fell out of the car, landing hard on my right ankle. My whole body hurt so bad that I didn't even feel the badly twisted ankle. It would just have to take a number and get in line. I lay there on the ground, looking at the race car. The pain from my ankle got to take its turn. I laid my head down and closed my eyes.

I guess the guys in the ambulance thought I had been thrown clean out of the car and was deader than a doornail. I heard one of them say, "Think there's any use of takin' him to the hospital?"

I raised up on one elbow and said, "Listen, guys, *you'll* have to; *my* car's broke."

They both jumped about a foot.

They examined me completely at the track hospital and taped my ankle. They couldn't find anything broken, so they let me go. I hobbled back to the pits, where Daddy was in his race car, ready to start the second race.

"They said you were okay," he said. "But I knew before they told me. You boys built that car strong."

"I reckon we did," I said.

He looked at me and grinned. "You wanna drive this here race, too?"

"Think I'll just get me a Pepsi and climb up on that pile of Goodyears over there," I said and got a can of pop from our little cooler.

He pulled out of the pits to line up for the start of the race. I put the pop can down and went back to the track hospital. I didn't want to tell Daddy, but my eyes were hurting real bad. The doctors said I had about a million itty-bitty pieces of glass in them.

"So that's where the windshield went," I said.

It must have taken them an hour to get all the tiny pieces out, but they said my eyeballs didn't appear to be scratched, so they let me go again.

I walked out of the track hospital just in time to hear the

public-address announcer say in an excited voice, "There's a crash over in turn 3. It looks like two cars are goin' over the wall."

I looked out toward the turn just in time to see Daddy's car going over, with Johnny Beauchamp's car T-boned right into the side of it. I held my breath for Daddy. Then I heard the crash. It was like distant thunder this time. It sort of rolled across the track to where I was standing and then rumbled right on past. It was an entirely different sound on the outside.

I couldn't hear the little sounds, but I hoped Daddy could. I hoped he could hear.

I found out later that Banjo Matthews' car had gotten sideways in front of Daddy. When Daddy backed off a little, Johnny must have froze or something, because people who saw it happen said that he hit Daddy full-throttle, right in the driver's door—square on the Number 42. Johnny's throttle was still wide open, they said, when the two of them went over the wall.

I ran as fast as I could, but I kept falling down, because of my ankle. By the time I got to where the two cars had crashed, I couldn't believe it. There wasn't anything left of either car. There was blood everywhere, and they had just taken Daddy out of the car and were putting him in the back of the ambulance.

He was lifeless.

I jumped in the ambulance and said, "I'm goin' too."

They didn't even stop at the little track hospital because they knew this one was serious. They went right through the tunnel and straight to the big hospital a few blocks away. The two guys in the back were trying to get the bleeding stopped, but the sheet he was laying on was rapidly turning from white to red.

They took him to Emergency, and after a quick examination, they took him to the operating room. I followed them. He was real still. He was cut up and bruised real bad, I could see that, but they had stopped the bleeding.

"You'll have to wait outside," one of the doctors said. "We'll let you know."

Chief and Mother and Dale and Lynda got there in a little while, and we waited together. Nobody said much.

"Where'd they take the race cars?" I asked.

"They're in the garage area," Chief said. "We'll get 'em loaded up tomorrow or the next day."

It seemed like a long time, I really don't know how long it was, but a doctor finally came out of the operating room. He said, "We won't know anything for quite a while. Maybe you all should go on back to your motel and get some rest. I understand you've been hurt, too," he said to me.

"I'm okay," I said.

"Go lie down," he said. "We'll call you."

Back at the motel, I took a shower and soaked my ankle for a while, but I couldn't stand it. There had been no word from the hospital. "Let's go back over there," I said to Lynda.

"I was waitin' for that," she said. "Come on, I'll drive."

Can you believe we ran out of gas? We had to walk about a mile to a service station—she walked, I hobbled—and it was only after we got there that we realized that neither of us had brought any money.

"Call Chief," I said.

"Okay, gimme a dime," she replied.

I just looked at her.

"You mean you don't even have a *dime*?" she asked.

"Look in your purse," I said.

She looked at me—no purse.

We talked the kid in the service station into giving us a dime, and we went outside to the phone. The phone ate the dime. There wasn't any use in trying to talk him out of another one, so we walked to the nearest house a couple of blocks away and asked if we could use their phone. Chief came and got us.

They were still working on Daddy when we got there. One leg was badly mangled, but they were working on internal bleeding and a punctured lung first. He had more cuts than they could count, and he had lost a lot of blood. He kept slipping in and out of consciousness, even after they took him to a room.

After two days he was conscious a little more, so I tried to talk to him.

"Daddy," I said quietly, "can you hear me?"

He was just lying there, hurt real bad. The doctors weren't even real sure he was going to make it. He opened his eyes a tiny bit and looked at me through the slits.

"You and Maurice go on home and get another car and start working on it. Me and your mother'll be home long about Friday."

I shook my head. There he was, about dead, and he was saying he'd be home long about Friday. I figured I might as well go on home. Right after the 500, which was the next day.

Bob Welborn was from Level Cross, so I was standing in his pit during the race. When he came in for a pit stop, he saw me standing there.

"You wanna drive, Richard?" he yelled. "I don't feel good."

I jumped over the wall, took his helmet, and dove into his Pontiac.

I had never driven a Pontiac before, but within a few laps, I was turning better times than Bob. The car felt good to me. It was completely different than my Plymouth, but I got used to it real fast.

In an hour or so, Bob got to feeling better, and he decided that he wanted to get back in his car. His crew held up the pit board for me, but I didn't see it. They held it up the next time I came around. I didn't see it again.

Dale had wandered over to Bob's pit when he heard I was driving. "Y'all want Richard in here?" he asked.

"That's the general idea," one of them said.

Dale took the sign and held it up. I came in the next lap. I just wasn't used to seeing anybody but him holding up a sign for me.

It was another three days before they set Daddy's leg. It took two operations, and the doctors told him that he would walk with a limp for the rest of his life. In fact, he would have to wear a brace. They were right. His leg had been caught between the door and the seat, so he's really lucky he didn't lose it.

After that, Petty race cars were set up inside so that if the car got hit from the side, the seat—driver and all—would move off the rails and away from the side of the car, so the driver wouldn't be trapped inside. There were also more bars in the roll cage assembly and more braces everywhere.

Daytona got our attention.

When Chief and I got home, there was a lot of work to be done. Here's another place where I was *given* something. I did take over Petty Engineering, there's no arguing that. But what did I have? I had two race cars that were totally destroyed, a Daddy in the hospital in traction, no sponsor, no money at all from the Daytona race—and that was one we always counted on—and a brother who immediately got into an argument with our crew. What I *didn't* have was a crew.

None of the Pettys had ever been known for keeping quiet about anything. If any of us thought something should be done differently, we said it, and we understood each other. We weren't thin-skinned. Not everybody understood this, which brings us back to Chief. He had more talent for the business of building race cars than any of us. And less tolerance for anybody who didn't do everything perfect. He wasn't the easiest person in the world to get along with, unless you knew him, of course, and then there wasn't any problem. It's just that not too many people got to know him.

But it was at this point, when we were between crews, that we made a decision that was one of the smartest ones we ever made. I had been building engines and Maurice had been setting up the chassis. That was all wrong, we decided. I was the one out there in the car, so I should be on the chassis-end, because I could tell immediately what the car needed in the way of setting-up. Maurice should be building engines. It was simple: We traded jobs.

We had more trouble running the business than we did anything else. Daddy had always done that, so a couple of nights a week, I went to King's Business College in Greensboro to learn something about debits and credits and profit and loss, although there sure wasn't much on the profit side at that point. While I was there, I also learned how to write.

My handwriting was so bad that nobody could read it, so one of the teachers suggested I take a course in penmanship. They taught that old Spencerian-script deal, you know, where you make all those letters with big loops and swirls. I liked it. In no time at all, I was writing like one of those cats who signed the Declaration of Independence. That's why, if you've ever seen my autograph, it's so fancy. I learned that in college.

Daddy was in the hospital four months. It would have been longer if he hadn't about driven everybody crazy to "get home and help my boys—they need me." Wasn't that something? Here he was a basket case and *we* needed *him*.

I ran all forty-two races on the NASCAR schedule that year, which took some real effort. I mean, picture two boys, twenty-three and twenty-one years old, running a business, when all they ever did before was bolt things together and drive. It is amazing to me, when I look back at it, that we got to all the races. It was tough at times, there's no doubt about it. There was so much to be done.

We expanded the shop. Earlier, we had built a much bigger building, right over the old reaper shed, and then we had torn down the shed, so the only thing that was left of the original building was the floor. We built an addition onto the big building and then we buried a gas tank underground—one of those tanks as big as a truck. Chief and I dug the hole with a pick and shovel. I had blisters on my blisters.

If anything, getting started was tougher for me than it had been for Daddy. When he started, everybody was new at it, but by the time I was running the show I was competing against many of the all-time greats—guys with years of experience like Junior Johnson and Joe Weatherly and Fireball Roberts and Ned Jarrett and Jim Paschal and Buck Baker and a bunch more. To make it worse, all those other guys did was drive. They didn't work on the car or dig holes. They drove somebody else's car. And some of them had other jobs, too, to bring in money. Some were one hundred percent drivers, some were fifty percent. All were zero percent car-builders. I was one hundred percent everything.

At the World 600 that year, I blew a motor in practice, so Chief and I worked all night building another one. Ronnie sat there and handed me parts, and it looked like it was going to pay off. During the race, that thing was running like a winner. In fact, I was leading at the 500-mile mark—it would have been the checkered flag at any other race. At mile 501, the engine ran out of oil and self-destructed.

At the end of the year, after we had paid all the bills—both race car and hospital—we had cleared $4,000.

There was one bright light in 1961. My daughter Sharon was born. It was really nice getting away from the business in the evenings. Being able to go home and play with the kids eased a lot of the mental strain. I don't know what I would have done if it hadn't been for Lynda and the kids.

14

You win races by being right; you get killed by being wrong.

When Daddy came home, he was supposed to stay in bed; that's the only way he ever talked the doctors into letting him out of the hospital in the first place. "Listen, Doc," he promised, "I'll spend every minute in bed and I'll take my medicine . . ."

"You don't have any medicine, Lee," the doctor said. "Just rest, that's your only medicine."

"Okay, Doc, I'll take my rest," he said.

It lasted about two days.

On the third day, Mother was tiptoeing around the house so that he could get his rest; it dawned on her that it had been awful quiet in there for a long time, so she decided to check on him. She opened the door quietly and peeked in. He wasn't even there. He had sneaked out the back door and he was over with us in the shop, telling us how to build a race car.

She was madder than a hornet when she got over there, but when she saw him lecturing to us, she threw up her hands. "Just make sure he stays off that leg, boys," she said. She knew it was hopeless trying to keep him in bed.

I'll have to say that he did teach me a lot about keeping the books and purchasing and dealing with Chrysler and track promoters and NASCAR, which was a full-time job in itself. And we set up a voting system—each one of us had a vote on all decisions. It was democracy in action. It didn't matter if I was the race driver or not, I still had only one vote.

Daddy didn't even talk about getting back in the race car that season, because his leg really hurt when he put any strain on it. As a matter of fact, the doctors had told him that he would never race again, but we all knew better than that. In fact, he said exactly what I expected:

"Whatta they know? Why they used to bolt Red Byron's leg to the pedal, so I reckon we can do that if we have to."

Just like trying to keep him in bed, it was a whole lot easier to just say, "Okay, Daddy," and see what happened. We had our hands full with trying to run a race car, so we just swept the problem of Daddy racing again under the rug until the next season. We figured we might have more time to deal with it then.

The trouble with driving a Plymouth in those days was that it didn't have as much horsepower as the other cars. We thought it did for a while, but the 1961 Daytona 500 convinced us it didn't. I think I had to drive a lot harder than the other drivers, but we had a long history of driving Plymouths, and Chrysler had been good to us, so we decided to stick with them. If nothing else, the Pettys were loyal, maybe to a fault.

I did good on the short tracks, but it was the long ones where I had to pedal a lot faster than the other cats, just to keep up. But, with the proper strategy and driving the banks, I managed to stay competitive, even on the superspeedways. People used to ask me why I didn't charge like Junior or Freddy Lorenzen or Fireball. They obviously didn't realize I *was* charging as hard. I guess it didn't look like it to the fans.

Sure enough, when the 1962 season opened, Daddy was ready to give it a try. Chief and Dale and I didn't think he could do it; he couldn't even walk without a cane, and it took him forever just to get in the race car, but we got one ready for him all the same.

"Don't you boys worry 'bout me," he said. "I know what I'm doin'."

But we did worry. He was trying to prove a point to the world and to himself. If he was going to quit, he wanted to do it on his own terms. Nothing as simple as a game leg was going to stop him. So he tried driving again. It was a little like the old story, "What does a 500-pound gorilla eat?" "Anything he wants to." So what did Daddy drive? You got it.

He finished way back in the pack in the first race. It sure wasn't the Lee Petty of old; he didn't charge into the turns and he wasn't smooth. That's the part I noticed most. After the race, he said, "It'll take me a race or two to get used to it, boys. Don't you worry."

He sat out the next two races. He wouldn't admit it, but his leg was hurting from the strain of the race he had driven. He drove one more race, but it was the same thing. His heart wasn't in it.

"Boys, I told you I'd hang 'er up when I didn't want to race anymore, didn't I?" He didn't wait for an answer. "Well, it ain't no fun anymore, so I'm gonna help you build cars, and Richard, you can race 'em."

He had proven his point; he could drive if he wanted to—as far as the rest of the world was concerned. We knew better, but I'll tell you this, he didn't quit out of fear or even out of pain: He quit because he knew he wasn't competitive anymore. And there never was a Petty that got into anything if he didn't think he would be the best at it. He was forty-seven years old when he put his helmet in the trophy case, alongside the fifty-four first-place trophies he had won in what had been the most successful racing career in NASCAR history—up to that point.

It was up to me from then on.

As far as my career was concerned, it was probably better that Daddy quit when he did. I mean, I don't want it to sound like I didn't want to share the driving responsibilities—or the glory—that wasn't it at all. I just don't think my career would have advanced as quick as it did if we were spreading our efforts out over two cars and two drivers. As it turned out, we could concentrate on my car and make it as good as we possibly could. He would be around to help us run the business, and we really did need him, so it worked out good for everybody.

My attitude toward racing and my career, in general, was good as we got into the season. I had run enough races to know that if you don't win, it's not the end of everything. There's always a race next week. Even then, the most important race to me was the one that was coming up; it didn't matter if it was a quarter-mile dirt track or the Daytona 500. And the most important race I'd ever won was the last one I won.

I think my positive outlook is why I won eight races in 1962 and fourteen in 1963. I not only won $100,000 in the two years but I finished second in the point standings both years. And I was voted "Most Popular Driver" by the fans; that meant a lot to me because I had always tried to treat everyone right and not to let success go to my head.

Things were on the move again; I guess you could say we were going into a new era. Maybe it was the changing of the guard. The factories were coming back strong, and a new group of drivers were coming into racing who hadn't gotten their start running 'shine. The dirt tracks of my youth were giving way to high-banked asphalt tracks—even some of the short ones had high banks. I guess racing was getting out of puberty.

It was better, I know that. The board fences had gone away with the dirt on most tracks; they had been replaced by steel guard rails or concrete walls. NASCAR was more organized. There was more money in racing.

I didn't miss the wild days, but I thought about them a lot. You see, I was looking over my shoulder at the "good ol' days" when they were hardly gone yet. I wondered if these newer, faster, more organized times would be any fun at all. Would the increased speed of the paved tracks add enough excitement to make up for the crazy incidents of the "dust-bowl" days?

I was sure it would.

I could see the handwriting on the wall; it was only a matter of time until all of the dirt tracks were gone. There would still be short tracks, but they would be paved. As much as we all complained about the dust, I hated to see them fading away. I guess I felt like a part of my heritage was slipping away. How could the Pettys live without dirt?

It didn't matter; I knew I would drive them the same way I always had—paved or dirt, high banks or flat. On a short track it takes more skill than it does horsepower, and that's what makes it fun for me.

There were lots of short-track races where I almost drove in the infield all the way around. I saved the high groove for the long tracks, but once in a while, I'd confuse them and drive low on long tracks and high on short. I've always been in search of a new groove. I mean, if you run the same groove as everyone else, then you're not going to go any faster than they do—simple logic. Racing is made up of a whole lot of experimenting and luck. You have to have luck in anything you do.

In a lot of ways, driving a short track is tougher than driving a long one. For one thing, there's never any time to make up for something you might screw up. On a long track in, say, a 500-mile race, you can make a mistake and still have plenty of room and time to make up for it. Man, there were long-track races when I blew a tire, and spun out, and did all kinds of wild deals, and won the race anyway. There are times when you're just meant to win.

You have to be on your toes every minute on every track.

Every racetrack has its good and its bad points. On a short track, you're turning all the time, and that wears you plum out. On a long one, the increased speed is hard on your nerves. You can't say that either one is easy.

How did I learn to drive all the tracks? Well, I learned most of the short-track stuff from following other drivers and learning from their skill and from their mistakes, just like I told you. I had some of the best teachers in the business. I got my "Dirt Degree" at the "Right Way/Wrong Way School of Racing."

As far as superspeedways and asphalt tracks in general are concerned, I taught myself. There weren't any experts, so I figured I might just as well hang out my shingle as a pioneer-on-pavement. I was ready to move on, and why not? There's no future to living in the past.

Another deal that helped me is that I found out real soon what a track was like, and I didn't get out there and run a lot of unnecessary laps in practice. Most of the races were long enough that I had plenty of time to practice when it counted—during the race. If I couldn't sort it out in a dozen or so laps before the race, I didn't think I could when the race was going on. My car was always a little fresher than most of them; I hadn't used it up in practice, like some of those cats.

There were drivers who got out there and ran lap after lap after lap, and, by the time the race started, their cars were plum wore out. For some reason, it just didn't take me that long to judge a track. I was never one to get out there and "go all out" to sit on the pole. If you want to know, I've never put that much stock in sitting on the pole in the first place.

If my car was fastest, I'd always try for the pole, don't get me wrong—there's nothing bad about being up front any time. It's just not worth tearing up your race car to get there.

Curtis and Little Joe were bad about that. Man, they loved being on the pole so much that they'd *destroy* a race car to get there. Then when the race started, they'd be in the pits in a dozen laps, with the hood up and oil all over the ground.

Knowing your car and what it's capable of is important, and when you drove as many races as we did back in those days, you learned a lot in a hurry. What's it called—total immersion?—whatever, that's what I was smack in the middle of. We ran fifty-two races in 1962 and fifty-four in 1963. And, man, if that's not total whatever-you-want-to-call-it, I don't know what it is.

I guess what I'm trying to say is that experience was starting to pay off for me. There's just no substitute for it in auto racing—if you expect to be the best. The more I ran against the other drivers, the quicker it was for me to figure out what they were going to do in any circumstance. I could immediately spot it when they were having a bad day or when their car was. And I took advantage of it.

Experience helps you make the right decisions, and that's maybe the single most important thing in racing. You win races by being right and you get killed by being wrong. I'm not trying to tell you for one second that all my decisions were right—listen, I still make stupid mistakes—but I found that I was making more and more right moves and less dumb ones. I've lost lots of races by making the wrong decision, and nobody in the stands ever knew; you see, the fans only notice when you crash.

My mental attitude was important to me. I knew I had to be able to relax and make the right decision and the right move every turn of every lap of the race, so while some of those cats were pacing up and down before a race, I was laid back on a stack of tires or up in front of the truck, sleeping. I learned to take it easy. Man, I've seen Freddy Lorenzen so nervous before a race that I thought they were going to have to chain him down. In fact, most of them were that way—not as bad as Freddy, but jumpy. And, you know, I think a lot of the drivers who raised so much cain and joked and laughed all the time were just as nervous as Freddy. It's just that they were trying to cover up their concern. Paul Goldsmith and David Pearson were about the only two I ever saw who could relax the way I could.

But when I got out on the track, I knew full well that the time for being a nice guy was over. I was never what you'd call a rough driver, but if some cat tried to lay it on me, well, man, I'd just lay it right back on him. I found out real quick that you can't take anything from anybody on a racetrack; if you let anybody knock you around without doing anything about it, the next thing you know, you've got everybody on the track running into you. So if somebody whammed me, I'd wham them back—harder.

My success coming when it did probably boils down to one thing: I ran 210 races in five years, which is more than Daddy had run in his whole racing life.

Racing cars is not an exact science, but I had a formula, at least. Think of this: You're out there with a lot of other guys, and you're never sure what they're going to do. You might have everything set up just right and the first thing you know, some cat has run over you. Racing is the kind of sport where things can turn on you real quick. If a part doesn't break, somebody else's does and he's heading right for you. When that happens—or when any unforeseen thing happens—it helps a whole bunch if you know the right thing to do. If it's happened to you before—in other races—the chances are you'll do the right thing. Once more, it's that experience deal.

There are so many things to learn about driving a race car. The car changes during a race as it gets hotter and the parts get worn down—tires change. The track changes, for crying out loud, as more and more rubber gets laid down on it and as the temperature goes up. It gets slick and bumpy and, well, unpredictable. If it can turn on you, it'll do it. I was always ready for it.

I like it when it gets slicker; I guess it's more like the dirt days. That's why I like my car set up a little "loose," so that it moves around more in the turns. It's the kind of car I learned on. You have to set up a car like that when you're underpowered, and the Pettys were always a little shy of horses.

There were a lot of good young drivers coming up with me in the early sixties—guys like Cale Yarborough and Bobby Allison and Buddy Baker—but I always thought the best of them was David Pearson. He had been running dirt tracks in Sportsman races for years before he came to NASCAR, so he had a lot of experience on short tracks, and he learned quick on the long ones. David drove a lot like I did: He thought about every move he made before he made it, and you could just about bet that it was going to be the right one. It started a period of Richard Petty/David Pearson battles that went on for many years. They may not be over yet, as a matter of fact. I know David hasn't given up—and I sure haven't.

Over the years, I guess David and I have raced against each other more than any two drivers in history. At first, we knocked each other out whenever we could, but, as time went on, we got more and more respect for each other, so we didn't do it. Oh, I've seen him knock other cats out of a race, and he's seen me do it, but we got so we didn't do it to each other. David always knew when to make his move, and he had himself in a position to do it. I'll guarantee you, that kind of driver is hard to beat.

Some drivers are impatient; they just can't wait to get in first place, no matter how long the race is. Cale Yarborough is a lot like that; I mean, there's one thing you always know about Cale: If he's following you, that's as fast as his car will run that day, otherwise he'd be in front of you. There's nothing wrong with that; in fact, Cale is one of the best drivers in history, but he just doesn't have the same style as I do. I guess it would be boring if everybody drove the same way.

I found out one thing real soon, running against some of those cats—both the new ones and the old ones; they weren't consistent. It's maybe the most important thing to do everything the same, every lap. You can't do it every lap, of course, because there are always other cars changing things for you, but you should always try to do it. I drive deeper in the corners than most of the other drivers. I get on the brakes later and then back on the gas pedal sooner, and I do it from start to finish. I noticed that a lot of those cats drove in deep with me early in the race, but by the end they were backing off way back there. The longer the race went, the farther back they hit their brakes.

As the track got slicker, they got more cautious, and I knew that wasn't how you won races. I won a lot of them by being quickest through the corners, slick or not. That's the way I made up for the tons of horsepower I didn't have. And it kept me competitive with everybody, particularly the new ones, who were learning fast on the fast tracks.

When you added this new group of drivers to the ones NASCAR already had, it may have been the best period for racing there ever was. You can imagine how tough the competition was. But, again, I think that helped me.

Nobody ever gets better in any kind of deal if he isn't challenged.

15

My hemi engine sounded like it was going to suck the hood in . . . I was ready for anything.

I could tell you that stock car racing was a sport of contrasts in the mid-sixties, let it go at that, and then move on to something else, but you wouldn't get the whole picture. It's important to understand this period because it set the stage for where we are today in racing. The mid-sixties was when Grand National racing did most of its growing. It grew right into national prominence. All of a sudden, you read about Grand National and its superstars in everything from *Grit* to *Sports Illustrated*.

I think it grew because of the contrasts—or maybe in spite of them—but, whatever, it prospered. You had big factory deals on one hand and little guys on the other. In between, you had about every size operation there could be. The only thing they had in common was the cheating they did from time to time.

Now don't get me wrong, we weren't lily-white either. I've already told you, cheating had always been a way of life with racers, but it had also been the main reason cars had gotten any better at all. I mean, if we had left it up to the guys at NASCAR, we would have been running Roman chariots. But we had sneaked enough things past them that the cars got better and better every year.

By the mid-sixties, stock cars were no more *stock* cars than they were airplanes. Let me give you an example: We built a frame for the car, which was something cars didn't have any more by then, and then we welded in more than 100 feet of 1¾-inch steel pipe to form a roll cage that would withstand the big, big crashes that happened once in a while. When it was completed, the car was as strong as a tank. It *was* a tank.

Then we bought what the factories called a "body in white," which was a complete body, painted in primer. Or, in most cases, they gave us the body. But the first thing we did was cut away all the "unit-body" frame that they all bragged about in their advertising. It was a joke, if you want to know the truth. It wasn't safe for going to the grocery store, let alone flipping down the racetrack at 180 mph.

When all the junk was cut away, we lowered the body over the superstructure and put in a motor that had been tweeked to 400 or 500 horsepower and *ta-da!*, we had a race car. Or, as the NASCAR guys said, a stock car. The tweeking of the motor and suspension was where a lot of the creative construction came in—borderline misdemeanors.

But I don't think it was really cheating, in most cases. Practically all of it was done to make the cars go faster and handle better and that, after all, was what we were out there for in the first place. The drivers and car-builders didn't get upset about it, it was the NASCAR guys who did. They were more worried about their "stock car" image than anything else.

You need to be stronger than the next guy if you expect to win a lot of races. That's what the deal was all about.

There were some classic examples of cheating that are worth repeating. At Atlanta one time, Cotton Owens showed up with a Dodge that he had built, and, I'll guarantee you, everybody knew there was something wrong with it. Nobody could put a finger on it, but the car just didn't look right. Besides that, it was faster than any other Dodge out there—a lot faster. Well, the inspectors were all over the car. They checked everything. They couldn't find a thing wrong.

In desperation, they hauled out the templates. You see, they had these devices cut out of aluminum that would conform perfectly to the shape of the particular car. They didn't want anybody changing the appearance of a car, because that's really the only thing they had going for them in their constant battle to fool the public into thinking that what we were driving were stock cars.

They put the template over Cotton's car, and it didn't touch anyplace. Man, they could have driven that car through the template at 150 mph and never hit a thing. Cotton had built a perfect Dodge body in seven-eighths scale. It was a masterpiece. The advantage was that the smaller body produced less wind resistance. The principle was simple: There was less of it to resist the wind, so it went faster.

They disqualified the car. I thought the dad-gum thing should have gone in a museum.

There was a certain amount of psychology used in cheating, too. I mean, some of the guys kept the rest of the group stirred up most of the time because they *said* they had a secret weapon, whether they did or not. Here's another example: Smokey Yunick brought a Chevy Chevelle from his garage in Daytona across town to the speedway and made sure that everybody saw that the rear-fender wells weren't cut out, like they were on all the other race cars. It made it harder to get to the big racing tires, but it also made the car more streamlined.

"He can't do that," all the guys said.

"Sure I can," Smokey replied. "The rules say I can cut out the fender wells if I *want* to. I don't want to."

They checked the rules. Smokey was right. Curtis got in the car and turned a record-qualifying average.

Then Smokey cut out the fender walls. Well, the other cats went into orbit.

"He can't do that!" they screamed.

"Sure I can," Smokey said. "The rules say I can cut out the fender wells if I want to. It doesn't say *when* I have to cut 'em out."

He was right again. As if that wasn't enough, Smokey told the other drivers that Curtis had qualified with his weak engine. "Just wait'll you guys see the *good* motor." He had them so psyched-out they were going around talking to themselves.

Curtis ran good in the race, but he broke the car.

Lots of times we did things to a car that didn't help at all, and then we might do some little deal to it that would make all the difference in the world.

Some of the mechanics did things they knew they might get caught at, but they figured those guys couldn't find everything. "Put a hundred changes in, and they can't catch but fifty, so you're fifty ahead" was their theory. It worked a lot of times, because the NASCAR inspectors were as happy as june bugs, even if they only caught you with one or two. It gave them a reason for being there in the first place.

I mentioned factories; well, factory help was important to all of us, and, if you charted the progress of NASCAR on a graph, the high points would be where the factories were in and the low ones would be where they were out.

The big battle started when Pontiac jumped into things. For a while, they won almost all the superspeedway races with Marvin Panch, Fireball, David, Little Joe, and Buck Baker all driving their cars. During those years, Pontiacs were rated at 465 horsepower, compared to 430 for Ford, despite the fact that Ford kept bringing out engine after engine. I mean, they were in it up to their ears. Chrysler was still at the drawing-board stage, but they finally came out with a 413-cubic-inch engine that kept us in the ball game—in a way. I had to drive my tail off to keep up, but I managed.

Ford worked out a deal with John Holman and Ralph Moody to build their race cars for them, and they put together one of the biggest racing operations the sport had ever seen. Man, Holman and Moody were cranking out Ford race cars like an assembly line.

The war was on.

It was on at trackside, too. Competition between all the manufacturers was fast and furious. It got hairy at times. At Martinsville, Virginia, for instance, Fireball got out front in his Pontiac and he intended to stay there. He used up every bit of the track. Well, Freddy Lorenzen didn't want to run in second place, so after trying to go high and low and everywhere else, he rammed into the back of Fireball, pretty hard. He did it time after time.

Fireball knew how to take care of that problem. The next time they went into a turn, Fireball slammed on his brakes. Freddy's car ran in under Fireball's rear bumper, wiping out the grill, the radiator, and the water that was in it. Freddy and his car steamed in the pits.

"Somebody slowed down in front of me, and I had to mash on my brakes," Fireball said after the race. The Holman and Moody crew loaded up Freddy's Ford and told Fireball: "There'll be other days, buddy boy."

There were.

Chevrolet got in the deal with the Junior Johnson cars and pretty soon everybody was so jacked up about engines and speed that you could expect anything to get an extra mile an hour or so out of a car.

Chevy always denied that they were officially involved in racing, but Vince Piggins, who was their technical man, was at every race. So was Ronnie Householder of Chrysler and Jacques Passino of Ford, but they admitted their involvement. I never did understand why Chevy denied it.

The tire companies were battling too, and the tire wars brought a lot more money to all of us. At first, Goodyear and Firestone just paid certain drivers to test their tires, giving them free tires. The next step was tires stuffed full of money. I'm not sure that's ever been brought out before, but it got so we found out who would make us the best deal before we decided which tires we were going to run. Oh, if one was definitely faster than the other, we'd run the fast one, but there usually wasn't that much difference in them. Some of the drivers were actually under secret contracts to run one tire or another. It's hard to imagine that Goodyear had come along so much that they were on almost equal footing with Firestone.

It hadn't taken them long. If you want to know, they may have been a shade ahead.

At times there was a difference. I know at Charlotte one year, Firestones were working better. A couple of weeks later at Atlanta, it turned out that Goodyears were faster. It had gotten real hot during the race and the Goodyear compound seemed to be the answer. Freddy had started on Firestones. Well, when he saw that the guys on Goodyears were blowing by him, he decided it was time for a change. It was before radio communication with the pits, so he fished around in his pocket for the grease pencil he had put there in case he needed to let them know anything during the race. He wrote a "G" backward on his side window at 135 mph. The guys got the message and tore over to the Goodyear tent and had a set of tires mounted for him. They changed them on Freddy's next pit stop. He won the race.

Did you ever try to write a "G" backward at 135 mph? I don't know how he did that. Listen, before King's Business College, I had trouble writing a "G" *forward*.

There's a reason for telling you all these car and tire-war stories, of course. I'm leading up to how Chrysler got in the battle, and how it shot me right into the absolute highlight of my racing career—the years from 1964 to 1967. It's what we call the "teaser" in the book-writing business.

In 1964 it was our turn. Chrysler took us to Goodyear's five-mile test track in San Angelo, Texas, to test the car with the new hemispherical combustion chamber engine—the "hemi," they called it. They also took along Junior Johnson and his Chevrolet, just so they would have a hot car to compare it to.

In all my racing career, I had never had a car that was faster than anybody else's—until then. I went past Junior like a rocket. Chrysler had produced a 426-cubic-inch bomb, and I couldn't wait to get it on the racetrack.

"You guys sure this motor's legal?" I asked. "I mean, anything this strong has got to drive them NASCAR dudes up the wall."

They assured me it was legal, and we all got ready to go racing in 1964. Junior went back and told all his G.M. buddies they might as well "go on back to the drawin' board, 'cause those 'MoPars' is strong." MoPar, which is short for Chrysler's Motor Parts Division, had arrived. We had waited a long time.

I could go on and on about races where the hemi blew everybody away—not only mine, but the other guys who were running them too; you see, Chrysler had a lot of friends now—but I promised you I wouldn't jump from race to race. You're going to get the interesting stuff, remember? So, I'll just pick out the significant hemi stories.

They began at Daytona. The feeling of the hemi was unbelievable on the high banks. Maybe you wonder how they came up with it, and why it took them so long—well, we did too. Chrysler had originally built the engine in 1951 for a street-version car, but it wasn't any good for that. It didn't run good at low speeds. Since Chrysler was a little-old-lady's car in those days, they ended up with a lot of cars with burned valves—and a lot of little old ladies who were burned up. They discontinued the engine, but when nothing else seemed to be able to combat the Fords and Chevys, they brought it out of mothballs, did some modifications and stuffed it back in a few street cars, just so it would be legal for racing. NASCAR rules said that anything that raced had to be available to the general public. We've been through all that.

The engine was so good that Chevy gave up. Ford didn't quit, but I'm sure they felt like quitting.

I had driven a lot of hot cars before, and I sure have since, but I've never been in anything that felt quite like the hemi. The power was there all the time; it didn't matter when you punched it, it socked you right back in your seat. It sounded like it was going to suck the hood in.

You might take one of today's hot turbos and get from point A to point B pretty quick, but you won't get the thrill you did with a hemi. They don't feel as good, and they don't sound as good. I've never forgotten how they responded. Man, if we knew back then what we know today about working on engines, we would have been getting 800 horsepower out of those hemis.

We were ready for anything.

I qualified on the outside pole at an average speed of 174 mph. Paul Goldsmith was on the inside pole in another hemi-powered Plymouth. From then on, it was all MoPar: Bobby Isaac and Junior won the twin qualifying races in Dodges. Junior wasn't anybody's fool—he had come straight back from San Angelo and worked out a Chrysler deal for himself.

You may have noticed that I haven't talked too much about my superspeedway victories up to this point. There's a very good reason: I didn't have any. You also may have the feeling that I'm going to tell you all of that changed with the hemi. I'll save you the "teaser"—it did.

I got out front right off the bat in the Daytona 500 and I won the most important stock car race in the world hands down. Goldie was somewhere behind me. I averaged 154 mph for the entire 500 miles—and that included pit stops and caution flags and everything. They gave me a check for $33,000.

Ford had started an advertising campaign a couple of years before that was built around its successful racing program. It was called "total performance." Right after the race, Dick Williford, Plymouth's public-relations man, passed out buttons that read "Total What?" I still have one of them.

I don't have to tell you that Ford was hopping mad over the hemi. They claimed there weren't enough of them built for the public to make it legal for racing. Bill France ignored them—for a while. After hemis won a couple more races, Ford came back and said, "You gotta let us run our overhead cam engine."

Nobody even knew Ford had an overhead cam engine. France said, "No."

We won some more races. Ford said, "The Plymouths and Dodges are shorter than our Galaxies. You gotta let us run the smaller Fairlane. It's the only fair thing to do." They got

another "no." Ford even lengthened the wheelbase of all pro-
duction Fairlanes to meet the 116-inch NASCAR minimum.
France said, "Okay." But the big 427-cubic-inch engine was
too heavy and the cars didn't handle.

Ford went back to the bigger Galaxie, lightened everything
they could, and improved the engine. Both Plymouth and Ford
had 500 horsepower engines. All of Ford's desperate work
didn't make much difference; I won the NASCAR championship and just a tad under $100,000 for the season. Maurice
was named "Mechanic of the Year" by NASCAR, and Dale
had developed into one of the most respected crew chiefs in
all of racing. It wasn't a bad showing for the "Three Musketeers from Pole Cat Creek."

My luck was good in 1964—everywhere. Lynda gave birth
to another daughter, Lisa. We had built a big, new brick house
over near Daddy's, and I got to spend some time there. I
played with the kids from after supper until they went to bed.
After they were tucked away, I built model cars. Can you
believe that? I built big cars all day, and little ones at night.
But it was relaxing for me.

By then, our lives had started to be typical Petty family
lives. We took all the kids to every race. The big difference
from my childhood days was that the age of the tourist cabin
was gone. We stayed at motels, where all the rooms were
hooked together, and we had our picnics there when I got
home from the track.

The kids didn't really care much for racing; they were much
happier playing around the motel pool or in the grass. I think
the noise of the race cars scared them—even Kyle. It was all
right with me; I was just glad to have them there, so I could
spend time with them in the evenings. When I got home from
the track, I never thought about the race car or qualifying or
anything about racing. That time was reserved for my family.
They never missed a race—or a town where the race was, at
least.

But, if there was ever anybody who had a shorter day in

the sun than I had, I'd like to know who it was. NASCAR pulled in their horns and ruled the hemi out for 1965. Chrysler was pretty upset, we were upset, the fans were upset, everybody . . . well, you get the picture. Chrysler went to the United States Auto Club, the group that sanctions the Indy 500 and the northern stock car circuit. Henry Banks, the USAC president, said, "Come on in, boys, and bring your hemi with you." They told NASCAR to have fun with their all-Ford show and then they left.

For the first time ever, I didn't have a ride. I had gone from the top of the heap to the breadline in one NASCAR minute.

"Why don't you come up North and run?" Chrysler said.

"I been up there," I told them, "and I ain't goin' back."

"Well, you could build a drag car," they said.

"A *what*?" I asked.

"A drag car," they repeated. "We'll work with you, and, who knows, you might like it."

That took some thinking. I mean, I had never even *been* to a drag race. But Chrysler called back and told us that they had been on the phone. "There's not a drag strip promoter in the South who wouldn't jump at the chance to have you run some match meets," they told us. "They'll pay you a lot of money."

That got my attention.

"Why not?" I said. "It beats workin' in the tobacco field."

We got a little Plymouth Barracuda and built it up strong, with a whole bunch of advice from Chrysler's drag car experts. When we got the suspension work done, we put a 426 hemi in it, and we painted it Petty Blue with a "43 jr." on the doors. Then, in big letters across both sides, we had it lettered "Outlawed."

I ran all over the South, and I was starting to like the feeling of drag racing. The car was quick—I was turning in 140-mph runs in the quarter-mile. I beat just about everybody. We got a ton of publicity, because nobody had ever gone from stock cars to drag cars before and been successful. None of this made the National Hot Rod Association drivers too happy, but they accepted us, in a cool sort of way, and we went on winning.

Nothing lasts forever: I had found that out too many times in racing. The fun came to an end in Dallas, Georgia, one Sunday afternoon.

I blasted off the line, and as I was going from first gear to second something broke up front—I don't know what. I had no control over the steering. I hit the brakes but nothing happened. The car swerved to the left and hit an embankment, sending it straight up into the air. It cleared a wire fence and landed on its nose—right in the crowd.

It was then I realized where it had landed. People were screaming, and a lot of them were lying on the ground, around the car. Somebody came running over to me and yelled, "Are you all right?"

"Don't worry 'bout me," I said. "Take care of the people I hit."

Six people were hurt and an eight-year-old boy was killed.

Seeing a race driver get killed is one thing, but that little boy was something else. I couldn't stand to think about it. I've never had anything in my whole life get to me like that.

We tried drag racing again, but my heart wasn't in it. I kept thinking about the boy, so I decided to quit. It had not been a good experience for me.

Shortly after I gave up drag racing, France said that we could run hemis in the smaller-bodied Plymouths—short tracks, in other words. It was better than nothing. We managed to get fourteen races in. I won four of them.

Ford won all the superspeedways, but the track owners were screaming their heads off. The crowds had dwindled: "So what," the fans were saying. It didn't mean a thing if Fords were running against Fords, so they stayed home in droves.

In 1966, we got to run the smaller 405 hemi and I won my second Daytona 500. Nobody had ever won two before. Ford demanded an answer on their overhead cam engine request.

NASCAR finally announced that Ford could run the engine but they would have to give up a weight penalty of one pound per cubic inch. What it amounted to was this: Our cars would weigh 4,000 pounds and theirs 4,427.

Ford walked out or, rather, *drove* out.

The crowds screamed about that. It was going to be another lopsided year without much competition. As it turned out, some of the drivers drove private-entry Fords, but it wasn't the same without Holman and Moody and the big Ford bucks in racing.

It was a strange year. It started out to be a big Ford rout again, and when they pulled out, some of their drivers moved over to the competition. Ford diehards LeeRoy Yarbrough and Marvin Panch won superspeedway races in Chrysler products; Jim Hurtubise came down from USAC and Indianapolis to win the Atlanta 500 in a Plymouth; Sam McQuagg won in a Dodge; Jim Paschal, who had driven a second car for us for a couple of years, won a couple of races in a Plymouth; Paul Goldsmith won a couple big ones in a Plymouth; and I won nine. The biggest victory Ford had was when Darel Dieringer won the Southern 500 in Bud Moore's Mercury.

I'll tell you what an unusual year it was: David Pearson only won the championship and two major races, but he won fifteen short track races. James Hylton, who didn't win a single race, but finished a lot of them, was second. I was third, but I won more money than anybody. I told you it was a strange year. And listen to this: Wendell Scott was sixth. That might not sound like much of an accomplishment, but it was. You see, Wendell was not only the first, he was the *only* black driver to run in NASCAR. He ran pretty good at times, but he didn't have any sponsorship, so it was hard for him to keep up. He ran down low most of the time and stayed out of trouble, but when the race was over, here would be Wendell in the top ten.

Wendell would actually stop working on his car to go help somebody else and, at times, some of the other guys would help him. There never was even a hint of racial prejudice. But

I'll tell you something I always figured: Those cats helped Wendell and said they weren't worried about the color of his skin because he wasn't that competitive—they weren't threatened by him. But if Wendell had found, say, 50 more horsepower, the help would have come to a screeching halt.

I've seen it happen a hundred times, everybody just helps you like mad until you get to within one tenth of a second of them on the track, and then the help stops—in a hurry.

Nineteen sixty-seven. Let me say it again: 1967. I like the ring of it. I've been building to this since the book started.

Ford was back. The MoPar forces were back. The battle lines were drawn. The shooting began at Riverside, California—the road course. Ford brought in USAC stars A. J. Foyt, Lloyd Ruby, Parnelli Jones, and Mario Andretti to add to their arsenal. They already had LeeRoy Yarbrough, Darel Dieringer, Cale Yarborough, and Freddy Lorenzen, not to mention Dan Gurney in a Mercury, who had won the race four times in a row. They had the horses and the riders.

Parnelli won the race. That was one for them.

Andretti won the Daytona after I blew an engine with five laps to go and Freddy got caught in traffic.

It was Lions, two; Christians, nothing.

Suddenly, for no known reason, things started to come together for us. The engines were stronger, the chassis better. It all meshed. Nobody paid any attention until I won three in a row. In the Rebel 400 at Darlington, I got my fifty-fifth career victory. It was a record for NASCAR—one that had been held by Daddy.

Then I broke the consecutive victory record by winning five, and then ten, in a row. We ran through the race victories so fast that what we were doing didn't even soak in. I mean, none of us ever sat down and said, "Man, look what we're doin' "—none of us.

Cars crashed in front of me, and I drove right around them.

At Nashville, I was leading when I blew a tire and hit the dang fence. My crew hammered the car out and said, "Go to 'er, boy." It looked awful, but I made up the eight laps I had lost and won the race. We didn't give up, because there was something that told us that just because you're eight laps down, it doesn't mean it's all over. Sure, some of the other cats dropped out, and that helped, but I won that race by five laps. Everything we did was like magic.

Things were going so well that it looked like I was never going to lose. The other drivers were flat psyched-out, and lots of times people talked about who was going to run *second* in the race—there wasn't any question in their minds who was going to win.

I got to thinking I could win every race. It wasn't an ego problem, it was just that everything was working so well and we had built up so much momentum that it didn't look like it would ever end. There were times when we didn't even unload the truck completely. That was unusual, because we usually took enough stuff to open up a parts store, but things were going so well that Chief would say, "Just get the jacks, and the gas cans, and the wheels, boys. That's all we'll need today." And he was right.

The consecutive string was broken at Charlotte when Paul Goldsmith blew a tire and crashed into me, and it was probably good for all of us. I know that sounds strange, but it brought us back to earth. And I went right back to the winner's circle the next race.

The record for victories in a single season was eighteen, which was set by Tim Flock in 1955. By the time the 1967 season was over, I had won twenty-seven of the forty-eight races, and what's even more impressive is I had completed an unbelievable forty-one of them, thirty-eight in the top five. I won the championship, the "Driver of the Year" award, and the Martini & Rossi "National Driver of the Year" trophy for all of motorsports.

I have no idea what made that season one that nobody ever

matched. I guess it's like Bill Walsh and his Forty-niners, or Bobby Knight and his Indiana basketball team, when they've had unbelievable years. One year they're just good but the next year they're great. They take movies of what they're doing, and it's exactly like they did the year before; it's just that they put everything together and *pow!* they're unbeatable.

I really believe you can overcome all obstacles but fate; there is no way to control that. Destiny is something that can't be changed, and luck, after all, is when *preparation meets opportunity*—maybe that sums up 1967. I know, I can't do it by concrete things, so I might as well get philosophical.

We took some of the $130,000 in winnings and built a huge addition onto the buildings we had added over the years to Petty Enterprises. We put some of the most modern equipment in the world in it and then we had an open house. More than 20,000 people came. I sat at the workbench and signed autographs for hours. I mean, people came from all over the country, and it took a whole bunch of the North Carolina Highway Patrol to control traffic.

When it was over and I was looking around, I couldn't help but think of the time when Chief and I helped with the cement floor in the reaper shed.

I still wish I had pushed him in.

16

We raced into the seventies from the bloodiest period in racing history.

There was one thing that ruined the sixties for all of us and it started at Riverside. Little Joe Weatherly came roaring into turn 6, which is an easy, uphill right-hander. For some reason his Number 8 Mercury lost traction and he slammed into the concrete wall. It wasn't the kind of wreck that should have hurt somebody, but, even though his shoulder harness was fastened, Little Joe's upper body came out of the window and his head was crushed between the car and the retaining wall.

Racing had lost its "Clown Prince." There wasn't any question, it wouldn't be the same around the racetracks.

When we got to Charlotte, things went well for us. Jim Paschal was driving our Number 41. He looked strong, and I felt real good about how Number 43 was running. Number 42, of course, had been retired.

I wasn't surprised about Jim. He was one of the best drivers from the good ol' days, so he knew his way around a racetrack. He and I were among the few left who had driven against most of the original heroes of Grand National racing.

Jim actually got out and read a racetrack. He drove each groove at every speed, seeing where and how the car felt at all times. It was one of the things that made him so smooth; he knew what the race car was going to do under any circumstance.

It was a fast race, with a lot of lead changes right off the bat.

For some reason, everybody was driving a lot harder than usual—everybody. I was told later that the announcers were predicting a record race speed.

The cars got through the first few laps without an incident, and that made me feel a lot better. There are always more accidents in the first few laps than at any other time in a race—except maybe the *last* few. But there's a big difference: The ones at the start are caused because the cars are all bunched up together. It only takes a slight bobble by someone and he's into another car, and then that car's into another car, and, the first thing you know, there are cars spinning and crashing everywhere. And if that doesn't cause it, you may have a fast car or two that's started way back, and he's streaking up through the pack when someone who doesn't see him pulls out and *wham!* there are more spinning cars everywhere.

The wrecks at the end of a race are usually one-car crashes. The cars and drivers are getting weaker; parts break and drivers make mistakes. But the cars are spread out, so most of the time, they don't hit anything but the wall. That's bad enough, but they don't take anybody else with them, at least.

That's why we all breath a little easier when we get a few laps in at the start.

But that bad period was out of the way in the World 600 when Junior spun coming out of turn 2. His car slid right into the path of Fireball and Ned Jarett. They both hit him. Fireball's car spun down across the track and smashed into the concrete inner wall, rear end first. The force drove the gas tank up into the driver's compartment and the car exploded.

There was fire everyplace. Fireball was trapped inside. We came around under caution, and I could see Fireball in there. It took another lap to get the fire put out. When they did, I could still see Fireball inside.

When something like that happens, I try with everything that's in me not to even think about it. I keep my mind occupied with what I am going to do. There's almost always a pit stop, so I get set up for that, and then I plan what my move is going to be once they start the race again.

It's not that I'm that insensitive, it's just that I have a job to do out there, and I can't let anything stand between me and that job. If you let your emotions take over, you're through, and you might just as well bring 'er in the pits and get out. Then you better think about finding another profession.

I mean, we know it's a dangerous sport; nobody has to tell us that. It's just that you can't dwell on the dangers of the deal any more than you can on the outcome—good or bad.

Fireball lived a few weeks, but he was burned so bad he would have been a vegetable. He died while we were qualifying for the Firecracker 400 at Daytona.

He had been sort of a loner. The crowd liked him, but they didn't know him because he never stayed around after a race to sign autographs or he never made public appearances. Still he had a following, because he was a colorful driver. And he was a good one.

In the next couple of months, Jimmy Pardue and Billy Wade were killed in stock car crashes, and Davy MacDonald and Eddie Sachs died in Indy cars. It was the worst period in the history of racing.

You might say that we raced into the seventies from the bloodiest period in racing history.

Lynda got on my case about racing. Everybody got paranoid. I know a lot of cats who overreacted when they got into trouble, and I think they crashed because of it. Their cars slid a little, just like they always had—those close calls that the fans never know about—but I guess they were thinking of all the bad wrecks, and they tried too hard to gather up the car. Maybe they turned the wheel too hard or got on their brakes at the wrong time, but instead of a simple little bobble like they usually had, they hit the wall like a ton of bricks. We were lucky we didn't have more fatalities. You know, it's sort of like plane crashes—how they come in groups.

It was as close a period to panic as I had ever seen in stock car racing, but I stayed calm. It was easy for me: I didn't think about the deaths. It wasn't that I didn't feel bad inside (I did). Man, I was one of the few drivers who went to the funerals. Listen, I know race drivers who have never been to a single funeral, and who never will. Most of them just don't even recognize death. At least, I know it's there. But I was still able to block it out of my mind when I was in a race car.

I hate to appear hard-hearted, but racing is what I do to make a living, and I know the risks. I don't need to be worrying myself about what might happen to me. Deep down, I know, and I intend to keep it deep down. I feel real bad for the family, and I really hate the whole situation, but I've still got my own life and my own career to think about. I have never gotten real close to any other drivers, just because of that. It makes it a little easier to block it out if something does happen. Man, I have to survive, and I can't do it if I'm losing a close friend out there on the racetrack. I try to feel like it didn't even happen. I guess it's this kind of deal with me: Yesterday's gone, and it will never be here again.

Not only was it a brutal period, but it marked the first mass exodus of top drivers in NASCAR history. Before that, it had been a sort of tapering off, with one driver retiring here and another one quitting there. But all of a sudden, at about the same time, a bunch of the greats hung it up—drivers like Junior Johnson, Ned Jarrett, Freddy Lorenzen, Marvin Panch, Jim Paschal, and Dick Hutcherson. When you added the four drivers who were killed, it meant that the new guard had really taken over in Grand National. Most of the familiar names were gone.

Along came another bunch of superstars, with names like Cale Yarborough, Bobby Isaac, LeeRoy Yarbrough, and Benny Parsons to take their places. Only a few made the transition from old to the new guard. You'll recognize some of the names:

Bobby Allison, Buddy Baker, David Pearson, and Richard Petty.

Before we leave the sixties, let me tell you about the year I switched to Ford. I know it's hard to imagine a Petty driving a Ford, but I did. It wasn't easy for me to imagine *not* driving a Chrysler, but it had gotten harder and harder to deal with them, so I could see something on the wall, I didn't know if it was writing or not, but there didn't seem to be much future with MoPar.

Ford had caught up with the hemis. They had Cale Yarborough and LeeRoy Yarbrough, who were burning up tracks everywhere. The races they didn't win in a Ford, David Pearson did. I still managed to win sixteen races during the 1968 season, but Chrysler didn't make it any easier come contract time. They wouldn't honor any of our requests, particularly to let me drive a Dodge, which was more aerodynamic, so we decided that it might be time to listen to Ford. They had been talking to us anyway, so we agreed to sit down with them in Michigan.

Jacques Passino made us a good offer. We went to Chrysler and asked once more for a Dodge. They said "no," so I said, in effect, "Look, fellas, we've had this offer from Ford, and. . . ." They didn't think we were serious.

We signed a one-year contract with Ford with a two-year option. It was a strange feeling when the parts began to arrive. I mean, here were these trucks from what had always been the "enemy camp," and they were unloading at our place. I felt like I should have told them, "Hey, you guys are at the wrong place. Holman and Moody is in Charlotte."

We moved a dynamometer in, just so we could better test our engines. All of us were pleased to know that Ford had a first-class racing deal. No wonder they had been so hard to beat.

We built two Petty Blue Ford Torinos—one race car and one backup car—and we headed for the road course at Riverside. I had never won there before. In fact, people couldn't believe we even ran those big stock cars on that course, because it had been designed for sports cars or little bitty Indy cars. But we ran them, right and left turns and uphill and downhill, and we ran almost as fast as the sports cars.

I was pleased with the performance of the Ford, but I spun out a lot at first in practice, because I just wasn't used to the way the new car handled, so I let it get away from me. The Ford was entirely different. For one thing, we had it sprung real stiff. With the torsion bar suspension on the Plymouths, we always had them a lot softer. Everybody called it the "Petty ambulance chassis."

It had been raining the day before we got there, so every time I spun I got the car covered with mud. Dale and Chief had to clean it before they could work on it. After I spun the third time, they made me wash it. "We're not runnin' a car wash," Chief said.

But I finally got the feel of it and I was running out front during the race. In fact, I thought I had it won until I looked in my rearview mirror and saw another Ford coming up on me like he was going to give me a ticket. It was A. J. Foyt. He went past me and it looked like he was whipping the car like a jockey whips a horse in the stretch drive. Turn 9 was coming up fast, a really hard right-hander, and Foyt was still on the gas. He had to slam on his brakes so hard that I guess he must have burned them out right there, because he slid wide coming out of the turn, and I went around him. When I took the checkered flag for the victory, A.J. was right on my tail. He had stayed right in there, without brakes—something you really need on a nine-turn road course.

A. J. Foyt can drive a race car.

It was a good start for our first year with Ford. It also was my ninety-second victory, and the only one that hadn't been in a Plymouth. I set a track record at Riverside, which wasn't bad for a basically roundy-round driver. It wasn't any big deal; it was just like driving on the back roads at home. There were just more people chasing me, that's all.

It took me to midseason to get back on the winning path, but I managed to win eight more races that year for Ford, including my one-hundredth victory, which came at Bowman Gray Stadium in Winston-Salem. Everybody had said it was impossible for a driver to win a hundred races. That was one of the great incentives I had to do it.

At the end of the season, Chrysler came to us and said, "Don't you guys think it's about time you come home?"

"Will you listen to some of our requests?" I asked.

"You name it," they said.

We went home.

We built a Plymouth SuperBird for the 1970 season. Glenn White, who was Plymouth's general manager, said, "It's about time. Do you know they've been flying flags at half-mast over the 3,400 Plymouth dealerships for the past year?"

One of the first things we did was to improve the ambulance chassis. We worked out a true geometry for the steering. Everybody does it now, but we're one of the teams who discovered that if you have a true arc at the pivot points, where the idlers come over, it made it easier to put the car where you wanted it. Our body rolled over more, but that didn't matter. On most of the other cars—the Fords included—the body didn't roll as much, but the car was always trying to steer itself. It would go where you put it, but the tires did all the work. So, when the track got slick, the car didn't handle as well.

It's the same kind of deal that Banjo Matthews builds and sells now. You can go out and buy a chassis set up like that. Things have changed: When we started, you had to make everything yourself. There were lots of times when we had to go borrow a bolt from one of the other car-builders.

Thanks to the good handling car and the strong engines, I won eighteen races in the Plymouth that year. And Pete Hamilton, who was driving our second car, won three.

That's an interesting story—Pete Hamilton. He came to NASCAR from Massachusetts, which is unusual in itself; most of our drivers came from the Southeast. But Pete had been so good up there in sportsman cars that we decided to give him a try.

He sat the racing world on its ear.

The three races he won in 1970 were the Daytona 500 and both 500-milers at Talladega, and that's the last thing anybody ever heard of him. Not many people know why, but I'm going to tell you. Right after the 1970 season, Chrysler called us and said, "We're cutting back on our racing program."

I thought, "Oh, no, here we go again."

"We're only going to run two cars this year, one Plymouth and one Dodge," they said.

"Well," I thought, "we may salvage one of the cars. Mine."

"We want you to build and manage both of them."

I breathed a big sigh. "With me and Pete driving," I said.

"No," he said, "we want you to drive one, but we want Buddy Baker to drive the Dodge. He's been driving a Dodge for us all along and we can't leave him out."

Pete was out of a factory ride. He could never put anything together as good as the ride he had, so he just quit Grand National and went to Norcross, Georgia, and set up a shop to build and race sportsman cars. He's still there.

The whole deal was something like the one with Freddy Lorenzen, who had brought his own car to Grand National from up around Chicago. He looked so good that Holman and Moody offered him a Ford factory ride. He had a lot of experience running USAC stock cars, so he took to it real quick down here. For three or four years, he was the "golden boy" of NASCAR.

But Freddy was nervous and he had real bad ulcers. He used to get deathly sick before almost every race. One year at

Daytona, he wrecked and went into shock. I mean, he didn't get hurt bad in the wreck, but he got out of the car and looked down and saw blood dripping on the track and he just about died—literally. I guess it was the first time he ever truly realized that he could get hurt in one of those things.

The race at Raleigh in 1970 was both significant and sad—not like there was anyone hurt or anything like that—but it was the last Grand National dirt track race ever run. When we lined up for the start, I couldn't help but think of my first race at Columbia, back in the days when I thought I was doing well if I got the car around the track for a complete lap without hitting the wall.

When the starter dropped the green flag, I thought, "Man, I'd really like to win this deal."

I did. It was about as important to me as winning the Daytona 500.

R. J. Reynolds Tobacco Company got involved in Grand National racing when they couldn't advertise their cigarettes on television anymore. They had millions of advertising dollars and nowhere to spend them, so they looked around and decided that stock car racing was as good a place as any. They were right.

Reynolds worked out a deal with NASCAR to become the prime sponsor of the Grand National series, and they agreed to establish a Winston Cup series that would pay the champion a bonus of more than $100,000 at the end of the season. I thought it was a wonderful idea, particularly since I won the first one. And the second one: I was the champion in both 1971 and 1972. Maybe the bigger carrot helped.

But Winston's entry into NASCAR made a big difference in more than just money—that was the most important thing, but the whole racing scene changed. For one thing, it was because of them that the dirt tracks were eliminated. They wanted to play to a much bigger audience, and they were willing to pay for it. They told NASCAR that if they dropped the little races, they would make the pot sweeter for everyone in the bigger races. Races of less than 250 miles were scratched.

It meant that instead of running forty-five or fifty races a year, we would only have to run twenty-eight or thirty. There would no longer be two or three races a week; instead, we raced once a week, and then there would be times when we actually had a weekend off. There had never been a time like that—except when it rained, and then we were usually already at the track, sitting in the back of the truck, watching it pour and talking about car racing. Or more likely, telling tales about the good ol' days.

With the new schedule, I could spend some time at home for a change. That made everybody happy. Besides, I had another daughter, Rebecca, who was born in 1972. It was one more good reason to be home. Man, I had four kids; I didn't need to be living in a motel for the rest of my life.

The whole deal was like getting a raise and more time off. There wasn't a thing wrong with that.

Let me tell you what a difference it made. I had another one of those unbelievable years in 1971. I won twenty-one races, including the Daytona 500 for the third time, the Atlanta 500 and both 500-mile races at Rockingham, North Carolina. You remember I said I won $130,000 for my twenty-seven victories in 1967? In 1971, I took home $309,000 for twenty-one wins. Having Winston around made that much difference.

I never smoked cigarettes, but I sure would have switched to their cigars or chewing tobacco if Reynolds made them.

Right on the heels of Winston came one of my biggest breaks ever. At the end of the 1971 season we knew that Chrysler was about to get out of racing, so we were scouting around for another sponsor. On the last race of the season, Andy Granatelli came to the track in Texas. He stopped by our pits and chatted for a while, but he didn't say anything about sponsorship. You see, Andy was president of STP at the time, and he made the decisions.

He called me at the shop one day after that and asked if I would be interested in coming to Chicago to talk about STP sponsorship. In my coolest manner, I told him I thought I could work it into my schedule. "In fact, I can stop next week, on my way to Riverside," I told him.

Chief and Dale and I went up to see what they had to say. We sent the rest of the guys on to California with the race car. The meeting we had scheduled for "an hour or so," stretched into the night. We finally had to take Chief and Dale to the airport so they could fly on out to get the car ready for me to practice and qualify. I stayed on for another day.

Andy and I dickered about this and that, but finally we had a deal put together—well, almost a deal. We agreed on everything but the color of the car. Andy wanted it red, which was STP's color, and I insisted on Petty Blue. He wouldn't give in, so I said, "Well, Andy, I gotta go race my blue car. Lemme know if you ever change your mind." And I got up to leave. I wasn't bluffing, there was no way I was ever going to drive a car that wasn't Petty Blue. There wasn't that much money in Chicago.

"Now wait a minute, Richard," Andy said. "We can work something out."

While we were talking, Andy was doodling. "What if we paint it red and blue?" he asked, and he showed me a rough sketch.

"You mean blue and red," I said.

He grinned. "We got a deal, partner?" Andy asked.

That's the nice thing about two bosses dealing: You can decide right on the spot. "We got a deal," I said.

I couldn't believe how quick Andy got things put together. The next day, he had a press conference set at the Ambassador Hotel in Los Angeles. He didn't tell any of the press what it was all about. STP had been very active in Indianapolis racing and the press guys knew that if Andy had something to say that it was probably pretty important.

Here's what they did: Ralph Salvino, one of Andy's top

men, was at the racetrack with the race car. At a specified time, he was going to plop huge STP stickers on my race car, and they figured all the people would go crazy. That's where most of the photographers were.

Andy got up on the stage in the ballroom of the Ambassador, and he said, "Ladies and gentlemen, STP has decided to enter NASCAR Grand National racing." And then he paused for effect (everybody knows what a showman Andy is) and said, "And here is our driver . . ."

I walked out from backstage, and the place went wild. It was a dramatic moment. Just as Andy said, ". . . the winningest driver in racing history, Richard Petty," Ralph, back at the track, plopped the STP decals on the car. All of racing was buzzing within minutes.

When I won the Riverside race, Andy was so happy he almost couldn't stand it—he kissed me. I said, "Andy, *that* ain't in the deal."

I heard one guy say, "There's no way it'll work. I mean, Andy and Richard, are you kidding? They're two of the hardest heads in racing. There's no way they can work together. No way."

The guy was wrong.

I can say this right now, there never was a time when Andy didn't bend over backward to try to please me. All of the STP people did. They let me run the show completely. Andy only came to Level Cross one time. He told someone, "Hey, those guys win races. There's no use to mess with them." He looked on us as pros, and I never had a cross word with him in all the years he was at STP.

It was just the opposite of what most people predicted. When we put the decals on the car the first time, for example, it wasn't exactly where he wanted them. It was two months before anybody at STP had the nerve to tell me they wanted it changed. He didn't want to make me mad, and despite the fact that he was paying me way up in six figures a season, he held back asking me to change the decals. Listen, I would have put them anywhere they wanted them. I did, in fact.

But I will say one thing about Andy: He never gave up. When the contracts came down the first time, there was one extra clause in them that said STP would pay me an extra $50,000 if I painted my car all red.

I smiled when I scratched out the clause.

17

Green means go and checkered means stop and no holds barred in between.

It must have been about my seven-hundredth race—1978 or so—when I realized there *was* real pain in racing. I was on ABC Television, explaining the thrills of victory and the agonies of defeat when it dawned on me. "Dang, this is a hard deal we do!" Before that I just took it for granted. I mean, I had always done it, so I didn't give it a second thought. It's like walking; you don't sit around and think about how you walk. The people I know don't, anyway. But I guess, unless you've done it, you would have no idea how much agony there is to driving a 3,700-pound stock car in a 500-mile race. Maybe I should tell you. Why do I feel like I'm on a psychiatrist's couch?

The stress alone that's placed on you in the race car, where the temperature may be 140 degrees, is unbelievable, and when you're drafting at, say, 200 mph, it keeps you so tense that you can feel it in every muscle. It wouldn't be too hard to drive one of those deals at that speed for a lap or two, but to do it for four or five hours is one of the most physically and mentally demanding things a man can do. It's a full day's work, I'll tell you that. I mean, compared to pro football or baseball or something like that, it's like a whole season wrapped up into one afternoon.

We don't have any two-platoon system or time-outs or

substitutes or even a little break between plays. It's a continuous journey, and it gets worse as the race goes on. It's a lot like rowing a boat, the longer you do it, the harder it gets. It starts to pyramid on you.

Running wide open would be hard enough on you, but when you do it with a whole track full of cars, lap after lap after lap, it wears you down. You see, we're doing this stressful thing in a car that's so hot inside you can't even move your hands from where you have them on the steering wheel. If you do, you have to put them right back where they were, because that's the only place that won't burn you.

The heels of my boots get gummy and melt to the floorboard and every once in a while I have to lift them up so they won't stick. My lips blister, and there have been times after a long, hot race when I had to have help to get me out of the car, because I was so plum wore out I couldn't do it by myself.

You can't let down mentally for a second either. I mean, if you lose your concentration, you might misjudge something, and then that's all she wrote. You take a wide receiver, if he takes his mind off his job for a second, the worst that can happen is the ball will go sailing over his head. The coach might be a little out of sorts with him—not to mention the quarterback—but everybody will forget it and go on to the next quarter. Make that kind of mistake in a race car at 200 mph and there might not even *be* a next quarter to worry about.

My neck gets tired from holding my head up straight with that heavy helmet on, when the G-forces are trying to pull it to the right. The pain goes all the way down your shoulders and back.

If you're leading, you don't much care about the pain. You don't even notice it, if you want to know the truth. It only hurts when you're back there in the pack and your car isn't running worth a hoot, and everybody's going by you. That's when I feel like going back to the tobacco field.

What you have to do is tell yourself, "This is nothing. It's not that hot in here. Stand on it!" But more than that, you have to listen to what you're trying to tell yourself. How I'm doin' Doc?

Oh, if it's Daytona or Talladega—one of those big, wide-open tracks, you don't have to tell yourself much of anything. You don't even have to do much getting ready, physically— you just get out there and race. Those tracks are easy, and even though you're going maybe 220 down the straights, it doesn't bother you. But at Darlington and some of the others, man, you better be all psyched-up and ready to go, because your work is cut out for you. It doesn't matter if you're hurting or not, you have to pull yourself up and go out there and get with it.

I've raced with broken ribs when I couldn't take a breath in the turns because the centrifugal force was pushing my ribs over against the side of the seat. If I breathed, the pain would be so great I'd nearly pass out. I'd have to wait until I came out of the corner before I took a breath, and then I'd have to take little gulps. There's pain at times that would make you scream if you were sitting at home in your living room.

The average guy would pull in and say, "See you, boys," and go on back to the farm, but a race driver is a different breed of cat. We're going to do it no matter how hot it is or how much we hurt. It's like the pro football player you see all bandaged up. The only difference is, we can't take any pain pills, because it would dull our senses too much. One thing is sure, we have to be as sharp as we can get mentally. We have to live with the pain. We've committed ourselves to it. All that stuff goes with the territory.

Les Richter was president of the Riverside International Raceway. He's also a former all-pro linebacker with the Los Angeles Rams; in fact, he's the only man that anybody ever traded a whole football team for. That's right, the Rams traded eleven players for him. Well, Les told me one time that the difference between a good football player and a great football player is that a great one can play when he's hurt. It's the same way with a race driver. If he's one-hundred-percent dedicated to it, he'll be driving no matter how much he would like to just go somewhere and lie down—and scream.

There are some races I should have won, but I was so sick that I wasn't as sharp as some of the other cats. And there are a lot of races when I had no business even being in the top ten, but I was so determined that I finished right up there. I ran one race after I had been up all night throwing up. I had the flu and was so weak I had trouble getting in the race car. But I went out and lapped half the field to build up a big enough lead so that I could come back in and get a relief driver. Dave Marcus got in the car and ran for a long time, and then I got to feeling strong enough to try it again, so I got back in. I still felt as weak as a kitten, but I finished second in the race.

If you have to boil it down to one word, it definitely would be *desire*. I probably run harder when I'm in tenth place than I do when I'm leading—pain or no pain—because I don't like to be in tenth place, and I do everything I can to improve my situation. Ninth isn't much to write home about, but it beats the tar out of tenth.

You may not always be able to drive as hard as you want to, but you sure can drive smart. No matter how you feel.

Another illness hit me one year at Augusta. They took me to the track and put me in the front seat of the truck to sleep until race time. I didn't even go to the driver's meeting. When they had the cars lined up, I got in mine and won the 500-lap race. And they look me back to the motel. I didn't even go to the winner's circle. I had a job to do, and I did it.

I think this had a lot to do with how my career turned out. But I'm not sure it did much for my health. I started getting severe migraine headaches, and I'd take everything I could get my hands on to stop the pain. There were lots of times that I'd pop a handful of aspirin before I got in the race car. Well, the aspirin would lay there in my stomach and the tension and heat and everything would end up making me sick, so I'd take some antacid after the race. Aspirin before, antacid after—it's no wonder I started having stomach trouble.

My stomach got worse and worse. I put it off for years—we call them my "aspirin and antacid days"—and I won some races while I was at it. I started getting more headaches and colds and flu and anything that was going around but I still raced. I wrote it off to heredity. The Pettys have always had weak stomachs; Daddy had trouble with his. I figured we just had a higher acid level than most people, and being in that pressure cooker made it worse.

I avoided what I knew had to be done for as long as I could, but it got so bad I couldn't concentrate well enough in the race car, and I figured I might as well get it fixed. I went to the hospital after the 1978 season. I was going to get killed out there on the track because I couldn't concentrate, so I listened to the doctor and let them put me in one of those drafty hospital gowns. I knew I had a real bad ulcer, and I was sure they were going to have to do more than put me on a diet. I didn't know they were going to have to take almost half of my stomach out. I guess the million or so aspirin I took over the years just ate it away.

I was racing again the following season, and most of the headaches and other problems had gone away. They've stayed away. Oh, I have to take a Goody's headache powder once in a while, but all of us do that, and I have some problems with my eyes, but that's because I have astigmatism. It's not from any normal cause: It's from the eye doctors grinding on my eyeballs over the years to get pieces of steel and junk out of them from the machining at the shop. They've just ground my eyeballs down until they're not round anymore.

My hearing has always been bad, so I have some trouble with that. I don't suppose living in a tin can that has the world's loudest motor hooked up to it has helped, but it's not the whole reason. I never did hear too good even when I was a kid, if you want to know the truth. Not too many people know that. Well, they didn't until now.

It sounds like I'm a mess, but I'm really not. I'm in pretty good shape for the shape I'm in. I can still race 500 miles—600 at Charlotte—and be as alert at the finish of the race as I was at the start. I know some twenty-year-olds who can't say that. Of course, I've been doing it a while. It's all part of the game I've been telling you about. It's not an easy life.

You have to have a positive attitude—in everything about racing. I tell myself: It's not over until the checkered flag, and whatever it takes in between is what I'm going to do. I don't let any of it bother me. If I have to work like mad to get up through the pack to first place, and then have to pit under green (which means all those cats I've just passed have gone by me again), I just shrug my shoulders and tromp down on the loud pedal. "You gotta pass 'em again, buddy boy," I tell myself. And I may have to do it several times before the race is over.

The Definition of Racing: Green means go and checkered means stop and no holds barred in between.

We've been through the crashing part a couple of times already, but it seems to be the thing that most people want to know about, so I'll just say one more thing about it: It all happens so fast that you don't have time to think when it's happening, and then, when it's over, it's too late to let it bother you. There's only one time when you can do anything about it and that's before it happens; that's why I said you can't let down for a second.

I've seen it happen a thousand times; somebody gets scared and then, the next thing you know, he's hit the wall. More than likely, it was that deal of letting whatever it was scare him that got him in trouble in the first place. He may have been so scared *after* he got in trouble that he couldn't get himself out of it: He just froze.

I've tried to condition myself from getting in that situation. As long as the car is moving—even after I've hit the wall—I always feel like there's a chance to get something hooked up. I think I have some control over it. Whether I do or not, doesn't really matter; I still have that belief.

Of course, there are times when none of it works. You hit the wall too hard at times to do anything about it. That's what happened to LeeRoy Yarbrough. It was at Texas and he hit the wall head on. It didn't seem to affect him much; he went to the hospital for a while, and he was back racing in a few weeks, but he never was the same. Not only didn't he charge as hard as he did before, he started to lose his memory. He didn't remember some people he'd known for years, and there were races he didn't even know he had run. He got real sloppy, and his hair turned gray in a matter of months. I heard that he started drinking heavy, and I do know that things went from bad to worse.

I didn't really know LeeRoy that well, so I can't say if the wreck caused the drinking or what, but he never won another race. He went from the top of the heap to the bottom in one year. Maybe it was fear after the bad wreck, I really can't say, but it wasn't long before he was completely out of racing. He had come up real quick and in 1969 he absolutely tore up the superspeedway circuit. We heard that he tried to kill his mother with a butcher knife, so they had to put him in a mental institution. It was in all the papers. He was in that place for years, and I guess most of the time he was almost like a vegetable.

LeeRoy died last year of a massive brain hemorrhage.

Anytime you crash, it could be serious, and it always hurts, but the head-on or backward crash is the one that does the most harm. I guess it's the sudden impact. When you hit a glancing blow or even when you flip, it's not as hard on you. You may have seen crashes where the car is just flipping and rolling and coming apart, like some I've had. Well, the car is built so strong, that it will more-than-likely stand that, but we do everything in our power to keep from hitting head-on.

Your personality when you get in a race car is going to be exactly the same as it is when you're sitting at home in front of the television or when you're driving your family car. Whatever your outlook on life is, it's going to be the same when you pull out of the pits to go to work. You can't really turn it on and off, so basically you're going to be *you*.

No matter how much you go to the White House or the country club or the local bar, you're going to be the same. You might appear to be different, but deep down, you're not. What's this have to do with race drivers? Well, the point I'm trying to make is that a race driver's true personality comes out in the race car. You get the real person. Man, they're themselves more than any other time. You can't hide it on the track.

David Pearson is easygoing when you talk to him; he's easygoing in the race car. I mean, he may be driving the fool out of that dude, but he's not taking chances and overextending himself. If you want to know the truth, he's like an old sheepdog: He'll work you all day and then he'll get you up in the corner and bite you. Dale Earnhardt is nervous and digging along when he's walking around in the pits, and he does the same thing in the race car. He's nervous, like Freddy Lorenzen. Don't get me wrong, I'm not saying they're not good drivers; Freddy was and Dale is—it's just that their personalities really show when they get in the car.

It's exactly like that plane crash in Japan in 1985. The passengers knew they were going to crash. They had half an hour to worry about it. After it crashed, and the rescue workers were sorting through the debris, they found a letter one of the Japanese passengers had written to his family. It was a short, warm note, telling them how much he loved them and how sorry he was that he was leaving them. I mean, here is this guy who knows he's going to die and he's writing home.

I'd be willing to bet that ninety percent of the passengers were screaming and wailing and carrying on, but not this guy. He wrote a calm, beautiful letter to his family. He had accepted his fate, and he was given half an hour to get things together.

Well, me and David would be writing home, while Dale and Freddy would be tearing up the airplane.

Let me tell you why I feel that way: Humpy Wheeler, who is president of the Charlotte Motor Speedway, got some scientist to come in one time to test the race drivers; they're always trying to find out why we do this thing we do. Well, this time it was to see what effect the whole thing had on our cardiovascular systems and our anxiety levels. They wired us all up like Christmas trees and sent us out on the track, and then they monitored us. I felt like an astronaut.

They were surprised to find that almost every driver's heart rate went up, a bunch of them as high as 150 beats per minute. They checked it before the race and during and after—the same thing: sky high. Mine was the only deal that didn't change at all. It was the same during the race as it was when I was sitting in the truck telling racing stories. There was one other driver that was right down near normal—David Pearson. I think that proves my point.

I told you they're always checking something; well, right after that, the Charlotte *Observer* did a survey on where the Congressional Medal of Honor winners from all wars had come from. They found out that more came from the Piedmont region of North Carolina than from any other place. Maybe it's why so many good race drivers have come from here, too. I mean, brave is brave. But not really—brave is the true personality coming out.

Some people might not be able to see your personality all the time in a race car, because you can't always run the kind of race you want to, but the other drivers see it. Someone may be blocking your groove, or your car may be bucking, or any number of things may be keeping you from where you want to be, so you have to try to run your kind of race as much as you can. If all else fails, you may have to draft your way to where you need to get, but you have to be careful when you're doing that, too.

Only a bad driver drafts a bad driver. That's Racing Rule Number Five—or Six. I lost count.

There are certain drivers I'd follow through any place. You know, you have to make that decision at times. If something happens in front of you and there's another car between you and the problem, you have to decide whether to follow the cat in front or find a route of your own. Well, if its somebody like Cale Yarborough or A. J. Foyt, I figure he's done the only thing there was to do, so I'll follow him, but if it's somebody I don't know too much about, I may start looking for my own escape road. I'd follow David Pearson into the infield, because I'd figure that's the only place there was to go.

You see, driving a race car is not just pure ability; it's a matter of knowing exactly where to put your car, and when to pass and when not to pass. In practice, I start slow and work up. I run it all the way up to where it doesn't feel good, and then I back off. If that's not fast enough, we work on the car until it does go fast enough.

In the race, it's a deal of knowing when to charge and when to hold back—you have to feel it. Then you have to set a pace for yourself, one that you can run all day. If they outrun you at that pace at the start of the race, fine. You know this is the pace you can keep up for 500 miles or whatever. It may be a half-second slower than the leader, but if you're smooth, you'll probably be a half-second quicker than anybody else at the end of the race. I mentally prepare myself for it and then I do it. But on the last lap, I pull out all the stops. I might take a chance I wouldn't take any other time in a race.

If you're a diehard race fan, you'll know that all of this is building up to the 1976 Daytona 500. It was, without a doubt, the wildest finish of any race ever, but I'm not sure if the whole story has ever been told. Here's what happened; I know— I had a front-row seat:

David and I had run close together on the last lap so many times over the years that people had started to expect it. I figured that it had to happen sometime. I mean, you just don't run bumper-to-bumper and wheel-to-wheel that many times without something going wrong at least once. You'd be surprised how many times it's come down to just me and David. But that day at Daytona, my Dodge was a little faster than David's Mercury—I think we both knew that. That doesn't matter with a cat like David; he'll work that car for all it's worth and he'll suck every second he can out of the draft. It's like I been telling you about driving smart.

We had raced the whole day, and we were a lap ahead of the field, so we were doing whatever we wanted out there—going high and low, all over. We came into the last lap. As we roared down the back stretch, David pulled out of the draft and slingshot past me. As we went into the third corner, his car didn't stick down low, like he had been running for the last few laps. He slid up in front of me in my high groove. I pulled back down on the inside of him, down low, where he didn't expect me. I'm going to tell you the truth, I really couldn't swear what happened from that point on. It's the hairiest part of the track anyway, and here we were, running flat-out and belly-to-the-ground. We both had our hands full. He pulled down low, and I went up high. He went up high. We got the place in the track where there's a bump, where the cars get squirrelly anyway. I know I was driving the car like it was on glare ice—I'm sure he was, too. I dropped down once more.

I got past him because I had the momentum of my slingshot, so I pulled in front of him and we touched. That was my mistake. I thought I was clear past him, but I guess I wasn't. David had gone up as close to the wall as he could without hitting it, trying to avoid my back bumper. Of course, he could have backed off and avoided the contact, but I knew he would never do that. That would have been like giving up, with a quarter-mile to go.

I wouldn't have backed off either.

He caught me on the left rear part of my bumper. Now,

keep in mind, that we're doing almost 200 mph at this point—maybe more. My car started sideways and the rear end kicked out to the left. I eased off the gas and turned the wheel to the left, trying to gather it up. It straightened out a little, but it took off again and I plowed into the dad-gum wall head-on. David was against the wall and it was ripping the whole right side off his car. I spun down into the grass. I could see David starting to spin, but he slid into Joe Frasson's Chevrolet, and that straightened him out enough that he didn't spin into the wall again.

There was smoke flying from David's tires and grass flying from mine. I was sliding, backward, toward the finish line. I knew that if I could just keep that rascal going that way, I would win the race. There wasn't any rule that said you had to be on the asphalt when you crossed the finish line. I figured I might just make a dirt track victory out of this one.

David's car kept sliding, until he got off in the grass, too. I was going slower and slower. My motor was dead and everything was real quiet. Finally the car stopped. I looked out my rear window. I was twenty yards from the finish line.

I tried to start the Dodge, but the starter just ground and ground. Then I looked out my windshield and I saw the grass and dirt flying from David's tires. I knew he was running. His tires were blown out and the car was a total wreck, but it was moving toward the track. I took my finger off the starter button, and I unhooked my shoulder harness. The 500-mile battle was over. Oh, well, easy come, easy go.

David limped across the finish line, dragging parts of his car behind him.

I went over to him after the race, and I said, "Sorry I got into you, David."

"Aw, that's okay, Richard," he said. "I know you didn't do it on purpose. Besides, it turned out all right."

It might have for *him*.

We were both as calm as if we had just finished a Ping-Pong game. Neither of us had been scared a bit. Listen, if those dudes had us all wired-up at that point, they might have found our anxiety deals hopped up a little, but I'll bet they weren't all that high even then.

A lot of not being afraid comes from having faith in your equipment. I know that my car is built so strong that it's going to take care of me. And I've got a whole lot of faith in my driving ability, so I really don't have anything to worry about. I tell myself that all the time.

I don't have nightmares of crashing and burning or bad vibes or any of those things that would make better reading. Oh, there have been times when I've been awake a lot at night—I mean, I've had some rough nights, some bad dreams, but I don't ever remember them when I wake up. Maybe I just block them out, like I block out the bad crashes. I don't really know. There have been times when I've had bad dreams, whatever they've been about, and I've gone right out there the next day and won the race. But there have been just as many times when I wake up feeling like I've had a good dream, and I think all I have to do is go to the track and stay out of everybody's way and I've got the race won—and I've lost. So I don't put much stock in dreams. Maybe that's a plus for me.

I don't believe much in superstitions and premonitions. There's even a Chapter 13 in this book. So we can go right on to the next category: *Strategy*.

As far as strategy is concerned, I save most of that for when the race starts. I really don't know what I'm going to do until the green flag drops and I see what all the other cats are doing. Oh, I have a general idea how I'm going to drive this track or that track; I've already told you a lot of that. In a hundred-mile race it was simple: You got out front as soon as you could, and you tried to stay there. But in the long races, I learned to take each lap as it came. And I knew not to make my move until the last hundred miles. So, you see, I was running long races, but I was only racing a hundred miles, every time.

Your car doesn't have to be the fastest, but you do have to stay in position to make your move, and then you have to use everything you can get. When the time comes, you have to draft anything that's moving. And you have to run anywhere the car will run or anywhere there's an opening. If it's necessary, you have to run up near the wall or down on the apron, where the track's a lighter color. They call it the grey matter. But if you try running like that early, you're asking for trouble.

When we really got into the strategy deal, Dale kept me informed on the radio; you know, where I was running and how fast the competition was going and where they were. And then we worked our strategy out from that. I don't know how we ever got along without the two-way radio. Well, I do, if you want to know. We depended on some very basic messages on the pit board. But, you know, I never could read those things that well at 180 or 190 mph. I guessed a lot of times.

One of the first things we learned was that strategy in the pits was as important as it was on the track. The Wood brothers taught us that you could win a race by sitting still. From that, we learned to use the caution flags to our advantage, so we could get a free stop as often as possible.

We started using a radio in 1969. It was just a CB then, and we got truck drivers and housewives and everybody on it. It was like listening to a soap opera. But I think it was Bud Moore who first tried radio in his cars; that was in the early sixties. In the seventies, they came up with the high-frequency deals. They worked good, but you still had a lot of static. Now they've improved them so much that it's like listening to your car radio. I have a speaker and a microphone wired right into my helmet and I can hear it. Listen, if I can hear it, it must be good. Of course, I have to turn the volume way up, but I hear most of what they tell me. I don't guess half as much any more.

The only time you ever get any crossover now is once in a while when a race starts and you've got all thirty-five or forty crew chiefs talking at the same time. It's not like it was in the sixties, when you had crew chiefs giving instructions to some other driver. Man, when we started using them, there were cars coming into pits when they weren't expected and others staying out there and running out of gas. It was a mess.

That's about all I can tell you about strategy. Oh, we work on some of it before the race. Things like tire stagger, which means the difference in size between tires. Even though the tires are all supposed to be the same size, there might be a slight variation. In fact, there always is. We measure the circumference of the tires; one might be 79¼ inches around the tread surface and the next one might be 80⅛ inches, and so on. It works best to have the bigger tires on the right side. If a crew made a mistake and put them on the left side, the car would push, or want to move to the right—where the *wall* is.

Each tire is measured and marked "RF" or "LR," or whatever, right front or left rear. The tires grow when they get hot, so you have to measure all of them the same way—either hot or cold. Hot is better. The perfect set up, say, at Charlotte, might be five-eighths stagger. Some teams like a half-inch on the back and a full inch on the front. We might find a really hot set up—a combination of tires that stick anywhere—and we usually save them for late in the race when I can go out there and surprise everybody on the track.

Tire strategy and things like setting up the car are usually left up to the crew chief, but then most of the drivers don't drive their own cars, so they don't care how it's done. They just want a car handed to them that handles. Drivers like A.J. and me want to know because neither of us is just a hired "shoe." We're driving our own cars. That may be an advantage, because we do get into that part of it. That's one of the things that's made Junior's cars so successful, particularly on a short track: He was so good himself as a driver, he knows how to set them up.

You remember I told you racing wasn't an exact science? Well, we prove that almost every week. And, with all I've told you, we might go out there in the next race and do every single thing different.

Exact? It's not a science at all.

18

Daddy and I watched Kyle in the winner's circle, while the photographers had a field day.

To begin with, I didn't think the day would come. Kyle had never said a word to me about ever wanting to drive a race car, but I turned on the television in Daytona in July 1978, when we were down there for the Firecracker 400, and there he was. He had been interviewed at the track that afternoon.

"And here's Kyle Petty, the eighteen-year-old son of the legendary King Richard," the announcer said. It wasn't unusual for the son of a race driver to be interviewed. What followed *was* unusual. For me, at least.

"Kyle," he continued, "what are you going to do with your life?"

"Well, Ken," he answered, "I'm gonna be a race driver."

I dropped the newspaper I was reading. "Lynda," I yelled, "you *have* to come in and hear this."

She came in from the bathroom, hair brush in hand. "What is it?" she asked.

"Well, your son just announced that he's gonna be a race driver."

Lynda sat down on the edge of the bed. The hairbrush dropped to the floor. "Oh, Lord," she said, "not another one."

Kyle was down at the swimming pool with his sisters, so I pulled my cowboy boots on, got a fresh cigar and a pouch of chewing tobacco, and went to the door. "I'll be back," I told Lynda, who was still sitting on the edge of the bed in a state of shock.

I found him at the Coke machine. "Boy, I wanna talk to you," I said.

He looked a little nervous. "They ran that thing on TV," he said.

"Yep," I answered.

All the way down to the pool, I had tried to think what I was going to say to him. I knew if I tried to talk him out of it, it would only make him want to do it more; but I didn't want just to say, "Go to it, kid," or, "Take the convertible over there." I wanted to *discuss* the matter. If you really want to know how a father feels when he learns that his son wants to be a race driver, I'll tell you: I felt a whole lot of concern.

We walked over to one of the umbrella-covered tables at the side of the pool. I sat down. Kyle stood there. "Well, sit down," I said. "I'm not gonna bite you." I don't think he believed me. But he pulled a chair over and sat down.

We were about to have a father-and-son talk. It wouldn't be the first one, but it would be the first one about the deal of him driving a race car.

"Want a chew?" I asked, holding the pouch out to him.

"You know I don't chew," he said.

"Well, I thought maybe you'd changed your mind about that, too," I said. He was looking around at the palm trees and the second-floor railings and the air conditioner units on the roof tops. "Who you been talkin' to?" I asked. He looked puzzled. "About drivin' a race car," I explained.

"Dale," he said, "and Wade."

Wade Thornburg was one of Dale's assistants. "Why didn't you talk to me about it?" I asked.

"Well, I figured you'd just try to talk me out of it," he said.

He was right, of course, but I wasn't going to admit it. "What about the football scholarship you were offered?" I asked.

"See, you're trying to talk me out of it."

"We're having a *discussion*," I said. "Anyway, you know your mother and I would like for you to go to college."

"I know, Daddy," he said, "but there's no use takin' a

scholarship that somebody else might be able to use better'n me, is there? I mean I wanna be a race driver."

"Well, if you don't wanna play football, just pick out a school. I'll pay for any school you pick," I said.

"It'd be a waste of your money, Daddy, because as quick as I would get outa school, I'd be racin' anyway, so why put it off?"

There wasn't much of an answer to that.

"Let me try racin' for four years, instead of college," he said. "I mean, it's four years of my life. And then I'll tell you if I want to go on or not."

I tapped the ashes off my cigar into the paper cup I had brought with me. You do that when you chew tobacco. You see, I was all set for a long talk, but the talk was over.

"Oh, boy," I said as I got up from the table.

"It's not that bad, is it Daddy?" he asked. "I mean, me being a driver . . ."

"It's not the drivin' part," I said. "I gotta go tell your mother. That's the hard part."

Lynda was still sitting on the bed when I got back. It was going to be even harder than I thought. "Look at it this way," I said, "we can bring Daddy's Number 42 out of retirement. He'd like Kyle usin' it."

"That's not high on my list of goals for Kyle," she said. Then she shrugged her shoulders and looked at me from over the top of her glasses. I shrugged back.

Nineteen seventy-nine was a year of changes for Petty Enterprises. I switched from Dodge to Oldsmobile. The car companies hadn't drifted back into racing yet, so it wasn't like it had been before. They weren't there to pick up all the bills and pay us a lot of money, like they had in the sixties. We were on our own—for a few years more—so it was up to the sponsor to pay the big money needed to run a team, and that kind of sponsor was hard to find.

It had gotten very expensive to put a competitive car on the track as we neared the eighties. The big rigs everybody used to haul the cars cost as much as $100,000. We had two of them—one for the two cars and one for parts and all the other things we couldn't get on the big truck.

It cost about $50,000 to build a race car, and we had a back-up car, a short-track car, and a back-up one there, and spare engines and, man, you name it, we had it. With the eight- or ten-man crew, travel expenses, motels, uniforms, and all that, we were looking at more than a million dollars a year, just to run NASCAR.

The General Motors cars had dominated Grand National for a while. I decided I couldn't beat 'em so I joined 'em. While we got the new Olds ready, I helped get one of the old Dodge Magnums prepared for Kyle. There is an ARCA—Automobile Racing Club of America—race the week before the Daytona 500, so that seemed like a good place for Kyle to get started. I figured he might as well start at Daytona, since his grandfather had won the first race they ever had there, and I had won my first superspeedway race there. That track meant a lot to the Pettys.

ARCA is an organization Bill France had a lot to do with getting started. He wanted something to compete with the Sports Car Club of America, because he had gotten into a feud with them a few years before, so he just got his own group started. They had replaced the old Sportsman races with ARCA races.

We went down to test the new Olds a couple of weeks before Daytona Speed Weeks, so we took along Kyle's Magnum, too. It was exactly the same car I had qualified in at 184 mph for the 1978 Daytona 500. After a couple of days of practice in it, Kyle went 184. I took the car out to see how it felt, and turned a 190.

Kyle was holding a press conference about every time he came in from practice. There was so much interest in the "Third Generation Racing Petty" that they swarmed all over him.

"Whatta'ya think about your Daddy's 190-mile-an-hour run?" one of the reporters asked him.

"Well, it looks like I'm gonna have to do a little better if I'm gonna run with him," he answered.

"And then he went out and ran 187.

"Whoa," I said. "That's quick enough."

When we got down there for Speed Weeks, we found that most of the drivers were doing exactly the same thing as Kyle. They were using year-old Grand National cars, and they were going like blue blazes. They were almost as fast as the NASCAR boys, but it was a much better place for him to start, because there were a lot of other rookies—at least, rookies as far as Daytona was concerned.

Kyle looked good in practice and he qualified well, so I wasn't too worried when he started his first race. I had a lot of faith in the car, and I figured he must have been watching me for years, and filing away all the driving tips that he could. I didn't know that for sure, but I had my own childhood to look back on, and that's what I had done. By the time I was ready to race, I knew a lot about it. Kyle looked like he did, too.

Kyle won that race.

He averaged 132 mph for the 200 miles. It was an absolutely unbelievable feat. It may not have been Grand National, but there were a lot of good drivers in there, and any time you win a race at Daytona, you've done something.

Daddy and I watched Kyle in the winner's circle, while the photographers had a field day. And then we moved in with him—after he had his own time in the limelight.

The following week, I won my sixth Daytona 500. I averaged 143 in the Oldsmobile. It was my first victory in anything other than a Chrysler product since 1969 when I sneaked over to Ford for a year. Right after Daytona we switched again; this time to Chevrolet. Might as well try 'em all. We would also try Buick before we finally settled down with a Pontiac.

It looked like Kyle was going to make it as a race driver, so we decided he might just as well move on up to Grand National. He could spend a few years in the minor leagues, but we figured he could learn a lot faster, running up there with the big boys, so we got a car ready for him.

There are two schools of thought on any training: one, you start somebody on the ground level, and two, you start them right on top. Kyle's first race had been at Daytona, which is one of the fastest tracks in the world, so he might as well go on to the fast cars, too. I figured he would be ready for the Talladega 500. The Alabama track is the fastest in the world.

Talladega was just the kind of place for a Petty introduction.

We began testing his car, and giving him some practice, at the Charlotte Motor Speedway, because it was close to home. And because it's one of the best tracks in the world. Kyle looked as good in practice as he had at Daytona. The first day.

About midway through the second day, Humpy Wheeler and I were sitting in the pits talking about the good ol' days— a racer never misses a chance to do that. I had just lit a fresh cigar when I heard the sound that is so familiar to me—the high-pitched wail of tires that have lost traction and are sliding across the asphalt.

It's not a nice sound.

We turned, just in time to see the car hit the wall in the second turn. It went about twenty feet in the air. It looked exactly like Fireball's crash in 1964, except there wasn't any fire this time. I had been glad a hundred times since '64 that Goodyear had developed the fuel cell. There hadn't been much fire since they did.

I looked at Humpy. He was white as a sheet. I knew he didn't know what to say. "Well, Kyle's made a mistake," I said. "Let's go look at it."

Humpy started his car, and he carried me over to where Kyle's car was sitting, down near the infield retaining wall. There wasn't much left of it. There were little rivers of water and oil running down across the track and wisps of steam coming out from under the hood. The whole rear end of the car was driven clear up to the driver's compartment.

The rescue squad had already gotten there—I had seen them take off before we did—and Kyle was out of the car. He was leaning against the wall with a worried look on his face.

"You okay, Kyle?" I asked.

"I'm all right, Daddy," he answered. "But the car . . . I'm sorry."

"Let's get 'er loaded up," I interrupted. "We gotta take 'er back and get started on another one." I had been in that same situation too many times. I knew that it sure wasn't the time to ask, "What happened?"

And I remembered Fireball's answer to the reporter: "It *is* possible to crash out there, you know."

I had been thinking a lot about Fireball that day. But then, that's not unusual—I always think of the guys that are gone.

"Maybe you made a mistake, Richard," Humpy said, "you know, putting Kyle in a Grand National car. Maybe he should run some more Sportsman races."

"Humpy," I said, "I think if I was learnin' to fly, I'd want to learn in a dad-gum jet, right off the bat. I don't think I'd wanna start with a little old Piper Cub." I really wouldn't.

"Guess he wouldn't be a Petty if he started at the bottom," Humpy said.

Kyle didn't run up front right away, but he improved steadily. But not winning races was a problem—the press and the fans expected too much out of him too soon. Just because he was Richard Petty's son and Lee Petty's grandson, they expected him to go right out there on those superspeedways and burn up the league. After all, he had done it at Daytona. But they were overlooking the fact that this was a far different league.

It's a whole lot harder for boys like Kyle and Davey Allison and Rickie Pearson and the other kids of race drivers than it is for any other new driver to come up. I mean a Terry Labonte or Bobby Hillen can jump right in, and if they don't win, or if they make a mistake, nobody notices. If they do, they say, "Well, he's new. Whatta'ya expect?"

It was the same way for the first five years he was running. But I'll tell you right now, Kyle is head and shoulders above those other people who started along about the same time he did. If you want to compare him, compare him with other drivers who have the same amount of experience; don't compare him with me. Don't compare Davey Allison with Bobby. It's not fair.

Of course, I didn't make it any easier for him in his first year; it was my twenty-second season, and it was also the year I won my seventh Grand National championship.

Dale left Petty Enterprises after the third race of the 1981 season. As much as I hated to see him go, I understood. He came to me one day, and he said, "Richard, I sorta feel like I've gone as far as I'll ever go here, you know, without actually being a Petty and all."

I couldn't really tell him he was wrong. "You got another offer?" I asked.

"Yeah, I do," he said. "They want me to be the crew chief on the Osterman car, and I think I'm gonna do it."

It was about that simple. At least, it seemed simple at the time. But I guess it started a chain reaction that completely destroyed Petty Enterprises.

Dale had left on a high note. I had won my seventh Daytona 500 in the first race of the season and had run third in the next two races. I was leading the race at Rockingham, when I ran out of gas. So Dale's decision wasn't based on any run of bad luck or hard feelings. It was just one of those career deals.

I named Wade Thornburg to take his place. The next step in the fall of the operation came when Chief's health started to deteriorate. It had been bad anyway, but trying to keep both Kyle and me running was making it worse. The untold hours of extra work and the strain of standing on the cement floor and asphalt of the racetrack had about ruined his legs and feet. It went all the way back to his polio when he was a kid. With age, he started to weaken again. He was going downhill.

He started to gain weight and his blood pressure went up. Well, when he went downhill, so did the engine program. He wanted to do just as good as he ever did, but his physical limitations prevented him from carrying it out.

And, besides that, I'll have to tell you, there were some family problems that might never have gotten worked out. All of a sudden, there were just too many Pettys trying to run things.

I decided that it would be better for everybody if I left Petty Enterprises. It might solve everybody's problems. I was tired of having the responsibility of driving and building cars anyway. Kyle had to be tired of living in the shadow of "King Richard," and Chief surely was fed up with trying to build engines for two Pettys, making each one as strong as the other—and not favoring either one.

It was an unbelievable coincidence that Mike Curb came to me and asked me if I would ever consider driving for someone else.

"You got anybody in mind?" I asked.

"I sure do," he said. "I want you to drive for me."

I went to both STP and Pontiac—my two sponsors—and talked it over, and they both said it was all right with them. So Mike and I worked out a deal. For the first time in my life, I would be a race driver *only*. I wouldn't have the worry of building the car and keeping it in parts. I could leave all of that at the track when I left at the end of the day. It would almost be like a nine-to-five job, I thought.

Kyle was pleased, too. He would be "on his own." Nobody knew better than I what it was like to live in the darkness cast by a giant.

Chief and Kyle got along pretty good in 1984. Kyle had a

good Seven-Eleven sponsorship, and the Ford Thunderbird he was driving ran well. He didn't win any races, but he was in the top ten several times, and he won $300,000, which was a little more than my winnings that year. But he wasn't happy.

He came to me at the end of the season and told me that he had an offer to drive for the Wood brothers.

"Daddy," he said, "I don't know what to tell Leonard and Glen."

"I think you oughta tell 'em you'll drive their car," I said.

Kyle didn't have the experience, and he wasn't really going to get it around Level Cross. He was too protected. I mean, he could have stayed there for the rest of his life, doing just what he wanted to. There might have been some ruffled feathers from time to time, but he was sure that nobody was going to fire him. That's not how you do it. You have to be hungry for success, and he wasn't going to ever get hungry with the Petty umbrella over his head.

I knew Kyle had to get out. The Wood brothers were a perfect answer. They had already told their driver, Buddy Baker, to look for another ride, so Kyle could take the Seven-Eleven sponsorship and leave the nest. It would work out well for everybody.

With the Wood brothers, he would have to produce. I was sure it would help him mature, and I was right.

"You said you wanted to spend four years racin' instead of goin' to college," I said. "Well, you've done that. Now you can go over there with Leonard and Glen. Look on it as graduate school."

Chief ran Petty Enterprises for a few months. He took a couple of Kyle's old Thunderbirds and built them up for Dick Brooks and Morgan Shepherd, but his heart wasn't in it—or his health. He came over to my house one night, and he said, "Richard, I wanna talk to you."

I knew what it was.

"I've decided to shut down Petty Enterprises," he said. "We're not doin' too good, and besides that, I'm flat wore out with racin'. I mean, I been in it all my life, and I'd like to have a normal life, for a change."

I understood—more than he knew. Maurice had always been the Petty in the background, that's what he preferred, of course. First Daddy and then me and finally Kyle always got all the spotlights, and here Chief was back at the shop or at the track, working his hind-end off, while the whole world was throwing roses at our feet.

"I don't blame you," I said. "Shut 'er down. What are you gonna do?" I asked.

"I got a job with National Warranty Corporation," he said. "I'm gonna dress up and live like the rest of the world."

On April 29, 1984, the doors to Petty Enterprises were closed.

I've had two good years with Mike Curb, but I'm going home.

On the day we started this book, I announced to the racing world that I would be going back to Level Cross to reopen Petty Enterprises. The reason I'm going home is I found out that when you're in somebody else's hands, you're no longer the master of your destiny. It's that simple.

I mean, if I was Kyle's age, it would be all right, but at forty-eight years of age, it's just too late to change. It's all so foreign to me, having somebody else run things. It would be like A. J. Foyt driving somebody else's car. He's like me—since he was a little bitty boy, all he ever knew was race cars, but they were either his daddy's or his. He's a businessman, too. He has a big Chevrolet dealership in Houston and a whole lot of other things, but I'd bet you that if his Chevy garage was burning down, and there was a race starting over across the street, he wouldn't even call the fire department—until after the race. That's how dedicated he is.

It's why both of us have done it for so long, and why we get so engrossed with what we're doing. We're the types that have to race, but we have to do it on our own terms.

A.J. and I get along well. You get him away from a race car, and he's a good fellow—he'll do anything in the world for you—but you put him in a car and, man, he's a holy terror. It goes right back to what I was saying at the beginning of the book. As tough as he is, he still has that light, smooth touch that only the very best race drivers have. He's never left his racing home.

I'll guarantee you, I'll never leave mine again. I may retire someday, and when I do I'll probably stay right in Level Cross and build race cars for somebody else to drive. Most drivers would be thinking of quitting right now, but I'm kind of like a schoolkid again. I've got a lot to look forward to. Of course, I've got a lot to look back on, too.

As for Kyle, I don't think he'll ever come back, at least, not until he's made a name for himself. Otherwise, I'm always going to be overshadowing him.

I was fortunate: When I came along, there wasn't much publicity, and outside of the circle of friends and followers, the early drivers weren't the superstars they are today. I didn't have as big a shadow to live under; it was big, don't get me wrong, but nothing like Kyle has had.

What happened during the 1984 season alone was enough to discourage anyone from moving into Petty Enterprises.

Before I won my one-hundredth race, I told you that people said it was an impossible feat, just because nobody had ever done it. Well, on July Fourth at Daytona—naturally, everything big has happened there—probably the major event of my racing life took place. I won my *two*-hundredth race.

The papers and magazines say it's a record that will never be broken. Maybe they're right, I don't know. All I know is that it seems like it took a couple of lifetimes to do it. There have been a lot of races and a lot of water under the dam. I'm just as glad that all of it has happened to me.

Two hundred.

When you look at it, it does seem like a lot. Maybe that's as good a place as any to stop—the book.

Epilogue

*Times are changing on me now. I
know that I'm as far as I'm ever going
to go.*

I've reached the point in my life where Fireball and Junior
and Ned were in the mid-sixties.

If Fireball hadn't gotten killed, he probably would have
retired, just like Ned and Junior and a bunch of the other old
guard did. They knew that they were as far as they were ever
going to go. Oh, they might have won some more races and
built onto their legends, but they were never going to be the
drivers that they once were. Times were changing on them.

Times are changing on me now. I know that I'm as far as
I'm ever going to go.

I'll never be as good as I was before—I mean, winning races
and setting records. There will never be another 1967 for me
or anybody. Racing has changed too much for that kind of
thing ever to happen again. As far as being a good driver is
concerned, I think I'm better right now than I've ever been.
But that's the experience deal.

In a few weeks, I'll start my one-thousandth race. *One
thousand!* That's a lot of experience, and it's probably the
major reason that I've done as much as I have. It only stands
to reason: If you drive more races, you're going to win more.

I went through a couple changings of the guard, and it looks
like I might go out with the next one. Me and Cale and Buddy
and David and Bobby caught the tail end of the old and the
front of the new one.

There's going to be another mass exodus in racing. A bunch

of us are going to step down, just like the other guys did in the mid-sixties. Darrell Waltrip will probably finish with us, too. We're going to walk away, and turn it over to the Bill Elliotts and the Terry Labontes—and the Kyle Pettys.

None of us really can tell you when that day will come; I know I can't. But I'll be the first one to know when that day comes for me. It will be the day when I sit in my car and worry about driving the track at Darlington. Or maybe I'll have a chance to slingshot past somebody at the end of a Daytona race and not take that chance. Or I'll give up hope of winning my eighth championship. Whatever it is, I'll know the signal, and I'll pull myself up out of that race car, and I'll go on back to Level Cross, and I'll strap myself in the rocking chair for a spell. This is the place, of course, where I take one last look over my shoulder at the good ol' days. Well, I'm not going to miss the opportunity.

You know, I don't think a lot of the drivers we have today would have made it back then. We're in an age where all you have to have is money to get a Grand National ride. Take a cat like Bobby Hillen: His Daddy's got plenty of money, so he sets him in a race car. Well, before that, Bobby didn't know a race car from an airplane. He's done all right, don't get me wrong. It's just that he didn't have to serve the tough apprenticeship that a lot of us "old-timers" did.

When a driver came up back then, he had to prove himself in what would be considered junk today, and then he had to prove himself again in good cars.

The days of working all night on a race car, to get it ready for a 200-lapper the next day at some scruffy track somewhere, and then hooking up and towing all the next night to get to another scruffy track are behind us.

The new kids just haven't paid their dues. I guess that's what bothers me more than anything. It's not their fault either. Some of them probably would be willing to do what we had to do—some of them. But they'll never have to, because racing doesn't demand it anymore. There's too much money, and too many people standing in line with bulging billfolds to take their place if they get disenchanted.

I'm not saying for one minute that there aren't still some good drivers today. There are as many as there ever were. I think the best are Cale Yarborough and Bobby Allison and Darrel Waltrip, but there are a lot of other good ones. And there are more good cars than there ever were. Again, that's where the money comes in.

There are specialists and people with computers and every kind of space-age technology to tell the driver's what their cars are doing. The seat-of-the-pants age is behind us, if you'll pardon the expression.

Times are so much different. I mean, NASCAR has improved so much over the years—they've learned from their mistakes and they've upgraded the entire sport. They know how to make rules work now. And the facilities are so much better. All of the old problems are gone. We have concrete walls everywhere and better grandstands and clean rest rooms; you don't have to go over behind a car anymore. And we have good traffic control, except at Atlanta—it hasn't changed much there.

Darlington used to be a disaster to try to get out of, now it's like coming home from the supermarket. And Charlotte, man, that's the track. Humpy has made so many improvements there that you'd never know it was the same track. They even have condos overlooking the racetrack. Can you imagine? Race cars in your front yard—I'm not sure even *I'm* ready for that.

Jimmy Cleveland was the first driver ever to get paid lap money in Grand National racing. It was in 1949 at Lakewood. He led just about the whole race, and he got $150. I'll use that as an example of how things have changed: In 1985, Bill Elliott won $2 million. It took me more than 500 races to win my first million dollars, and more than fifty races to win my fifth million dollars. And here comes Bill in a Thunderbird and takes away one million in one race.

I'm not trying to take a dang thing away from Bill—the money's out there and he deserves it. He out-drove us about all season, but I'm going to tell you, it's not the only time when one driver totally dominated a season. There were years when the Wood brothers' car used to be so much faster than everybody else's car that it wasn't funny. But David, or whoever was driving it, didn't run away from everybody, like Bill did in 1985. He held back and made it look hard. He was smarter about it. But we all knew that he could have lapped us if he had wanted to.

For one thing, we knew that if we got out there and showed off too much, Bill France would have changed the rules so that we couldn't do it again. I mean, if you won two in a row, they tore down your car to check it.

I'll tell you now, there were many times in 1967 when I could have lapped the whole field, and I didn't do it. I was smart enough to know they'd change things on me. Besides that, I didn't want to make the other cats look that bad.

In the sixties, the Elliotts wouldn't have showed up for the third race, because they would have penalized them so much, they couldn't run. I don't mean for this to sound like sour grapes. It isn't—I promise. There's no question in my mind that the Elliotts have found something the rest of us don't know about. Think about it: They were almost never in competition before Harry Melling came along and bought their racing operation. Harry's got all kinds of engineers working for his company—they manufacture oil pumps for Ford and GM and a lot of other big companies.

They've got computers and people who are so smart they don't know enough to come in out of the rain. Well, the reason I know anything about it is that I know they went to Bud Moore and offered to "help him out." Don't ask me how I know. He told Bud something like, "We can build your car by computer, and run every race on every track by computer, and blow everybody's doors off." But I guess Bud had been building cars too long.

"We'll do it ourselves," he told Harry.

So Harry went to the Elliotts, who had been running at the front of the second pack of cars, and they jumped at the chance. It obviously worked.

What it actually is, or what the combination is, I don't know, but I do know that the Elliotts didn't just stumble across it. It came from the outside. You can look at the car and tell that: It shows that there hasn't been a whole lot of work done on it. It has to be the way I told you, otherwise Waddell Wilson, who builds Cale's Thunderbirds, and the Ford people would have discovered the "secret part."

I'm glad they were able to pull it off. They're nice guys, and if the big money's out there, they've got as much right to it as any of us. It still goes to the guy who crosses the finish line first—it doesn't make much difference how he got there. And if they don't have to do it anymore by hard, dirty, back-breaking work, well, more power to them.

Dale Inman is coming back to be my crew chief again and that makes me feel good. In fact, a lot of my old crew will be back when we open the doors of Petty Enterprises again. The one I'll really miss is Chief. I guess he meant it when he said he'd had enough of racing. It's not going to be quite the same deal with one of the musketeers gone, I'll tell you that.

There are lots of times now when I'm sitting at a track talking—or maybe just *thinking*—about the days when Chief and Dale and I got started. So much has happened since then: Dale won all those championships as crew chief (he won another championship while he was away from us, with Terry Labonte), Chief won so many awards, and there are all those races I won. We've got a rich past.

It was just the other day when I was looking over where we're going to be working again. I was thinking how big the complex is now. It looks like an automobile factory—I mean, one where they build passenger cars, like something in Detroit.

I was standing in the building where the reaper shed had once been, just looking around. I looked up at the rafters, and I remembered when we put them up, right over the old shed. I was afraid of climbing up there. And then we tore down the old building.

I looked down at the old cement floor, the one that remained after all the rest of the shed was gone. I brushed away a layer or two of dust that had collected while Petty Enterprises was closed and I saw the initials in the cement: "RP," "MP," "DI." I could almost hear Daddy's 1953 Dodge idling as we tinkered with it.

Those old race cars had a different sound, even when they sat still and idled. They popped and skipped and kind of gurgled. And when you moved the throttle linkage back, the RPMs jumped up and the engine came to life.

I could hear the sound of summer thunder. It was the sound of my youth.

I cut off the lights. It was dark. And quiet.

Major Events Won by Richard Petty

1959

July 18	Columbia, SC	½ d	100 miles	Oldsmobile

1960

February 28	Charlotte, NC	½ p	100	Plymouth
April 10	Martinsville, VA	½ p	250	Plymouth
September 19	Hillsboro, VA	9/10 d	100	Plymouth

1961

April 23	Richmond, VA	½ d	100	Plymouth
May 2	Charlotte, NC	1½ p	100	Plymouth

1962

April 15	North Wilkesboro, NC	⅝ p	100	Plymouth
April 22	Martinsville, VA	½ p	250	Plymouth
July 14	Greenville, SC	½ d	100	Plymouth
August 8	Huntsville, AL	¼ p	50	Plymouth
August 15	Roanoke, VA	¼ p	50	Plymouth
August 18	Winston-Salem, NC	¼ p	50	Plymouth
August 21	Spartanburg, SC	½ d	100	Plymouth
September 30	North Wilkesboro, NC	⅝ p	200	Plymouth
November 11	Tampa, FL	⅓ p	66⅔	Plymouth

1963

March 2	Spartanburg, SC	½ d	100	Plymouth
March 3	Weaverville, NC	½ p	100	Plymouth

Legend: d-dirt; p-paved; rc-road course, paved.

April 14	South Boston, VA	⅜ p	56¼	Plymouth
April 21	Martinsville, VA	½ p	250	Plymouth
April 28	North Wilkesboro, NC	⅝ p	160.6	Plymouth
May 2	Columbia, SC	½ d	100	Plymouth
May 18	Manassas, VA	⅜ p	112½	Plymouth
June 9	Birmingham, AL	½ p	100	Plymouth
July 21	Bridgehampton, NY	2.8 p	100	Plymouth
July 30	Greenville, SC	½ d	100	Plymouth
August 8	Columbia, SC	½ d	100	Plymouth
October 5	Randleman, NC	¼ p	50	Plymouth
December 29	Savannah, GA	½ d	100	Plymouth

1964

February 23	Daytona Beach, FL	2½ p	500	Plymouth
May 17	South Boston, VA	⅜ p	100	Plymouth
June 11	Concord, NC	½ d	100	Plymouth
June 14	Nashville, TN	½ p	100	Plymouth
June 26	Spartanburg, SC	½ d	100	Plymouth
August 2	Nashville, TN	½ p	200	Plymouth
August 16	Huntington, WV	⁷⁄₁₆ p	218.75	Plymouth
October 25	Harns, NC	³⁄₁₀ p	100	Plymouth

1965

February 11	Atlanta, GA	(NHRA drag races)		Barracuda
June 6	Bristol, TN	(NHRA)		Barracuda
July 31	Nashville, TN	½ p	200	Plymouth
August 8	Weaverville, NC	½ p	100	Plymouth
September 10	Hickory, NC	⁴⁄₁₀ p	100	Plymouth
September 17	Martinsville, VA	½ p	150	Plymouth
November 14	Augusta, GA	½ p	150	Plymouth

1966

April 30	Darlington, SC	1⅜ p	400	Plymouth
May 7	Hampton, VA	⁴⁄₁₀ d	100	Plymouth
May 10	Macon, GA	½ p	100	Plymouth
June 12	Weaverville, NC	½ p	150	Plymouth
July 30	Nashville, TN	½ p	200	Plymouth
August 7	Atlanta, GA	1½ p	400	Plymouth
November 13	Augusta, GA	½ p	150	Plymouth

1967

March 5	Weaverville, NC	½ p	150	Plymouth
April 6	Columbia, SC	½ d	100	Plymouth
April 9	Hickory, NC	⁴⁄₁₀ d	100	Plymouth
April 23	Martinsville, VA	½ p	250	Plymouth
April 30	Richmond, VA	½ d	125	Plymouth
May 13	Darlington, SC	1⅜ p	400	Plymouth
May 20	Hampton,VA	⁴⁄₁₀ d	100	Plymouth
June 6	Macon, GA	½ p	150	Plymouth
June 18	Rockingham, NC	1 p	500	Plymouth
June 24	Greenville, SC	½ d	100	Plymouth
July 9	Trenton, NJ	1 p	300	Plymouth
July 13	Fonda, NY	1 p	100	Plymouth
July 15	Islip, NY	½ d	100	Plymouth
July 23	Bristol, TN	½ p	250	Plymouth
July 29	Nashville, TN	½ p	200	Plymouth
August 12	Winston-Salem, NC	¼ p	62½	Plymouth
August 17	Columbia, SC	½ d	100	Plymouth
August 25	Savannah, GA	½ d	100	Plymouth
September 4	Darlington, SC	1⅜ p	500	Plymouth
September 8	Hickory, NC	⁴⁄₁₀ p	100	Plymouth
September 10	Richmond, VA	½ d	150	Plymouth
September 15	Beltsville, MD	½ p	150	Plymouth
September 17	Hillsborough, NC	⁹⁄₁₀ d	150	Plymouth
September 24	Martinsville, VA	½ p	250	Plymouth
October 1	North Wilkesboro, NC	⅝ p	250	Plymouth
November 26	Montgomery, AL	½ p	100	Plymouth

1968

April 7	Hickory, NC	⁴⁄₁₀ p	100	Plymouth
April 13	Greenville, NC	½ d	100	Plymouth
May 31	Asheville, NC	⅓ p	100	Plymouth
June 6	Maryville, TN	½ p	100	Plymouth
June 8	Birmingham, TN	⅝ p	100	Plymouth
June 22	Greenville, SC	½ d	100	Plymouth
July 9	Oxford, ME	⅓ p	100	Plymouth
July 11	Fonda, NY	½ d	100	Plymouth
July 25	Maryville, TN	½ p	100	Plymouth
August 23	South Boston, VA	⅜ p	100	Plymouth
September 8	Richmond, VA	⅝ p	187½	Plymouth
September 15	Hillsborough, NC	⁹⁄₁₀ p	150	Plymouth
September 22	Martinsville, VA	½ p	250	Plymouth

September 29	North Wilkesboro, NC	⅝	p	250	Plymouth
October 27	Rockingham, NC	1	p	500	Plymouth
November 17	Macon, GA	½	p	250	Plymouth

1969

February 1	Riverside, CA	2.7	rc	500	Ford
April 27	Martinsville, VA	½	p	250	Ford
June 19	Kingsport, TN	⁴⁄₁₀	p	100	Ford
July 6	Dover, DE	1	p	300	Ford
July 15	Beltsville, MD	½	p	150	Ford
July 26	Nashville, TN	½	p	200	Ford
July 27	Maryville, TN	½	p	100	Ford
August 22	Winston-Salem, NC	⅝	p	62½	Ford
September 28	Martinsville, VA	½	p	250	Ford

1970

March 8	Rockingham, NC	1	p	500	Plymouth
March 15	Savannah, GA	½	p	100	Plymouth
April 18	North Wilkesboro, NC	⅝	p	250	Plymouth
April 30	Columbia, SC	½	d	100	Plymouth
June 14	Riverside, CA	2.62	rc	400	Plymouth
June 26	Kingsport, TN	⅓	p	100	Plymouth
July 7	Malta, NY	⅓	p	90½	Plymouth
July 12	Trenton, NJ	1½	p	300	Plymouth
July 24	Maryville, TN	½	p	100	Plymouth
August 2	Atlanta, GA	1½	p	500	Plymouth
August 11	Huntington, WV	⁷⁄₁₆	p	132.25	Plymouth
August 28	Winston-Salem, NC	¼	p	62½	Plymouth
August 29	South Boston, VA	⅓	p	100	Plymouth
September 13	Richmond, VA	½	p	270	Plymouth
September 20	Dover, DE	1	p	300	Plymouth
September 30	Raleigh, NC	¼	d	100	Plymouth
October 18	Martinsville, VA	½	p	250	Plymouth
November 8	Macon, GA	½	p	275	Plymouth

1971

February 14	Daytona Beach, FL	2½	p	500	Plymouth
March 7	Richmond, VA	½	p	270	Plymouth
March 14	Rockingham, NC	1	p	500	Plymouth
March 21	Hickory, NC	⅓	p	100	Plymouth
April 8	Columbia, SC	½	d	100	Plymouth
April 15	Maryville, TN	½	p	100	Plymouth

April 18	North Wilkesboro, NC	⅝ p	250	Plymouth
April 25	Martinsville, VA	½ p	250	Plymouth
May 21	Asheville, NC	⅓ p	100	Plymouth
June 26	Greenville, SC	½ p	100	Plymouth
July 14	Malta, NY	⅓ p	90½	Plymouth
July 15	Islip, NY	⅕ p	46	Plymouth
July 18	Trenton, NJ	1½ p	300	Plymouth
July 24	Nashville, TN	½ p	250	Plymouth
August 1	Atlanta, GA	1½ p	500	Plymouth
August 8	Huntington, WV	⁷⁄₁₆ p	218.75	Plymouth
August 27	Columbia, SC	½ d	100	Plymouth
October 17	Dover, DE	1 p	500	Plymouth
October 24	Rockingham, NC	1 p	500	Plymouth
November 14	Richmond, VA	½ p	270	Plymouth
December 5	College Station, TX	2 p	500	Plymouth

1972

January 23	Riverside, CA	2.62 rc	500	Plymouth
February 27	Richmond, VA	½ p	270	Plymouth
April 23	North Wilkesboro, NC	⅝ p	250	Plymouth
April 30	Martinsville, VA	½ p	250	Plymouth
June 25	College Station, TX	2 p	500	Plymouth
September 10	Richmond, VA	½ p	270	Plymouth
September 24	Martinsville, VA	½ p	250	Plymouth
October 1	North Wilkesboro, NC	⅝ p	250	Plymouth

1973

February 18	Daytona Beach, FL	2½ p	500	Dodge
February 25	Richmond, VA	½ p	270	Dodge
April 8	North Wilkesboro, NC	⅝ p	250	Dodge
June 10	College Station, TX	2 p	500	Dodge
July 29*	Pocono, PA	2½ p	500	Dodge
September 9	Richmond, VA	½ p	270	Dodge
September 30	Martinsville, VA	½ p	250	Dodge

1974

February 17	Daytona Beach, FL	2½ p	450	Dodge
March 3	Rockingham, NC	2 p	450	Dodge
April 21	North Wilkesboro, NC	⅝ p	225	Dodge
May 11	Nashville, TN	½ p	238	Dodge

* United States Auto Club race

June 16	Brooklyn, MI	2 p	360	Dodge
July 28	Atlanta, GA	1½ p	500	Dodge
August 4	Pocono, PA	2½ p	480	Dodge
August 11	Talladega, AL	2.66 p	500	Dodge
September 8	Richmond, VA	½ p	270	Dodge
September 15	Dover, DE	1 p	500	Dodge

1975

February 23	Richmond, VA	½ p	270	Dodge
March 16	Bristol, VA	.533 p	266½	Dodge
March 23	Atlanta, GA	1½ p	500	Dodge
April 6	North Wilkesboro, NC	⅝ p	250	Dodge
April 27	Martinsville, VA	½ p	250	Dodge
May 25	Charlotte, NC	1½ p	600	Dodge
June 8	Riverside, CA	2.62 rc	400	Dodge
July 4	Daytona Beach, FL	2½ p	400	Dodge
August 24	Brooklyn, MI	2 p	400	Dodge
September 14	Dover, DE	1 p	500	Dodge
September 21	North Wilkesboro, NC	⅝ p	250	Dodge
October 5	Charlotte, NC	1½ p	500	Dodge
November 2	Rockingham, NC	1 p	500	Dodge

1976

February 29	Rockingham, NC	1 p	500	Dodge
August 1	Pocono, PA	2½ p	500	Dodge

1977

February 17	Daytona Beach, FL	2½ p	500	Dodge
March 13	Rockingham, NC	1 p	500	Dodge
March 20	Atlanta, GA	1½ p	500	Dodge

1979

February 18	Daytona Beach, FL	2½ p	500	Oldsmobile
April 22	Martinsville, VA	½ p	250	Chevrolet
August 19	Brooklyn, MI	2 p	400	Chevrolet
September 16	Dover, DE	1 p	500	Chevrolet
October 21	Rockingham, NC	1 p	500	Chevrolet

1980

| April 20 | North Wilkesboro, NC | ⅝ p | 250 | Chevrolet |
| May 10 | Nashville, TN | ½ p | 250 | Chevrolet |

1981

February 15	Daytona Beach, FL	2½ p	500	Buick
April 5	North Wilkesboro, NC	⅝ p	250	Buick
August 16	Brooklyn, MI	2 p	400	Buick

1983

March 13	Rockingham, NC	1 p	500	Pontiac
May 1	Talladega, AL	2.66 p	500	Pontiac
October 9	Charlotte, NC	1½ p	500	Pontiac

1984

| May 20 | Dover, DE | 1 p | 500 | Pontiac |
| July 4 | Daytona Beach, FL | 2½ p | 400 | Pontiac |

(Richard Petty's two-hundredth career victory)

Index

ABC Television, 220
Akron, 87
Alexander, Ed, 170
Allen, Johnny, 137, 140
Allison, Bobby, 190, 211, 247, 249
Allison, Davey, 241
Andretti, Mario, 204
Arizona, 122
Asheboro (N.C.), 16, 42, 112
Asheville (N.C.), 133, 149
Atkins, Chet, xiv
Atkins, Turk, 62
Atlanta, 43, 44, 59, 60, 146, 150, 151, 165, 167, 169, 194, 197, 249
Atlanta 500, 203, 216
Automobile Racing Club of America (ARCA), 238

Bailey, H. B., 7
Baker, Buck, 68, 123, 125–26, 134, 141, 157, 181
Baker, Buddy, 4–5, 7, 190, 211, 214, 244, 247

Banks, Henry, 201
Bay Meadows (Oakland), 120
Beam, Herman, 149–50
Beauchamp, Johnny, 159, 160, 176
Blair, Bill, 89, 100
Blue Mist (Asheboro, N.C.), 114
BMX courses, 33
Bowman Gray Stadium (Winston-Salem), 213
Branson Mill Road (Level Cross, N.C.), 15
Brooks, Dick, 244
Buick, 239
Buick Roadmaster, 64, 65, 66, 68, 70, 129
Byron, Red, xiii, 59–60, 61, 63, 68, 69, 71, 86, 89, 90, 91

Cadillac, 86, 89, 91, 92
California, 122, 123, 161
Callahan, Tex, 62

Charlotte, 43, 48, 63, 65, 66, 67, 68, 80, 128, 146, 153, 165, 167, 197, 205, 207, 211, 225, 234, 249

Charlotte Motor Speedway, 228, 240

Charlotte *Observer*, 59, 228

Chevrolet, 64, 116, 127, 196, 197, 198, 231, 245

Chevy Chevelle, 194

Chevy coupe, 20, 129

Chicago, 217

Chrysler, viii, 49, 106, 109, 110, 114–15, 120, 125, 129, 182, 183, 195, 197–99, 201, 211, 213, 216, 239

Circle-In (Randleman, N.C.), 114

Cleveland, Jimmy, 249

Colorado River, 122

Columbia, v, 80, 81, 133, 134–35, 146, 147, 161, 168, 215

Curb, Mike, 243, 245

Dallas (Ga.), 202

Dallas, 121, 123

Danville (Va.), 50

Darlington (S.C.), 1, 2, 3, 4–6, 7–10, 11, 81, 82, 83, 91, 92, 93, 102, 123, 130, 144, 156, 169, 204, 222, 238, 249

"Darlington Stripe," 8

Daytona Beach, 58, 59, 60, 129, 130, 155–61, 169, 171, 172, 179, 194, 198, 215, 240

Daytona 500, v, 158, 183, 185, 199, 202, 204, 214, 215, 216, 229, 238, 239, 242

Daytona International Speedway (Daytona Beach), 155–61, 165, 169, 198, 222, 246

Detroit, 102–103, 105, 120, 167, 251

Dieringer, Darel, 8, 203, 204

Dodge, 43–44, 73, 101, 102, 115, 116, 117, 120, 129, 193, 194, 199, 211, 214, 230, 231, 237, 252

Duke University Medical Center, 25

Dunnaway, Glenn, 67, 69

Earnhardt, Dale, 2, 227–28

Earnhardt, Ralph, xii, 2, 3

East St. Louis, 83

Elliott, Bill, 2, 248, 249–51

Ethridge, Jack, 62

Firecracker 400 (Daytona Beach), 209, 235

Firestone tires, 87, 169, 170, 196–97

Flock, Bob, 44–45, 49, 63, 67–68, 100

Flock, Fonty, 62–63, 68, 69, 100, 126

Flock, Julian (Tim), 67, 68, 69, 99–100, 123, 126, 139, 205

Flock brothers, xiii, 80, 89, 100

Florida, 60

Fonda (N.Y.), 146

Ford, 64, 67, 72, 73, 85–86, 88, 109, 127, 195, 198, 199, 200, 201, 202–203, 204, 211–12
Ford coupe, 20, 46, 47, 63, 116
Ford Fairlane, 199–200
Ford Galaxie, 199–200
Ford Model T, 17, 18
Ford Thunderbird, 249
Ford Torino, 212
Ford V-8, 114
Foyt, A. J., vi, 204, 212, 229, 234, 245–46
France, Bill, Sr., v, 58, 63, 88, 155, 156, 159, 199, 202, 238, 250
Frasson, Joe, 231
French, Max, 62
Fricks, J. F., 63

Gaffney (S.C.), 121
General Motors (GM), 127, 173, 197, 238, 250
Goldsmith, Paul, 130, 157, 188, 199, 203, 205
Goode, Gilmer, 65, 70, 129
Goodyear, 169, 171, 196–97, 240
Granatelli, Andy, 216–19
Grand National racing, ix, xi, 66, 80, 82, 104, 109, 192, 207, 214, 215, 218, 238, 239, 240, 241, 242, 248
Grand Prix, viii
Grange, Red, vii
Grant, Harry, 2
Greensboro, 15, 19, 26, 34, 37, 42, 48, 80, 103, 119, 120, 135, 180

Greensboro News, 58, 59
Greenville (S.C.), 146, 147
Grit, 192
Gurney, Dan, 204

Hamilton, Pete, 214
Harrisburg (N.C.), 123
Heidelberg (Pa.), 75
High Point (N.C.), 16, 80, 98, 120
Hillen, Bobby, 242, 248
Hillsboro (S.C.), 146, 147
Hollywood (Fla.), 169
Holman, John, 195, 196, 203, 211, 214
Householder, Ronnie, 196
Hucks, Ronnie, 111, 112, 113, 115–16, 127, 171–72, 181
Hudson Hornet, 72, 127, 155
Hurtubise, Jim, 203
Hutcherson, Dick, 5, 210
Hylton, James, 203

Illustrated Speedway News, 62
Indianapolis, 217
Indianapolis 500, 3, 19, 64, 87, 91
Indianapolis Speedway, 155
Inman, Dale, 26, 28–31, 33, 60, 78, 111, 112, 113, 114, 117, 133–34, 137, 138, 178, 183, 200, 212, 217, 233, 236, 242, 251
Iowa, 101
Ireland, 17
Isaac, Bobby, 7, 199, 210

Jarrett, Ned, 149, 181, 208, 210, 247

Johns, Bobby, 165
Johnson, Junior, x, 141, 143–
    44, 153, 166, 173–74, 181,
    183, 196, 197–98, 199,
    210, 234, 247
Jones, Alan, viii
Jones, Bobby, vii
Jones, Parnelli, 204
Jones, Possum, 139

Kansas, 69
Kansas City (Mo.), 156
Kentucky Derby, 3
Kiekhafer, Carl, 124–27
King's Business College
    (Greensboro),180,
    197
Knight, Bobby, 206

Labonte, Terry, 241, 248, 251
Lakewood Speedway (Atlanta),
    44, 150, 249
Langley, Elmo, 7
Las Vegas, vi
Latford, Bob, 146
Level Cross (N.C.), vii, 15, 17,
    19, 60, 65, 168, 179, 218,
    244, 246, 248
Level Cross Methodist
    Church, 103
Lewallen, Jimmy, 100, 169
Liberty (N.C.), 116
Lincoln, 86
Lombardi, Vince, 112, 115
Lorenzen, Freddy, 183, 188,
    196, 197, 204, 210, 214–
    15, 227–28
Los Angeles, 217
Loulan, Jim, 170

Lund, Tiny, 135, 153–54, 169
Lynchburg (Va.), 55

MacDonald, Davy, 209
Madison Square Garden, vi
Mantz, Johnny, 83, 87–89, 91–
    92, 93
March of Dimes, 26
Marcus, Dave, 223
Martinsville (Va.), 40, 195
Matthews, Banjo, 213
McQuagg, Sam, 5, 203
Meadowlands Arena (N.J.), vi
Melling, Harry, 250–51
Mercury, 203, 207, 230
Mercury outboard engine, 124
Milliken, Tommy, 26
Moody, Ralph, 195, 196, 203,
    211, 214
Moore, Bud, 203
Myers, Bobby, 130, 144
Mylar, Red, 133, 136
Myrtle Beach (S.C.), 148

Namath, Joe, v
NASCAR (National Association
    for Stock Car Auto Racing),
    xii, 2, 58–59, 63, 65, 66, 69,
    73, 78, 79–80, 92, 94, 99,
    101, 104, 105, 123, 124,
    126, 127, 128, 129, 133,
    140–41, 144, 146, 151, 152,
    153, 155, 162, 164, 165,
    166, 172, 180, 182, 184,
    185, 190, 191, 192, 193,
    195, 197, 198, 200, 201,
    202, 203, 204, 210, 214,
    215, 218, 238, 239, 249
Nashville, 147, 205

National Hot Rod Association, 202
National Warranty Corporation, 245
Nebraska, 101, 102
New York, 95
Norcross (Ga.), 214
North Carolina, 67, 77, 121

Oakland, 120
Ohio, 101
Oklahoma City, 125
Olds 88, 67, 86, 89, 114
Oldsmobile, 72, 127, 129, 130, 131–32, 135, 136, 150, 162, 164, 237, 239
Owens, Cotton, 80, 142, 152, 158, 193–94
Owens, Lynda. *See* Lynda Owens Petty
Oxford (Me.), 97

Palmer, Arnold, vi, vii
Panch, Marvin, 123, 173, 195, 203, 210
Pardue, Jimmy, 209
Parsons, Benny, 210
Paschal, Jim, 101, 181, 203, 207, 210
Passino, Jacques, 196, 211
Peachhaven Speedway (Winston-Salem), 80
Pearson, David, 5, 190, 195, 203, 211, 227–28, 229–31, 247, 250
Pearson, Rickie, 241
Pee Dee River region, 134
Peeler, Hoppy, 26
Peeler, Nathan, 26

Peeler, Wade, 26
Pennsylvania, 95
Pepsi-Cola, 21, 37, 116, 175
Petty, Elizabeth Toomes (*mother*), 12–13, 22, 23, 24, 25, 26, 34, 36, 38, 39, 50, 51, 55–56, 60, 61, 66, 70, 80, 85, 90, 98, 102, 106, 108, 112, 118, 153, 154, 177, 182
Petty, Grandmother, 18, 37–38
Petty, Great-granddaddy, 17–18
Petty, Judson (*grandfather*), 18
Petty, Kyle (*son*), x, xii, xiii–xiv, 163–64, 235–46
Petty, Lee (*father*), x, xii, 12–13, 18–21, 22, 23, 24, 26, 32, 34, 35, 38, 39–40, 41–45, 49–54, 55–58, 59, 60, 61, 63, 64–72, 73–82, 83–93, 94–105, 106–109, 110–15, 117–18, 120, 122–30, 131–34, 135, 138, 141–43, 145, 150–52, 154, 159, 161, 165–66, 168–69, 175–80, 182–84, 200, 224, 241, 245, 252
Petty, Lisa (*daughter*), 200
Petty, Lynda Owens (*wife*), 117–18, 119–20, 154–55, 163–64, 177, 181, 200, 209, 235
Petty, Maurice "Chief" (*brother*), 12–13, 21, 22, 23, 24, 25–26, 28, 31, 32–33, 35, 38, 50–52, 57, 60, 61, 65, 66, 71, 78, 84, 85, 90, 98, 101, 102, 107, 108–109, 111, 113, 133, 149, 153, 168–69, 172,

Petty, Maurice "Chief" (cont.)
174, 177, 178, 179–81,
183, 200, 205, 206, 212,
217, 242–43, 244–45, 251
Petty, Rebecca (daughter), 216
Petty, Richard:
and back-road racing, 39–48
and bike racing, 31–35
closes Petty Enterprises, 245
and car crashes, 6–7, 11, 30–
31, 130, 173–76, 209, 240–
41
daughter Lisa born, 200
daughter Rebecca born, 216
daughter Sharon born, 181
at Daytona track, 155–61
development as stock car
racer, 140–45, 146–54
early driving experiences,
109–18
early years, 15–27, 28–38,
39–54, 55–72, 73–82, 83–
93, 94–105, 106–110
education, 15, 25, 107–108
family ties, 14, 21–25, 37–38,
107, 144, 200
and fear, 11–14, 232
first race, 131–39
on the future of stock car
racing, 247–51
life on the road, 95–98, 101–
102, 200
marries Lynda Owens, 154–
55
as mechanic, 57–58, 71, 105
named Rookie of the Year,
162
philosophy of, 10–11, 106,
206

plans to reopen Petty Enterprises, 245
popularity of, v–x, 185
on racetrack strategy, 186–
89, 232–34
on rebuilding stock cars,
192–203
relationship with brother. See
Maurice "Chief" Petty
relationship with father, 55–
72, 73–82, 83–93, 94–105,
106–109, 132–33, 141–42,
151–52. See also Lee Petty
son Kyle born, 163
and Southern 500, 1–5, 6, 7–
9
on stress of racing, 220–25
and tobacco cutting, 35–37
and toughness, xiii, xiv, 141
voted Most Popular Driver,
185
and wagon racing, 28–31
wins Driver of the Year
award, 205
wins first race, 161–62
wins National Driver of the
Year trophy, 205
Petty, Sharon (daughter), 181
"Petty Blue," 133, 168, 201,
212, 217
Petty Engineering, 132, 133,
179
Petty Enterprises, 15, 132, 133,
179, 206, 237, 242, 243,
244, 245, 251, 252
Petty Racing Team, 78
Piedmont region, xiv, 16, 17,
134, 228
Piggins, Vince, 196

Pistone, Tom, 158
Pittsboro (N.C.), 116
Plymouth, 4, 64, 77, 81–82, 88, 91, 92, 93, 98, 150, 164, 167, 168, 171, 172, 173, 178, 183, 199, 200, 202, 203, 213–14
Plymouth Barracuda, 201
Plymouth coupe, 49, 52, 70, 72, 73, 75, 84, 85, 87–88
Plymouth SuperBird, 213
Pole Cat Creek, 26
Pontiac, 64, 77, 127, 157, 173, 178, 195, 196, 239, 243
Pontiac STP, 2, 216–19, 243
Purser, Smokey, 130

Raleigh, 22, 43, 60, 80, 100, 215
Randleman (N.C.), 15, 16, 25, 42, 109, 112, 113, 119, 171
Randleman High School, 108
Randolph County (N.C.), 34
Reed, Jim, 101, 169
Rice, Sam, 69
Richmond, 80
Richter, Les, 222
Riverside, 204, 207, 213, 217
Riverside International Raceway, 222
R. J. Reynolds Tobacco Company, 215
Roanoke, 53, 103
Robbins (N.C.), 116
Roberts, Glenn "Fireball," x, 62, 80, 89, 90, 92, 138, 143, 159, 173, 181, 183, 195–96, 208–209, 240, 247

Rockingham (N.C.), 216
Rollins, Shorty, 160
Root, Chapman, 155
Roper, Jim, 69
Ruby, Lloyd, 204
Ruth, Clay, 114–15

San Angelo (Tx.), 197, 199
Sachs, Eddie, 209
Salvino, Ralph, 217
Savannah, 143, 146
Scott, Wendell, 203–204
Seagrove (N.C.), 116–17
Sears All-State tires, 87
Seven-Eleven, 244
Shaw, Wilbur, vii
Sheeler, Ralph "Three Wheel," 62
Shepherd, Morgan, 244
Shuman, Buddy, 48–49
Smith, Jack, 162
Snead, Sam, vi
South Carolina, 2
South Carolina Highway, 34, 83
South Dakota, 101
Southern 500 (Darlington, S.C.), 1, 3, 4–6, 83, 89, 91, 169
Spartanburg (S.C.), 146, 147
Sports Car Club of America, 238
Sports Illustrated, 192
STP. *See* Pontiac STP

Talladega (Ala.), 240
Talladega 500, 214, 222, 240
Teague, Marshall, 62–63, 155–56

Tennessee, xiv
Texas, 226
Thomas, Herb, 80, 100, 109, 140–41
Thomas, Lowell, 60
Thompson, Speedy, 101, 153
Thornburg, Wade, 236, 242
Tommy's Drive-In (Asheboro, N.C.), 114
Toomes, Granddaddy, 21–22, 27, 108
Toomes, Grandmother, 21–22, 37
Toronto, 139
Tri-City Speedway (High Point, N.C.), 98
Turner, Curtis, 68, 80, 86, 88, 89, 90, 91, 92, 99, 100, 135, 139, 141, 144, 187, 194–95
Tuthill, Bill, 63, 92

Uncle Bob, 19, 109
Uncle Bud, 19, 75
Uncle Julie, 19, 40, 41, 42, 46, 49–50, 53, 55, 56, 58, 63, 65, 66, 69, 90, 124
United States Auto Club (USAC), 201, 203, 204, 214
U.S. Route 200, 84
U.S. Route 220, 15, 16, 19

Valdosta (Ga.), 146
Virginia, 22, 46, 60, 68
Vogt, Red, 60, 63, 89, 92

Wade, Billy, 209
Walker, Otis, 46–48, 49, 115

Walker's Mill Road (Level Cross, N.C.), 114
Walsh, Bill, 206
Waltrip, Darrell, 248, 249
Weatherly, Joe "Little Joe," 99, 134, 135, 137, 138, 139, 156, 158, 181, 187, 195, 207
Welborn, Bob, 101, 138, 139, 158
West Virginia, 110
Westmoreland, Hubert, 67
Wheeler, Humpy, 228, 240, 249
White, Glenn, 213
White, Rex, 101, 126, 164, 166, 168
Wilkerson Boulevard (Charlotte), 66, 67
Williford, Dick, 199
Wilson (N.C.), 146, 148
Wilson, Waddell, 251
Winston Cup, 215, 216
Winston-Salem, 80, 88, 103, 120, 126, 139, 213
Wood brothers (Leonard and Glen), 167, 233, 244, 250
World Series, 3
World 600 (Charlotte), 165, 181, 208
Wyoming, 26

Yarborough, Cale, x, 190, 204, 210, 211, 229, 247, 249, 251
Yarbrough, LeeRoy, vi, 203, 204, 210, 211, 226
Yates, Doug, 164
Yunick, Smokey, 130, 194–95

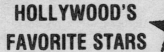

FREE!!
BOOKS BY MAIL
CATALOGUE

BOOKS BY MAIL will share with you our current bestselling books as well as hard to find specialty titles in areas that will match your interests. You will be updated on what's new in books at no cost to you. Just fill in the coupon below and discover the convenience of having books delivered to your home.

PLEASE ADD $1.00 TO COVER THE COST OF POSTAGE & HANDLING.

- -

BOOKS BY MAIL

320 Steelcase Road E.,
Markham, Ontario L3R 2M1

210 5th Ave., 7th Floor
New York, N.Y., 10010

Please send Books By Mail catalogue to:

Name _____
(please print)

Address _____

City _____

Prov./State _____ P.C./Zip _____

(BBM1)